Transatlantic Crossing

Other books by Walter Allen

All in a Lifetime
The English Novel
Tradition and Dream
Writers on Writing
George Eliot
The Urgent West

Transatlantic Crossing

American Visitors to Britain and
British Visitors to America
in the Nineteenth Century

selected and with an introduction by
Walter Allen

William Morrow & Company, Inc.
New York

Contents

Acknowledgments

Introduction

Americans in Britain

Nathaniel Parker Willis (1806–1867)   25
From Dover to London
Breakfast in Scotland
Partridge Shooting
English aristocracy
'The true philosophy of Life'
Brighton
Elephant and Castle

James Fenimore Cooper (1789–1851)   39
English order
From the dome of Saint Paul's
Anti-American Prejudice
London streets
English proprieties
The tall and the short
Windsor
Servants in England
London street music
English independence
Leaving England

William Cullen Bryant (1794–1878)   53
Railway travel in England
The police—and the poor
Edinburgh

Bayard Taylor (1825–1878)   59
Unemployed miners
Crime in London
Greenwich Fair
London fog

Herman Melville (1819–1891)   63
From Melville's Journal

William Hickling Prescott (1796–1859)   67
English society and English gentlemen

Francis Parkman (1824–1893)   73
Impressions of London

Ralph Waldo Emerson (1803–1882)   77
From Emerson's Journal

Harriet Beecher Stowe (1811–1896)   89
Why English ladies keep their beauty
Staying with the Duke of Argyll at Inveraray

Nathaniel Hawthorne (1804–1864)   93
The Liverpool poor
Liverpool street-scenes
Peculiar behaviour of the English
An English beggar
Letters to the Editor
Fruit and sunshine
In a Law-court
At the Mayor of Liverpool's soirée
The Englishman's contemptuous jealousy of Americans
Time telescoped
Meekness of the unemployed
English restraint breaks down
London street-scenes
Christmas in England
Dung-collectors
In the House of Commons
Reflections on Hampton Court
Reputation of Americans in England
In Manchester Cathedral
Leamington
York Minster
In the British Museum

Henry Brooks Adams (1838–1919)   113
Arriving in England
London society
The American Civil War and the English
The marriage of the Prince of Wales
In the Hebrides

Elihu Burritt (1810–1879)   125
Farm wagons and farm-labourers' boots

Joaquin Miller (1841–1913)   129
Living in the slums

James Russell Lowell (1819–1891)   133
The advantages of a great capital
The Lord Mayor's Show
The attractions of fog

Oliver Wendell Holmes (1809–1894)   137
Some first impressions
Waiting for the carriage
A party at the Rothschilds'
Windsor Castle
In the Abbey
Afternoon tea
Bond Street and Oxford Street
England's chief product

William James (1842–1910)   147
On the bus to Hampton Court

Henry James (1843–1916)   149
London during the Season
James at the Derby

Britons in America

William Cobbett (1762–1835)   163
Long Island
Lancaster, Pennsylvania
Absence of bird song and wild flowers
Versatility and independence of American workers

Basil Hall (1788–1844)   169
New York: first impressions
American self-praise
American restlessness
Rochester, N.Y.

Frances Trollope (1780–1863)   175
American spitting
On a Mississippi steamboat
Refuse-disposal in Cincinnati
A frontier farm in Ohio
Southern attitudes to slaves
Cooking, parties and women's dress
'A lovely and noble city'

Thomas Hamilton (1789–1842)   187
Breakfast in a New York hotel
Negro children in New York

At President Andrew Jackson's levée
Men and manners on an Ohio River steamboat
Yankees and southerners compared

Fanny Kemble (1809–1893)   197
New York City
Street-behaviour in New York
Freedom of American girls
'A darling country for poor folks'
Charleston, South Carolina
Why slaves are dirty
On a Georgia plantation
Poor whites

Harriet Martineau (1802–1876)   213
Life on a Southern plantation
Chicago
Milwaukee: population 400
Advantages of the Northern working man
Pampering of American women
Evil effects of boarding-house life

Frederick Marryat (1792–1848)   225
Luxury in the new towns
Whittling
Spirits and chewing-tobacco
The prairie
A camp meeting
American prudery

Charles Dickens (1812–1870)   235
'This is not the republic I came to see'

Laurence Oliphant (1829–1888)   239
Paddling down the Mississippi
Driving from Dubuque, Iowa, to Illinois

Thomas Richard Weld (1813–1869)   245
Financial advice to the travellers
Ladies in New York
Contrasts in Richmond, Virginia

William Makepeace Thackeray (1811–1863)   253
From Thackeray's letters

Isabella Bishop (1832–1904)   261
Railway travelling in the West
Chicago
American passion for oysters
American temperance

Thomas Colley Grattan (1792–1864)   265
Boston
American street-scenes
The perils of central heating
The inauguration of President William Henry Harrison
Mysteries of childbirth
American servants

Anthony Trollope (1815–1882)   277
Rhode Island
American hotels
Milwaukee and the frontier mind
American workmen
New York—and the American face
New York schools
New York: Central Park
Washington D.C.
Thirsting after civil words
Slaves in Kentucky
The Westerner
The immigrant transformed

Windham Thomas Wyndham-Quin,   295
fourth Earl of Dunraven (1841–1926)
Squaw-men in Montana

Robert Louis Stevenson (1850–1894)   299
Notes by the Way to Council Bluffs
San Francisco

Matthew Arnold (1822–1888)   311
Civilization in the United States

Sir Henry Lepel Griffin (1840–1908)   323
Niagara

Oscar Wilde (1854–1900)   327
Impressions of America

Acknowledgments

The author and publishers would like to express their gratitude to the following for permission to reprint the work of some of the contributors to this book:

Harvard University Press for *Journal of a Visit to London and the Continent* by Herman Melville (ed. Metcalf) Cohen & West Ltd.
Houghton Mifflin Co. for *The Letters of Henry Adams* (ed. Chauncey Ford).
Harper & Row and Eyre & Spottiswoode for *The Journals of Francis Parkman* (ed. Mason Wade) Copyright 1947 by Massachusetts Historical Society.
University of Oklahoma Press for *The Literary Memoranda of William Hickling Prescott* (ed. C. Harvey Gardiner).
Mrs B. Norman Butler for *The Letters and Private Papers of W. M. Thackeray* (ed. Gordon Ray).
The Modern Language Association of America for *The English Notebooks of Nathaniel Hawthorne* (ed. Randall Stewart).

Introduction

POLITICIANS—BRITISH ADMITTEDLY more often and more enthusiastically—are fond of invoking what they call the 'special relation' between Britain and the United States. The relation is real enough; but it is something much more complex and considerably less cosy than appears in the politicians' speeches. Naturally, during the almost two centuries that have passed since the original thirteen rebellious colonies turned themselves by victory into the United States of America, the relation has changed. For example, whereas nothing struck early-nineteenth-century American visitors to London so much as the ostentation of its wealth and luxury, those of us who are middle-aged have seen in our lifetime British claims for the special relation become depressingly like the claims of a poor man to kinship with a millionaire. Yet, as I think this book shows, fundamentally the nature of the relation has remained remarkably constant, and, fundamentally, it may be defined as the exaggerated awareness each party to it has of the other.

But this needs qualification, since, as an Englishman, I have to make the conscious effort to remember that, whereas Britain has a special relation with the United States, the United States has a special relation with other countries besides Britain. So far from having an exaggerated awareness of Britain, the majority of Americans have probably no awareness of her at all, at any rate of her as a country differing in a significant way from other countries. Why should they? They have no links with Britain; which means that for them Britain is a foreign country that can be visited, appreciated or not appreciated, enjoyed or not enjoyed, just like any other, without intervention of ancestral prejudice.

But this is a relatively new situation, and it seems worth pointing out that most if not all of the visitors to nineteenth-century Britain I quote from were what today would be called WASPs—White Anglo-Saxon Protestants—WASPs, moreover, who had come to inspect the aboriginal WASPs, which is what the British, or most of them, are. The waspier the visitors were, the more critically they came to inspect. They came prepared to take offence because expecting to be slighted, and ready to go over to the offensive themselves because, it seemed plain to many of them, they felt the need to justify their immediate ancestors' repudiation of Britain. They were still fighting a war of independence, which was also a civil war; there were old scores to be paid off, and they were as quick to patronize the British as the British were to patronize them. In many ways they were extraordinarily like some of the British visitors to the States at the same time. Both were supremely confident in the superiority of their own culture, and almost everything that came their way in the other could be construed as evidence of it.

But the intensity of feeling was, I think, stronger on the American side. For good reasons. England was the hereditary enemy, indeed America's only hereditary enemy, apart from the country's original inhabitants. Then, the United States had to prove herself as a nation, not only to the outside world but also to Americans themselves. Culturally, the country was still a province of England. It was all very well for Edgar Allan Poe, writing on American literature in the 1830s, to announce, 'We have snapped asunder the leading-strings of our British Grandmamma': it did not seem like that to many Americans or to many British, and the British could afford to be smug about it: 'Why should the Americans write books, when a six weeks' passage brings them in our own tongue, our sense, science and genius, in bales and hogsheads?' That was Sidney Smith writing in 1818. The *cri de cœur* of Philip Freneau, the poet of the Revolutionary War, is understandable enough:

> Can we never be thought
> To have learning or grace
> Unless it be bought
> From that damnable place?

How the visitors reacted to the situation depended, of course, on temperament, training, bent of interest and perhaps even on class. And almost the earliest visitor I quote, N. P. Willis, contradicts all the generalizations I have made by his enthusiastic and awed appreciation of England and English life. But much more typical of American attitudes are those of Cooper, Parkman and Henry Adams, and I suspect a sense of social status enters here. Cooper was an old-fashioned American even during his lifetime; he was also consciously an American gentleman and a patriot, but a patriot increasingly critical of the United States of his day. He judges life and society in Britain and America alike from an ideal standard, and when he finds things to praise in Britain, as he often does, it is usually to point the moral for

America, as when he writes, of the 'greater independence of personal habits' in Britain: 'The besetting, the degrading vice of America, is the moral cowardice by which men are led to truckle to what is called public opinion.' But he picks out, as most of the American visitors do, the weaknesses of nineteenth-century British life, in particular the glaring contrast between rich and poor.

Parkman's attitude towards the British scene was much more one of contempt. When he visited Britain he was, it is true, a much younger man than Cooper. As he looks down on London from the dome of St Paul's, 'Was there ever such a cursed hole?' he asks himself, and we are reminded that in those days for the American England could easily represent an alternative and infinitely more depressing future to that which America promised, a future of vast urban agglomerations in which the masses were conditioned to what seemed to many to be industrial slavery. Cooper believed that, their servitude apart, Negro slaves were better off than the servant-class in England. Indeed, if the British visitor to the States was horrified by the spectacle of slavery, the American visitor to Britain tended to be just as horrified by the spectacle of working-class poverty. The America of the time, of course, was still a predominantly rural country. Henry Adams writes in *The Education* of the impression that what he calls the 'Black District' made on him when he first passed through South Staffordshire on the train from Liverpool to London:

> The plunge into darkness lurid with flames; the sense of unknown horror in their weird gloom which then existed nowhere else, and never had existed before, except in volcanic craters; the violent contrast between the dense, smoky, impenetrable darkness, and the soft green charm that one glided into, as one emerged,

all this represented a future that a young American, who 'had no idea that Karl Marx was standing there waiting for him', could, at that time, be pardoned for assuming was not an American future. It was nothing like any American future the founding fathers had envisaged.

And as a young American in London, Adams, by virtue of his office of secretary to the American Minister, who was his father, and by virtue also of his ancestry, grandson of the sixth President of the United States and great-grandson of the second, was even closer to the spirit and traditions of the founding fathers than Cooper had been. Moreover, both time and place must have sharpened his sense of national identity, his Americanness. The United States was at civil war with itself, and Britain was divided in its sympathies: generally, the upper classes, fashionable London, the people with whom a young diplomat would be in closest contact, supported the South. Relations between Whitehall and Washington were often strained; as late as March 1863, we have Adams writing:

> We are in a shocking bad way here. I don't know what we are ever going to do with this damned old country. Some day it will wake up and find itself at war with us, and then what a squealing there'll be. By the Lord, I would almost be willing to submit to our sufferings, just to have the pleasure of seeing our privateers make ducks and drakes of their commerce.

Young Adams in London was not only campaigning in the War between the States, he was also still, and perhaps consciously, fighting the War of Independence, which had been a civil war too. He was not without English friends in London; indeed, he knew everybody; but he found his friends among members of the Liberal Party, on which he pinned his hopes for Britain. If they triumphed, Britain would become, as it were, more American. His contempt for the traditional trappings of English life, for Society, comes out in his letters very plainly.

Adams was unassailable by Britain. He could see it from the outside, as a huge laboratory illustrating the workings of social processes. He was unassailable partly by temperament, which was very much that of the detached scientist, but also by upbringing, by family. He was an aristocrat, with the unselfconscious confidence in himself of the aristocrat. His heritage had made him so. His British equivalent would have been a Russell, a Cecil or a Churchill.

The situation of the imaginative writers who visited Britain was rather different, simply because they *were* imaginative writers. Emerson is one of the great American spokesmen; from one point of view, he can be seen almost as a cultural chauvinist. But when he made his first visit to Britain, in 1832, it was as though he were making a pilgrimage, for he came to meet his great heroes, Wordsworth, Coleridge and Carlyle. For all that he gave them a uniquely American cast, the essentials of his doctrine are essentially Wordsworthian. His journals show him an acute and sympathetic observer of Britain. He is impressed by her power, her richness, her technology, her prodi-gality of talent. There is the fascinating passage at the end of his account of his second visit in which he lists the eminent writers and scientists he has met. It is an impressive array and it carries with it, I think, an implication on Emerson's part of 'I came, I saw, I conquered.' London is the place where one 'lives in extremes', and he confesses: 'If I stay here long, I shall lose all my patriotism and think that England has absorbed all excellences.' But of course he doesn't stay.

The case of Hawthorne, a much greater writer, was considerably more complex. His family was as old as any in America, and in himself and in his works he enshrined the quintessence of the New England spirit as it had evolved during two centuries. Some years after his stay in England he wrote to a friend: 'Have you ever read the novels of Anthony Trollope? They precisely suit my taste—solid and substantial, written on the strength of beer and through the inspiration of ale, and just as real as if some giant had hewn a great lump out of the earth and put it under a glass case, with all its inhabitants going about their daily business, and not suspecting that they were being made a show of. And these books are just as English as a beef-steak.' This sounds like a rich appreciation of England: in fact, as his journals show, Hawthorne's attitude towards England was thoroughly ambivalent. But then Hawthorne's attitude towards everything was thoroughly ambivalent. He was to write, after his stay in England, in the preface to *The Marble Faun*: 'No author can conceive of the difficulty of writing a romance about a country where there is no shadow, no antiquity, no mystery, no picturesque and gloomy wrong, nor anything but a commonplace prosperity, as is happily the case with my dear native land.' It is a curious—and characteristic—sentence: Hawthorne seems to be at least half-regretting too its commonplace prosperity. And a similarly mixed attitude dictates his responses to Britain.

He was in England for four years, as U.S. Consul at Liverpool; he was also probably the most famous American writer of his time. As one reads his account of England in *The English Notebooks*, the journal out of which he carved the much less lively and much less provocative *Our Old Home*, one sees his uncertainty, his veerings between admiration and hostility, where Britain is concerned. The hostility strikes one as genuine, and the admiration, which is also genuine, as reluctant. England is certainly picturesque enough, but there is a distressing absence of commonplace prosperity. After walking through the slums of Liverpool shortly after his arrival, he notes:

I should not have conceived it possible that so many children could have been collected together, without a single trace of beauty, or scarcely of intelligence, in so much as one individual; such mean, coarse, vulgar features and figures, betraying unmistakably a low origin, and ignorant and brutal parents. They did not appear wicked, but only stupid, animal and soulless. It must require many generations of better life to elicit a soul in them. All America could not show the like.

And then there are the paupers and the beggars. But at the same time he cannot fail to be struck by the independence, even the insouciance, that the paupers and the beggars display. Beggars don't consider themselves outlaws, as they would in America. But how the English delude themselves! They talk of their oak-trees: he has seen vaster oaks in Massachusetts. As for their fruit, they have no more idea of what fruit is than of what sunshine is. The climate is unspeakable; they can only bear it because 'they keep up their animal-heat by means of ale and wine'. And the women! Grim, red-faced monsters every one, whom a man would surely be justified in murdering! They look as if they have fed on the fat of meat.

Beneath all this is the ancestral hostility. Hawthorne is thoroughly aware of this: 'There is an account to settle between us and them for the contemptuous jealousy with which (since it has ceased to be unmitigated contempt) they regard us.' And yet—'There are some Englishmen whom I like—one or two for whom, I must almost say, I have an affection—but still there is not the same union between·us, as if they were Americans... In this foreign land, I can never forget the distinction between English and American.' All the same, there is the English countryside, the cathedrals, the charm of living in Leamington Spa, the British Museum, the art, the history and historical remains:

> Palaces, pictures, parks! They do enrich life; and kings and aristocracies cannot keep these things to themselves—they merely take care of them for others. Even a king, with all the glory that can be shed around him, is but a liveried and bedizened footman of his people, and the toy of their delight. I am very glad that I came to see this country while the English are still playing with such a toy.

There's Hawthorne having it both ways. England as the picturesque raree-show for the Great American Tourist. But, as he's already told us, it will soon all be over: help is on the way:

> My ancestor left England in 1635. I return in 1853. I sometimes feel as if I myself had been absent these two hundred and eighteen years—leaving England just emerging from the feudal system, and finding it on the verge of Republicanism . . .

The English Notebooks is crammed with perceptions and ideas and with the vivid renderings of life in action of a great novelist. Altogether, it presents a superb panorama of mid-Victorian England and at the same time it is a superb piece of autobiographical writing. If there is a single image that dominates it it is, I think, the one I began with, that of beefsteak and ale, which for Hawthorne seems to be the source at once of England's glories and of her defects. The obvious defects are those of poverty, inequality, the rigidity of the classes. But beneath and beyond these is something else, a materialism, a coarseness, a grossness that has something to do with unshakable self-confidence and unconscious arrogance. To the English today it might well seem that American visitors were discovering the eighteenth century in the nineteenth. One gets a distinct impression that visitors from New England to old England were more refined, more thin-skinned, more thin-blooded than their British counterparts. Perhaps they were merely more genteel. There is an amusing account by James Russell Lowell of meeting Trollope in the company of Emerson and Oliver Wendell Holmes. 'I dined the other day with Anthony Trollope, a big, red-faced, rather underbred Englishman of the bald-with-spectacles type. A good roaring positive fellow who deafened me.' The effect of Holmes's famous witticisms on him Lowell compares to 'pelting a rhinoceros with seed-pearls'. Trollope's heartiness, exuberance and assertiveness were plainly disconcerting to the New England sages. I get the impression that Trollope knew exactly what he was doing.

In the last decades of the century, after the Northern victory in the war, I think, a change in American attitudes towards Britain becomes apparent. Criticism is much less evident as the American sense of inferiority diminishes. Appreciation takes over, as in the delightfully spritely account of his visit to England by the octogenarian Holmes. But the great appreciator, of course, is Henry James, who responded to the English scene with no reservations but with a connoisseur's acceptance of a rich spectacle. His finest rendering of it is *The Princess Casamassima*, which is one of the great London novels, but his powers of sympathetic evocation are equally evident in the travel pieces which he wrote for American magazines and which I have anthologized from.

Americans came to Britain to see the old, the country their forbears had repudiated. British visitors went to the United States to see the new. Like the Americans, they took with them their prejudices and rarely had difficulty in confirming them. In *Pencillings on the Way* N. P. Willis quotes Christopher North as saying:

[17]

. . . What a strange thing it is that nobody can write a good book on America! The ridiculous part of it seems to me that men of common sense go there as travellers, and fill their books with scenes such as they may see every day within five minutes' walk of their own doors, and call them American. Vulgar people are to be found all over the world, and I will match any scene in Hamilton or Mrs Trollope, any day or night, here in Edinburgh.

And this, I think, remains the feeling one has after a prolonged diet of Basil Hall, Frances Trollope, Captain Marryat and Thomas Colley Grattan. Their observations of the American scene are amusing enough and their unanimity is such that they all seem to see the same things; but for all the accuracy of their observations, what most strikes one is their lack of generosity and their lack of imagination. We are in the presence of thoroughly undistinguished minds. How bored one becomes with their constant British superiority and how understandable that Americans should have resented their criticisms. Harriet Martineau's is the appropriate comment:

> The popular scandal against the people of the United States, that they boast intolerably of their national institutions and character, appears to me untrue; but I see how it has arisen. Foreigners, especially the English, are partly to blame for this. They enter the United States with an idea that a republic is a vulgar thing; and some take no pains to conceal their thought. To an American, nothing is more venerable than a republic. The native and the stranger set out on a misunderstanding. The English attacks, the American defends, and, perhaps, boasts.

Certainly no English visitor to nineteenth-century America produced anything that can be mentioned in the same breath as Tocqueville's *Democracy in America*, and partly, perhaps, because the English were too emotionally implicated in the country they were visiting. Even today, it seems to me, Englishmen visiting the United States judge it by standards they would not dream of applying to, say, Germany or Italy or Sweden or Holland. They take Britain as the norm; and certainly few, if any, of the nineteenth-century visitors had the flexibility of mind, the imagination, to see America as Laurence Oliphant advised in his *Minnesota and the Far West*:

> The impressions of a traveller visiting the United States of America for the first time are so totally unlike those which he has experienced in the course of his rambles in the Old World, that he at once perceives that, in order to the due appreciation of the country he is about to explore, an

entire revolution must be effected in those habits of thought and observation in which he has hitherto indulged. He finds that, instead of moralising over magnificence in a process of decay, he must here watch resources in a process of development—he must substitute the pleasures of anticipation for those of retrospection—must be more familiar with pecuniary speculations than with historical associations—delight himself rather in statistics than in poetry—visit docks instead of ruins—converse of dollars, and not antique coins—prefer printed calico to oil paintings, and admire the model of a steam-engine more than the statue of a Venus. He looks on scenery with an eye for the practical, as well as the picturesque; when gazing on a lovely valley or extensive plain, he discerns at a glance the best line for a railway; and never sees a water-fall without remembering that it is a mill-site.

But Oliphant's 'entire revolution' in habits of thought and observation was very difficult to achieve, for reasons put forward by Henry Adams in 1884 in his *History of the United States during the Administrations of Thomas Jefferson and James Madison*. It is from this book that, so far as I can tell, the notion of the American Dream stems. What the rest of the world did not realize, according to Adams, was that 'the hard, practical, money-getting American democrat, who had neither generosity nor honour nor imagination, and who inhabited cold shades where fancy sickened and where genius died, was in truth living in a world of dream, and acting out a drama more instinct with poetry than all the avatars of the East, walking in gardens of emeralds and rubies, in ambition already ruling the world and guiding Nature with a kinder and wiser hand than had ever yet been felt in human history'. A world of dream, and from its very nature the dream was all but incommunicable. Adams imagines a dialogue between an American and a foreign visitor:

'Look at my wealth,' cried the American to his foreign visitor. 'See these solid mountains of salt and iron, of lead, copper, silver, and gold! See these magnificent cities scattered broadcast to the Pacific! See my cornfields rustling and waving in the summer breeze from ocean to ocean, so that the sun itself is not high enough to mark where the distant mountains bound my golden seas! Look at this continent of mine, fairest of created worlds, as she lies turning up to the sun's never-failing caress her broad and exuberant breasts, overflowing with milk for her hundred million children! See how she glows with youth, health, and love!' Perhaps it was not altogether unnatural that the foreigner, on being asked to see what needed centuries to produce, should have looked about him with bewilderment and indignation. 'Gold! cities! cornfields! continents!

Nothing of the sort! I see nothing but tremendous wastes, where sickly men and women are dying of homesickness or are scalped by savages! mountain-ranges a thousand miles long, with no means of getting to them, and nothing in them when you get there! swamps and forests choked with their own rotten ruins! nor hope of better for a thousand years! Your story is a fraud, and you are a liar and a swindler!'

This passage from Adams places the American practice of boasting, to which the British visitors reacted so strenuously, in a new light. I don't think the British visitors can be blamed for reacting as they did. They saw the actuality; Americans were more impressed by the possibility. Dickens, in *Martin Chuzzlewit*, saw the Eden settlement for what it was, a malarial swamp, and therefore for him its promoters were cynical exploiters of innocent immigrants. But perhaps Dickens was not telling the whole story.

As always, however, Dickens is a special case. *Martin Chuzzlewit*, *American Notes* and his letters from America to friends at home are the index of his extreme disillusionment with the United States. He went with the highest hopes, as to a country much more accordant with his notions of a just society than the England of his time was. He did not find what he expected. He seems to have felt, to judge from his letter to Macready, personally betrayed, and his reaction expressed itself in the savage satire of *Chuzzlewit*.

Just as American visitors to nineteenth-century Britain tend to fasten on to the same aspects of English life, the tyranny of class, the contrast between what Disraeli called the two nations, so in the books of British visitors to America certain aspects of America recur again and again— the phenomenon, then novel, of the American hotel, eating and drinking habits, the universal pastime of spitting, the freedom of women and the tyranny exercised by women. The cuspidor is no longer the most conspicuously ubiquitous item of furniture in the United States; but many of the things that caught the visitor's eye more than a century ago are exactly those that attract the visitor's attention today.

Travel writing is a form of autobiography. A man who writes about a foreign country reveals as much about himself as he does about the country he has visited. And the most rewarding accounts of the two countries included in this book come, it seems to me, from precisely those writers we would expect to provide them: Cooper, Hawthorne, Emerson, Adams and James on Britain; Cobbett, Fanny Kemble, Harriet Martineau, Thackeray, Trollope and Stevenson on the United States. They are the better writers, and that they are the better writers seems to have something to do with the fact that they have the more generous, the more hospitable, in Arnold's word the more *interesting* minds. It is not a question of enthusiasm for the other country. Trollope in America is as obstinately English as Hawthorne is obstinately American in England. As his introduction shows, he seems to have had misgivings about his mother's famous book on America. 'The writings which have been most popular in England on the subject of the United States have hitherto dealt chiefly with social details; and though in most cases true and useful, have created laughter on one side of the Atlantic, and soreness on the other.' In fact, though Trollope wrote of his mother:

> No observer was certainly ever less qualified to judge of the prospects of even the happiness of a young people. No one could have been worse adapted by nature for the task of learning whether a nation was in a way to thrive—

he wasn't, on the face of it, in a much better position himself to judge America. He liked a great many Americans but, as he writes in *An Autobiography*: 'They among Englishmen who best love and most admire the United States, have felt themselves tempted to use the strongest language in denouncing the sins of Americans ... In the midst of it all the stranger, who sees so much that he hates and so much that he loves, hardly knows how to express himself.' And then Trollope was no democrat, and however much he wanted to 'mitigate the soreness' that books like his mother's had caused in Americans, he does not spare his criticism. Yet—and this was his triumph—he knew, better, I think, than any other British visitor of his time, what the United States was all about and proclaimed it generously, in the last paragraph of his book especially, when he describes how the immigrant from Ireland is changed in America:

> It is right that all this should be acknowledged by us. When we speak of America and her institutions we should remember that she has given to our increasing population rights and privileges which we could not give—which as an old country we probably can never give. That self-asserting, obtrusive independence which so often wounds us is, if viewed aright, but an outward sign of those good things which a new country has produced for its people. Men and women do not beg in the States—they do not often offend you by tattered rags; they do not complain to heaven of starvation; they do not crouch on the ground for half-pence. If they are poor they are not abject in their poverty. They read and write. They

walk like human beings made in God's form. They know that they are men and women, owing it to themselves and to the world that they should earn their bread by their labour, but feeling that when earned it is their own. If this be so—if it be acknowledged that it is so—should not such knowledge in itself be sufficient testimony of the success of the country and of her institutions?

Not that the minor writers represented in this book don't have their moments of perception: Elihu Burrit, for instance, with the fascinating relationship he makes between the weight of the English farm wagon and the weight of the English farm-labourer's boots. And there is Isabella Bishop.

Arnold's 'Civilisation in the United States' deserves a word to itself, since it is the most considered attempt at a judgement made by a visitor to either country. Arnold had the unfortunate experience of being forced to run the gauntlet of the American press; and in some of his writings on America he seems to me disingenuous, as when, in his review of the memoirs of General Grant, he pronounces on American literature as though Hawthorne, Emerson, Melville, Thoreau, Whitman and Twain had never written. But in 'Civilisation in the United States' his appraisal in my view is very fair, given Arnold's critical position. He is subjecting American society and its institutions, the quality of American life, to the kind of scrutiny that he had subjected England to in *Culture and Anarchy*, and for similar reasons. He is taking America with the highest possible seriousness and, in doing so, paying her the highest possible compliment he can make.

Americans in Britain

Nathaniel Parker Willis

poet and editor, was born in Maine in 1806, brought up in
Boston and educated at Yale. According to Oliver Wendell
Holmes, 'he was something between a remembrance of
Count D'Orsay and an anticipation of Oscar Wilde'.
He travelled in Europe, from Turkey to Britain, from
1832 to 1836, publishing *Pencillings by the Way*, an account
of his journeys, in the latter year. He died in 1867.

From Dover to London

I WAS LYING on my back in my berth when the steamer reached her moorings at Dover, and had neither eyes nor disposition to indulge in the proper sentiments on approaching the 'white cliffs' of my fatherland. I crawled on deck, and was met by a wind as cold as December, and a crowd of rosy English faces on the pier, wrapped in cloaks and shawls, and indulging curiosity evidently at the expense of a shiver. It was the first of June.

My companion led the way to an hotel, and we were introduced by *English* waiters (I had not seen such a thing in three years, and it was quite like being waited on by gentlemen) to two blazing coal fires in the coffee room of the Ship. Oh what a comfortable place it appeared! A rich Turkey carpet snugly fitted; nicely rubbed mahogany tables; the morning papers from London; bell-ropes that *would* ring the bell; doors that *would* shut; a landlady that spoke English, and was kind and civil; and, though there were eight or ten people in the room, no noise above the rustle of a newspaper, and positively rich red damask curtains, neither second-hand nor shabby, to the windows! A greater contrast than this to the things that answer to them on the Continent could scarcely be imagined.

Malgré all my observations on the English, whom I have found everywhere the most open-hearted and social people in the world, they are said by themselves and others to be just the contrary; and, presuming they were different in England, I had made up my mind to seal my lips in all public places, and be conscious of nobody's existence but my own. There were several elderly persons dining at the different tables, and one party, of a father and son, waited on by their own servants. Candles were brought in; the different cloths were removed, and, as my companion had gone to bed, I took up a newspaper to keep me company over my wine. In the course of an hour, some remark had been addressed to me, provocative of conversation, by almost every individual in the room! The subjects of discussion soon became general, and I have seldom passed a more social and agreeable evening. And so much for the first specimen of English reserve!

The fires were burning brilliantly, and the coffee-room was in the nicest order when we descended to our breakfast at six the next morning. The tea-kettle sung on the hearth, the toast was hot, and done to a turn, and the waiter was neither sleepy nor uncivil—all, again, very unlike a morning at an hotel in *la belle* France.

The coach rattled up to the door punctually at the hour; and, while they were putting on my way-worn baggage, I stood looking in admiration at the carriage and horses. They were four beautiful bays, in small, neat harness of glazed leather, brass mounted; their coats shining like a racer's; their small blood-looking heads curbed up to stand exactly together, and their hoofs blacked and brushed with the polish of a gentleman's boots. The coach was gaudily painted, the only thing out of taste about it; but it was admirably built—the wheel-horses were quite under the coachman's box, and the whole affair, though it would carry twelve or fourteen people, covered less ground than a French one-horse cabriolet. It was altogether quite a study.

We mounted to the top of the coach; 'all right,' said the ostler, and away shot the four fine creatures, turning their small ears, and stepping together with the ease of a cat, at ten miles in the hour. The driver was dressed like a Broadway idler, and sat in his place, and held his 'ribands' and his tandem-whip with a confident air of superiority, as if he were quite convinced that he and his team were beyond criticism —and so they were. I could not but smile at contrasting his silence and the speed and ease with which we went along, with the clumsy, cumbrous Diligence or vetturino, and the crying, whipping, cursing, and all-appointed postillions of France and Italy. It seems odd, in a two-hours' passage, to pass over such strong lines of national difference —so near, and not even a shading of one into the other.

England is described always very justly, and always in the same words—'it is all one garden'. There is scarce a cottage between Dover and London (seventy miles), where a poet might not be happy to live. I saw a hundred little spots I coveted with quite a heart-ache. There was no poverty on the road. Everybody seemed employed, and every-body well-made and healthy. The relief from the deformity and dis-ease of the way-side beggars of the Continent was very striking.

We were at Canterbury before I had time to get accustomed to my seat. The horses had been changed twice—the coach, it seemed to me, hardly stopping while it was done; way-passengers were taken up and put down, with their baggage, without a word, and in half a minute; money was tossed to the keeper of the turnpike-gate as we dashed through; the wheels went over the smooth road without noise, and with scarce a sense of motion—it was the perfection of travel.

The new driver from Canterbury rather astonished me. He drove into London every day, and was more of a '*swell*'. He owned the first team himself, four blood horses of great beauty, and it was a sight to see him drive them. His language was free from all slang; very gentle-manlike and well-chosen, and he discussed everything. He found out that I was an American, and said we did not think enough of the memory of Washington. Leaving his bones in the miserable brick tomb, of which he had read descriptions, was not, in his opinion, worthy of a country like mine. He went on to criticize Giulia Grisi (the new singer just then setting London on fire), hummed airs from '*Il Pirata*', to show her manner; sang an English song like Braham; gave a de-cayed count, who sat on the box, some very sensible advice about the management of a wild son; drew a comparison between French and Italian women (he had travelled); told us who the old count was in very tolerable French, and preferred Edmund Kean and Fanny Kemble to all actors in the world. His taste and his philosophy, like his driving, were quite unexceptionable. He was, withal, very handsome, and had the easy and respectful manners of a well-bred person. It seemed very odd to give him a shilling at the end of a journey.

At Chatham we took up a very elegantly dressed young man, who had come down on a fishing excursion. He was in the army, and an Irishman. We had not been half an hour on the seat together, before he had discovered, by so many plain questions, that I was an American, a stranger in England, and an acquaintance of a whole regiment of his friends in Malta and Corfu. If this had been a Yankee, thought I, what a chapter it would have made for Basil Hall or Madame Trollope! With all his inquisitiveness I liked my companion, and half accepted his offer to drive me down to Epsom the next day to the races. I know no American who would have beaten that on a stage-coach acquain-tance.

Breakfast in Scotland

MY FRIEND HAD determined to have what he called a 'flare-up' of a Scotch breakfast, and we were set down the morning after our arrival,

[28]

at nine, to cold grouse, salmon, cold beef, marmalade, jellies, honey, five kinds of bread, oatmeal cakes, coffee, tea, and toast; and I am by no means sure that this is all. It is a fine country in which one gets so much by the simple order of 'breakfast at nine'.

Partridge Shooting

THE NOMINAL ATTRACTION of Scotland, particularly at this season, is the shooting. Immediately on your arrival, you are asked whether you prefer a flint or a percussion lock, and, supposing that you do *not* travel with a gun, which all Englishmen *do*, a double-barrelled Manton is appropriated to your use, the gamekeeper fills your powder and shot-pouches, and waits with the dogs in a leash till you have done your breakfast: and the ladies leave the table, wishing you a good day's sport —all as matters of course.

I would rather have gone to the library. An aversion to walking, except upon smooth flag-stones, a poetical tenderness on the subject of 'putting birds out of misery', as the last office is elegantly called, and hands much more at home with a goose-quill than a gun, were some of my private objections to the 'order of the day'. Between persuasion and a most truant sunshine, I was overruled, however, and, with a silent prayer that I might not destroy the hopes of my noble host, by shooting his only son, who was to be my companion and instructor, I shouldered the proffered Manton and joined the gamekeeper in the park.

Lord R — and his man looked at me with some astonishment as I approached, and I was equally surprised at the young nobleman's metamorphosis. From the elegant Oxonian I had seen at breakfast, he was transformed to a figure something rougher than his Highland dependant, in a woolen shooting-jacket, that might have been cut in Kentucky; pockets of any number and capacity; trowsers of the coarsest plaid; hob-nailed shoes and leather gaiters, and a manner of handling his gun that would have been respected on the Mississippi. My own appearance in high-heeled French boots and other corresponding gear for a tramp over stubble and marsh, amused them equally; but my wardrobe was exclusively metropolitan, and there was no alternative.

[29]

The dogs were loosed from their leash, and bounded away, and, crossing the Esk under the castle walls, we found our way out of the park, and took to the open fields. A large patch of stubble was our first ground, and with a 'hie away!' from the gamekeeper, the beautiful setters darted on before, their tails busy with delight and their noses to the ground, first dividing, each for a wall-side, and beating along till they met, and then scouring towards the centre, as regularly as if every step were guided by human reason. Suddenly they both dropped low into the stubble, and with heads eagerly bent forward and the intensest gaze upon a spot, a yard or more in advance, stood as motionless as a stone. 'A covey, my Lord!' said the gamekeeper, and, with our guns cocked, we advanced to the dogs, who had crouched, and lay as still, while we passed them, as if their lives depended upon our shot. Another step, and whirr! whirr! a dozen partridges started up from the furrow; and the while Lord R — cried 'now!' and reserved his fire to give me the opportunity, I stood stock-still in my surprise, and the whole covey disappeared over the wall. My friend laughed, the gamekeeper smiled, and the dogs hied on once more.

English aristocracy

I HAVE BEEN struck everywhere in England with the beauty of the higher classes, and as I looked around me upon the aristocratic company at the table, I thought I had never seen 'Heaven's image double-stamped as man, and noble', so unequivocally clear. There were two young men and four or five young ladies of rank—and five or six people of more decided personal attractions could scarcely be found; the style of form and face at the same time being of that cast of superiority which goes by the expressive name of 'thorough-bred'. There is a striking difference in this respect between England and the countries of the continent—the *paysans* of France, and the *contadini* of Italy, being physically far superior to their degenerate masters; while the gentry and nobility of England differ from the peasantry in limb and feature, as the racer differs from the dray-horse, or the greyhound from the cur. The contrast between the manners of English and French gentlemen is quite as striking. The *empressement*, the warmth, the shrug and gesture of the Parisian; and the working eye-brow, dilating or contracting eye, and conspirator-like action of the Italian, in the most common conversation, are the antipodes of English high breeding. I should say a North American Indian, in his more dignified phase, approached nearer to the manner of an English nobleman than any other person. The calm repose of person and feature, the self possession under all circumstances, that incapability of surprise or *dérèglement*, and that decision about the slightest circumstance, and the apparent certainty that he is acting absolutely *comme il faut*, is equally 'gentlemanlike' and Indianlike. You cannot astonish an English gentleman. If a man goes into a fit at his side, or a servant drops a dish upon his shoulder, or he hears that the house is on fire, he sets down his wine-glass with the same deliberation. He has made up his mind what to do in all possible cases, and he does it. He is cold at a first introduction, and may bow stiffly (which he always does) in drinking wine with you, but it is his manner; and he would think an Englishman out of his senses, who should bow down to his very plate, and smile, as a Frenchman does on a similar occasion. Rather chilled by this, you are a little astonished when the ladies have left the table, and he closes his chair up to you, to receive an invitation to pass a month with him at his country-house; and to discover, that at the very moment he bowed so coldly, he was thinking how he should contrive to facilitate your plans for getting to him, or seeing the country to advantage on the way.

'The true philosophy of Life'

THE GREAT SPELL of high life in this country seems to be *repose*. All violent sensations are avoided, as out of taste. In conversation, nothing is so 'odd' (a word, by the way, that in England means everything disagreeable) as emphasis or startling epithet, or gesture, and in common intercourse nothing so vulgar as any approach to 'a scene'. The high-bred Englishman studies to express himself in the plainest words that will convey his meaning, and is just as simple and calm in describing the death of his friend, and just as technical, so to speak, as in discussing the weather. For all extraordinary admiration the word 'capital' suffices; for all ordinary praise the word 'nice'; for all condemnation in morals, manners or religion, the word 'odd'. To express yourself out of this simple vocabulary is to raise the eyebrows of the whole company at once, and stamp yourself under-bred or a foreigner.

This sounds ridiculous, but it is the exponent not only of good breeding, but of the true philosophy of social life. The general happiness of a party consists in giving every individual an equal chance, and in no one's self-love. What is called an 'overpowering person', is immediately shunned, for he talks too much, and excites too much attention. In any other country he would be called 'amusing'. He is considered here as a monopolizer of the general interest, and his laurels, talk he never so well, shadow the rest of the company. You meet your most intimate friend in society after a long separation, and he gives you his hand as if you had parted at breakfast. If he had expressed all he felt, it would have been a 'scene' and the repose of the company would have been disturbed. You invite a clever man to dine with you, and he enriches his descriptions with new epithets and original words. He is offensive. He eclipses the language of your other guests, and is out of keeping with the received and subdued tone to which the most common intellect rises with ease. Society on this footing is delightful to all, and the diffident man, or the dull man, or the quiet man, enjoys it as much as another. For violent sensations you must go elsewhere. Your escape-valve is not at your neigbour's ear.

There is a great advantage in this in another respect. Your tongue never gets you into mischief. The 'unsafeness of Americans' in society (I quote a phrase I have heard used a thousand times) arises wholly from the American habit of applying high-wrought language to trifles. I can tell one of my countrymen abroad by his first remark. Ten to one his first sentence contains a superlative that would make an Englishman imagine he had lost his sense. The natural consequence is—continual misapprehension, offence is given where none was intended, words that have no meaning are the ground of quarrels, and gentlemen are shy of us. A good-natured young nobleman, whom I sat next at dinner on my first arrival at G — — Castle, told me he was hunting with Lord A —, when two very gentlemenlike young men rode up and requested leave to follow the hounds, but in such extraordinary language, that they were not at first understood. The hunt continued for some days, and at last the strangers, who rode well and were seen continually, were invited to dine with the principal noblemen of the neighbourhood. They turned out to be Americans, and were every way well-bred and agreeable, but their extraordinary mode of expressing themselves kept the company in continual astonishment. They were treated with politeness, of course, while they remained, but no little fun was made of their phraseology after their departure; and the impression on the mind of my informant was very much against the purity of the English language as spoken by Americans. I mention it for the benefit of those whom it may concern.

Brighton

BRIGHTON IS LIKE a great city, built entire, and at one job, to order. It is fresh and modern all over. It looks finished too; for there is no sign of building, and in that it is unlike an American city. Wallack did the honours of the town with great kindness, lionizing us in his 'leathern convenience' from end to end of the superb 'cliffs'—which cliffs are broad streets, beautifully Macadamised, with rows of palaces on one side, and the surf of the sea on the other. I think the two cliffs, which form a crescent with the Queen's pavilion, and the chain-pier in the centre, are something more than three miles long. The most magnificent feature in this long terrace, is a succession of squares receding from the beach, and with one side open to the sea: the houses are of a very ornamental style of building, and surmounted with balconies, low windows and belvideres, so as to command from every room and chamber a prospect of the sea. These three-sided squares are all large, with an inclosed park at the centre, and in such a windy place as Brighton, form very snug and sheltered promenades to the slender-legged invalid, and the sail-carrying-dame. Kemp Town, as it is called, forms the eastern extremity of the horn, and the square last built, though standing a hundred feet above the beach, has subterranean passages under the street, and connecting every house with baths on the sea. This is the finest bit of Brighton in point of architecture, and in one of its plainest houses lives the Duke of Devonshire.

The other features of the cliffs are small phaetons to let, for children, drawn each by a pair of *goats*, well groomed and appointed; hand-carriages for invalids; all sorts of pony-chaises sputtering about with fat ladies, and furnished invariably with the smallest conceivable boy behind; any quantity of lumbering 'double flys', or two-horse coaches, drawn by one wretched skeleton of an animal, and occupied usually

[33]

by a fat cit and his numerous family; great numbers of remarkably single-looking ladies, hanging to their parasols with one hand and fighting the wind out of their petticoats with the other; yellow-visaged East Indians forgetting their lives while they watch the struggles of these unwilling aeronauts; here and there a dandy, looking blue and damp with the chill of the salt air; and, all along the beach, half in the water, and half in the sand, in singular contrast to all this *townishness*, groups of rough sailors cleaning their boots, drying their nets, and cooking their messes on cross sticks, apparently as unconscious of the luxury and magnificence on the other side of the street, as if it were a *mirage* on the horizon.

The royal pavilion is not on the sea, and all you can see of it from the street, is a great number of peaked balloons, some small and some large, which peer above the shrubbery and wall, like the tops of the castors beyond a dish of salad. Whether it was this appetizing spectacle, or the chill of the air in a very agreeable though a very dampish drive, I was never more pleased at the conclusion of a day than with the turtle-soup, turbot, and turkey, with which Wallack wound up the wonders of Brighton. I know what the critics think of travellers who venture to acknowledge that they eat, but I must summon up courage to record the fact, that this was a glorious dinner, gloriously done justice to, and the critics may take their will of me.

The seed of this great flower upon the sea-side, was a whim of George the Fourth's, and to the excessive fright of the Brighthelmstonians, little Victoria has taken a particular dislike to it, and makes her visits briefer and briefer. The population, with the exception of the tradespeople, and a small circle of professional persons, and invalid families, is as transient as that of Saratoga and if her Majesty should succeed in making the place unfashionable, Persepolis and Thebes will be a joke to it.

Elephant and Castle

THE 'ELEPHANT AND CASTLE' is perhaps the most amusing point on this side of London; but having omitted to describe it, before it became familiarized to me, I am at a loss how to convey to you the features which strike a stranger, and which indeed, are the only ones by which any idea of it could be conveyed in a description. The inn (of which the sign is an elephant with a castle on his back,) stands at the confluence of all the roads which lead southward out of London. It is about a mile from Charing Cross, and a mile from London-bridge, the two *wrists* of the great metropolis. The west-end and city coaches for Brighton and Dover have branch coaches, which bring passengers from the opposite end of London to this point; and for the purpose of meeting these, and taking up passengers who come hither from every point in the cabs and private carriages, every coach makes a stop here of twenty minutes. This is the great starting point also of innumerable omnibuses to every quarter of town and city, a great stand for jarveys, cabs, &c. and a nest of eating-houses, ale-houses, and gin-shops. Of course here assemble all itinerant vendors of cheap razors, cheap pen-knives, ballads, oranges, soda-water, and watch-guards, and of all these articles, as you sit in the coach, you have the offer in the most eloquent Cockney and Irish, for prices ridiculously trifling. The two aristocratic races of loungers at the 'Elephant' however, are news-boys—who carry in one hand the Times, Herald, and other respectable papers, and in the other the Paul Pry, Satirist, Crim Con Gazette, &c.—and the cads and helpers to the coaches, who live by sixpences for putting up baggage, calling cabs, and arresting distant omnibuses, and by picking up what 'gentlemen' drop out of their pockets in the hurry of departure. The Elephant and Castle is the High College of slang, and those two last classes are its professors. Here originate all those brilliant expressions characteristic of 'Life in London', the 'All round my hat', 'Does your mother know you're out?' &c., familiar to all readers of flash papers, sporting chronicles, &c.

The dresses and manners of these two classes of slang makers are widely different. The newsman wears the worst possible hat, usually decorated with a crape, a black coat of the highest polish by grease and rain, no shirt, but a very smart black glass breast-pin, holding together the stringy ends of his cravat and the remains of a silk pocket-handker-chief, stuck in his breast when it does not rain—spread over his news-papers when it does. The moment the coach stops, four 'daily's' arranged like a fan are thrust before your eyes, entirely closing the coach-window, (if you are conversing with a friend, or watching the purloining of your carpet-bag, it is all one,) and immediately follows the one speech for the day, conned as regularly as a school-boy's lesson, and intended to convey an inviting picture of the news within. ' *'Osspipper*, Sir! Buy the morning pippers, Sir! Times, Herald,

Crinnicle, and Munning Post, Sir!—contains Lud Brum's entire innihalation of Lud Nummanby—Leddy Flor' Esting's murder by Lord Milbun and them maids o' honour—debate on Croolty—Hannimals Bill, and a fatil catstrophy in conskens of Loosfer matches! Which'll y'have Sir? Sixpence, only sixpence!' Here he pauses for a reply, getting a look at your face between the spread corners of his fan, which proving unpromising, he raises the contents of his left hand, another expanded fan, ingeniously exposing the names of all the scandal chronicles of the metropolis. His recommendation of these is invariably in a suppressed and confidential tone. 'Vot do you say to the Paul Pry, Sir! Here they be—Crim Con Gazette, Age, Satirist. You can't conceive, Sir! 'Vy all the sins o' the vest end—are there, Sir! with the most hinteresting partiklers! See that picter! Ain't that vell done? There's Bochsa, Sir, a-making o'love to Missus Bishop—natural as life! I've seed 'em often! Buy it, Sir! Take 'em all for sixpence! *Do*, Sir.' This touching appeal having failed at both windows, he commences the first speech again to the outside passengers, usually designating the individual, at whose attention he aims by some personal peculiarity. 'You, Sir, with that werry genteel pattern of veskit,'—or 'the gemman the bar-maid is a-oglin out o' the vinder. Yes, Sir!—she's smit with your gold spectacles, and no mistake! Buy the Munning Post, Sir!'

The *cad* is quite another style of person. He is dressed in a drab, slashy-looking, painfully-shabby driving coat, made originally for a man of twice his stature, and having one solitary and superb relic of its former glory, in a single huge mother-o'-pearl button, left somewhere on the breast. His hat is rigidly small-rimmed, and pulled over his left eye as pertinaciously as if he were taking sight by the hollow and well-worn crescent of felt, which shows the pull of his thumb. His nose is purple, the carbuncles of the gin and beer contending with the lividness of perpetual chill, from standing out of doors; and the most worn spots in his coat, oddly enough, are the two shoulders, either from his habit of always nudging the next cad with his 'I say, Bob!' when he is about to say something witty, or from leaning by the hour against the post of the gin-shop. As he never takes his hands from his coat pockets, except to receive sixpence, or square away for a fight, his shoulders naturally do all the reminding, shoving, and leaning, besides most adroitly supplying the place occasionally of both hand and pocket-handkerchief to the above-mentioned purple organ. The cad is never a fool; indeed he requires to have great quickness, uncommon impudence, wit, and courage. He is usually some turned-off tiger, who proved too wicked for a recommendation, or a second-rate boxer who is within one, of Molyneux and Dutch Sam, and probably has seen life in many shapes, and the inside of most prisons before he is sufficiently reduced and accomplished to be willing to turn cad, and steal and bully under the very noses of the police. I should have mentioned, that amid the crowd at 'the Elephant' are constantly seen perambulating three or four policemen in their blue coats and glazed hats, ready to pounce upon every offender; but meanwhile on joking and drinking terms with the undetected cads and newsmen. It is very unwise to be savage with the cad, and it is rather uncomfortable to decline his services when he sees that you might get on the better for them. The best way is to accept his offer at once, to tell him exactly what you want, and so be rid of all his fraternity, and your own embarrassment. It is a kind of sixpenny toll levied in favour of the brotherhood, which is best paid without grumbling, unless you are very well acquainted at 'the Elephant'.

James Fenimore Cooper

The practice of appointing distinguished writers to consulates
abroad that were largely sinecures was one of the most amiable
features of American government in the 19th century. As the author
of *The Last of the Mohicans*, James Fenimore Cooper was the
most famous living American writer when he was made U.S. Consul
at Lyons in 1826. He was then 37 and already a notably prickly
and cantankerous observer of the contemporary scene both native
and foreign. During his seven years in Europe, he spent many
months in London, publishing his impressions of English life
and society, *England*, in 1837. He died at Cooperstown, New York,
in 1851.

English order

ONE OF THE merits of England is the perfect order in which everything is kept, and the perfect method with which everything is done.
One sees no cracked cups, no tea-pots with broken noses, no knives
thin as wafers, no forks with one prong longer than the other, no coach
wanting a glass, no substitute for a buckle, no crooked poker or tongs
loose in the joint, no knife that won't cut, no sugar cracked in lumps
too big to be used, no hat unbrushed, no floor with a hole in it, no
noisy servants, no bell that won't ring, no window that won't open,
no door that won't shut, no broken pane, nor anything out of repair
that might have been mended. I now speak of the eyes of him who can
pay. In France, half of these incongruities are to be met with amid
silken curtains and broad mirrors, though France is rapidly improving
in this respect; but, at home, we build on a huge scale, equip with cost,
and take refuge in expedients as things go to decay. We are not as bad
as the Irish are said to be, in this respect; but he who insists on having
things precisely as they ought to be, is usually esteemed a most un-
reasonable rogue, more especially in the interior. We satisfy ourselves
by acknowledging a standard of merit in comforts, but little dream of
acting up to it. We want servants, and mechanical labour is too costly.
The low price at which comforts are retailed here, has greatly surprised
me. I feel persuaded that most of the common articles of English
manufacture come to the consumer in America at about thrice their
original cost.

From the dome of Saint Paul's

NOT SATISFIED WITH the whispering-gallery, we ascended to another
on the exterior of the dome, where we found one of the most extraordinary bird's-eye views of a town I remember ever to have seen. The
day was clear, cool, and calm, and, of course, the vapour of the
atmosphere floated at some distance above the houses. The whole

panorama presented a field of dingy bricks, out of which were issuing thousands of streams of smoke, ascending in right lines to the canopy of murky vapour above. The effect was to give this vast dusty-looking cloud the appearance of standing on an infinity of slender vapoury columns. In a small district around the cathedral there also arose a perfect *chevaux de frise* of spires and towers, the appendages of the ordinary parish churches, of which London proper contains an incredible number. Some one said that three hundred might be counted from the gallery, and really it did not strike me that there could be many less.

Seen in this manner, London offers little to be mentioned in comparison with Paris. It has no background, wants the grey angular walls, the transparent atmosphere, the domes and monuments, for we were on the only one of the former, and the general distinctness, necessary to satisfy the eye. It was not always easy to see at all in the distance, and the objects were principally tame and confused. I like mists, feathery, floating, shadowy mists, but have no taste for coal smoke.

Anti-American Prejudice

IT IS NOT easy for an American to imagine the extent of the prejudice which exists against his country in England, without close and long observation. One of its effects is frequently to cause those who were born on our side of the water, or who have connections there, to wish to conceal the fact. Two anecdotes connected with this feeling have come to my knowledge, and I will relate them.

A gentleman of one of our well-known families was put young in the British army. Circumstances favoured his advancement, until he rose early to a situation of high honour, and of considerable emolument. Speaking of his prospects and fortune, not long since, to a near relative, who mentioned the anecdote to me, he felicitated himself on his good luck, adding, that 'he should have been the happiest fellow in the world had he not been born in America!'

An Englishman married an American wife, and their first child was born in the country of the mother. Alluding to the subject, one day, an American observed, 'But you are one of us; you were born in the United States.' Observing his friend change colour, he asked him if he really had any feeling on the subject; when the other frankly admitted, 'there was so strong a prejudice against America in England, that he felt a reluctance to own that he was born there!'

London streets

WHEN WE FIRST arrived here from Paris, I was disposed to deny that the streets of London were as crowded as it is usual to pretend. My opinion was formed too soon. What was then true, is so no longer. London, or rather Westminster, in the height of the season, and Westminster out of the season, so far as the movement in the streets is concerned, are not the same town.

When I was here in 1826, I saw no essential difference between Regent-street and Broadway, as regards the crowd; but now that we have passed the Easter holidays, every one appears to be at his post, and so far from having ever seen anywhere else the crowds of people, the display of rich equipages, the incessant and grand movement that adorn and bewilder the streets of London, I had never even pictured such a sight in my imagination. They who have not been here at this season of the year know nothing of the place. There is a part of the day, between one and six, when it is actually a matter of risk for a pedestrian to cross the streets.

I live near Piccadilly, which is not wider than Broadway, if quite as wide, and I have occasion to cross it frequently. You know I am no laggard, and am not deficient in activity; and yet I find it convenient to make my first run towards a stand of coaches in the middle of the street, protected by which I take a fresh departure for the other side. Regent-street is still worse; and there is a place at Charing-cross that would be nearly impracticable, but for a statue of Charles I, which makes a capital lee for one on foot. As for Broadway, and its pretended throng, I have been in the current of coaches in what is called the city here, for an hour at a time, when the whole distance was made through a jam, as close as any you have ever seen in that street, for the space of a hundred yards. Broadway will compare with the more crowded streets of London, much as Chestnut-street will compare with Broadway.

I frequently stop and look about me in wonder, distrusting my

[42]

eyes, at the exhibition of wealth and luxury that is concentrated in such narrow limits. Our horses have none of the grand movement that the cattle are trained to do in Europe generally, and these of London seem, as they dash furiously along, as if they were trampling the earth under their feet. They are taught a high carriage, and as they are usually animals of great size as well as fleetness, their approach is sometimes terrific. By fleetness, however, I do not mean that you, as a Queen's county man, and one who comes of a sporting stock, would consider them as doing a thing 'in time', but merely the fleetness of a coach-horse. As to foot, I have little doubt that we can match England any day. I think we could show as good a stock of roadsters, both for draught and the saddle; but we appear to want the breed of the English carriage-horse; or, if we possess it at all, it is crossed, dwindled and inferior.

English proprieties

ENGLAND IS A country of proprieties. Were I required to select a single word that should come nearest to the national peculiarities, it would be this. It pervades society from its summit to its base, essentially affecting *appearances* when it affects nothing else. It enters into the religion, morals, politics, the dwelling, the dress, the equipages, the habits, and one may say, all the opinions of the nation. At this moment I shall confine the application of this fact to the subject before us.

It would not be easy to imagine more appropriate rules than those which pervade the whole system of the stable in England. It is so perfect, that I deem it worthy of special notice. One might possibly object to some of the carriages as being too heavy; but the excellence of the cattle and of the roads must be considered, and the size of the vehicles give them an air of magnificence. What would be called a *showy* carriage is rarely seen here, the taste inclining to an elegant simplicity; though, on state occasions at court, carriages do appear that are less under laws so severe.

The king is seldom seen; but when he does appear, it is in a style as unlike that of his brother of France as may be. I have witnessed his departure from St James's for Windsor, lately. He was in a post-chariot, with one of his sisters, another carriage following. Four horses were in harness, held by two postilions, while two more rode together, on horses with blinkers and collars, but quite free from the carriage, a few paces in advance. Four mounted footmen came in the rear, while a party of lancers cleared the way, and another closed the *cortége*. There was no *piqueur*. He went off at a slapping pace. On state occasions, of course, his style is more regal.

Five-and-twenty years since, families of rank often went into the country with coaches and six, followed by mounted footmen. I have seen nothing of this sort now. Post-chariots and four are common, but most people travel with only two horses. The change is owing to the improvements in the roads. It is only at the races, I believe, that the great 'turn outs' are now made . . .

You have not the smallest conception of what a livery is. A coat of some striking colour, white, perhaps, covered with lace, red plush vest and breeches, white stockings, shoes and buckles, a laced round hat with a high cockade, a powdered head and a gold-headed cane, constitute the glories of the footman. A shovel-nosed hat and a wig, with a coat of many capes spread on the hammercloths, in addition, set up the Jehu. Two footmen behind a carriage seem indispensable to style; though more appear on state ceremonies. Chasseurs belong rather to the Continent, and are not common here. But all these things are brought in rigid subjection to the code of propriety. The commoner, unless of note, may not affect too much state. If the head of an old county family, however, he may trespass hard on nobility. If a *parvenu*, let him beware of cockades and canes! There is no other law but use in these matters; but while an Englishman may do a hundred things that would set an American county in a ferment of police excitement, he cannot encroach on the established proprieties with impunity. The reckless wretch would be cut, as an Ishmaelite. Vanity sometimes urges an unfortunate across the line, and he is lampooned, laughed at, and caricatured, until it is thought to be immoral to appear in his society.

The tall and the short

ENGLAND IS THE country of the wealthy. So far as the mass can derive benefits from the compulsory regulations of their superiors (and positive benefits, beyond question, are as much obtained in this manner as fleets, armies, and prisons are made more comfortable to their *personnels* by discipline,) it may expect them; but when the interests of the two clash, the weak are obliged to succumb.

The celebrated division of labour, that has so much contributed to the aggrandizement of England, extends to the domestic establishments. Men are assorted for service, as in armies; size and appearance being quite as much, and in many cases more, consulted, than character. Five feet ten and upwards, barring extraordinary exceptions, make a footman's fortune. These are engaged in the great houses; those that are smaller squeeze in where they can, or get into less pretending mansions. All the little fellows sink into pot-boys, grooms, stable-men, and attendants at the inns . . .

The upper classes of the English are, as a whole, a fine race of people; and, as they lay so much stress on the appearance of their dependants, it is not unusual to see one of diminutive stature, or ungainly exterior near their dwellings. The guards, the regiments principally kept about London, are picked men, so that there is a concentration of fine forms of both sexes to be met with in the streets. The dwarfs congregate about the stables, or mews as they are called here; and, now and then, one is seen skulking along with a pot of beer in his hand. But in the streets, about the equipages, or at the doors of the houses, surprisingly few but the well-looking of both sexes are seen.

As strangers commonly reside in this part of the town, they are frequently misled by these facts, in making up their opinions of the relative stature of the English and other nations. I feel persuaded that the men of England, as a whole, are essentially below the stature of the men of America. They are of fuller habit; a consequence of climate, in a certain degree, but chiefly, I believe, from knowing how and what to eat: but the average of their frames, could the fact be come at, I feel persuaded would fall below our own. Not so with the women.

England appears to have two very distinct races of both men and women; the tall and the short. The short are short indeed, and they are much more numerous than a casual observer would be apt to imagine. Nothing of the sort exists with us. I do not mean that we have no small men, but they are not seen in troops as they are seen here. I have frequently met with clusters of these little fellows in London, not one of whom was more than five feet, or five feet one or two inches high. In the drawing-room, and in public places frequented by the upper classes, I find myself a medium-sized man; whereas on the Continent, I was much above that mark.

In America it is unusual to meet with a woman of any class who approaches the ordinary stature of men. Nothing is more common in England, especially in the upper circles. I have frequently seen men, and reasonably tall men too, walking with their wives, between whose statures there was no perceptible difference. Now such a thing is very rare with us, but very common here; so common, I think, as to remove the suspicion that the eye may be seeking exceptions, in the greater throngs of a condensed population; a circumstance against which it is very necessary to guard, in making comparisons as between England and America.

Windsor

WE TOOK ANOTHER day to go to Windsor, which is twenty miles from town. Here the Thames is scarcely larger than the Susquehannah at Cooperstown, flowing quite near the castle. The town is neat but irregular, and as unlike Versailles as England is unlike France. This is a snug, compact, beef-and-beer sort of place, in which one might enjoy a sea-coal fire and a warm dinner while waiting for a stage-coach; the other awakens the recollections of Burgundy and made dishes, and of polite life. One may expect a royal *cortège* to come sweeping down the stately avenues of Versailles at any moment, whereas the appearance of style in the streets of Windsor excites a sense of unfitness. One leaves an impression of a monarch who deems a kingdom erected for his use, who forces nature and triumphs over difficulties to attain the magnificent; the other, of the head of a state, profiting by accident to obtain an abode in which his comforts are blinded with a long chain of historical images.

Servants in England

THE POOR OF this country appear to me to be overworked. They have little or no time for relaxation; and instead of exhibiting that frank, manly cheerfulness, and heartiness of feeling that have been so much extolled, they appear sullen, discontented, and distrustful. There is far less confidence and sympathy between classes, than I had expected to see; for, although a good understanding may exist between the great landholder and the affluent yeoman who pays him rent, and farms the soil, the social chain appears to be broken between those below the latter and their superiors. I do not mean that the rich are obdurate to the sufferings of the poor, but that the artificial condition of the country has choked the ordinary channels of sympathy, and that the latter, when known at all, are known only as the *poor*. They are the objects of duties, rather than fellow-creatures living constantly within the influence of all the charities, including those of communion and rights, as well as those which are exhibited in donations.

There is one large class of being, in England, whose condition I should think less enviable than that of Asiatic slaves. I allude to the female servants of all-work, in the families of those who keep lodging-houses, tradesmen, and other small house-keepers. These poor creatures have an air of dogged sullen misery that I have never seen equalled in any other class of human beings, not even excepting the beggars in the streets. In our lodgings at Southampton there was one of these girls, and her hand was never idle, her foot seemed to know no rest, while her manner was that of wearied humility. We were then fresh from home, and the unmitigated toil of her existence struck us all most painfully. When we spoke to her kindly, she seemed startled, and looked distrustful and frightened. A less inviting subject for sympathy could scarcely be imagined, for she was large, coarse, robust, and even masculine, but even these iron qualities were taxed beyond endurance.

I should not draw a picture like this, on the authority of a single instance. I have seen too much to corroborate the first impressions, and make no doubt that the case of the woman at Southampton was the rule, and that instances of better treatment make the exceptions. In one of my bachelor visits here, I had lodgings in which there was a still more painful example. The mistress of this house was married and had children, and being a lazy slattern, with three sets of lodgings in the house, her tyranny exceeded all I had ever before witnessed. You are to understand that the solitary servant, in these houses, is usually cook, housemaid, and waiter. When the lodger keeps no servant, she answers his bell, as well as the street-door knocker, and goes on all his errands that do not extend beyond a proper distance. The girl was handsome, had much delicacy of form and expression, and an eye that nature had intended to be brilliant and spirited. She could not be more than twenty-two or three, but misery had already driven her to the bottle. I saw her only at the street-door, and on two or three occasions when she answered my own bell, in the absence of my man. At the street-door, she stood with her eyes on the carpet, and when I made my acknowledgements for the trouble she had taken, she curtsied hurriedly, and muttered the usual 'Thankee, sir'. When she came into my room, it was on a sort of drilled trot, as if she had been taught a particular movement to denote assiduity and diligence, and she never presumed to raise her eyes to mine, but stood the whole time looking meekly down. For every order I was duly thanked! One would think that all this was hard to be borne, but, a day or two before I left the house, I found her weeping in the street. She had disobliged her lazy exacting mistress, by staying out ten minutes too long on an errand, and had lost her place. I took the occasion to give her a few shillings as her due for past services, but so complete was her misery in being turned away without a character, that even the sight of money failed to produce the usual effects. I make little doubt she took refuge in gin, the bane of thousands and tens of thousands of her sex in this huge theatre of misery and vice.

The order, method, and punctuality of the servants of England are all admirable. These qualities probably contribute quite as much to their own comfort as to that of their masters and mistresses. It is seldom that well-bred persons, anywhere, are unkind to their menials, though they are sometimes exacting through ignorance of the pain they are giving. The tyranny comes from those who always appear to feel a desire to revenge their own previous hardships on the unfortunate creatures whom chance puts in their powers. I do not know that the English of condition are unkind to their domestics; the inference would fairly be that they are not; but there is something, either in the system that has unfortunately been adopted, or in the character of the people, which has introduced a distance between the parties that must be injurious to the character of those who serve . . .

The comparison between the condition of the common English

house-servant and that of the American slave is altogether in favour of the latter, if the hardship of compelled servitude be kept out of view. The negro, bond or free, is treated much more kindly and with greater friendship, than most of the English domestics; the difference in colour, with the notions that have grown up under them, removing all distrust of danger from familiarity. This is not said with a view to turn the tables on our kinsmen for their numberless taunts and continued injustice; for, with such an object, I think something more original and severe might easily be got up; but simply because I believe it to be true. Perhaps the servants of no country have more enviable places than the American slaves, so far as mere treatment and the amount of labour are concerned.

London street music

SPEAKING OF THE music of England, you are not to understand that there is no good music here. The gold of the country attracts the first artists of Europe, as a matter of course; but even the cultivated English have, quite obviously, not much more feeling for the art than we have ourselves. As a greater portion travel, their tastes are a little more cultivated than those of our people; but nothing strikes one sooner, than the obvious difference in feeling between an English audience at the opera, and one on the continent of Europe.

Still, the street music of London is positively the best in the world. The improvement in the last few years, even, is quite apparent. Respectable artists, such as would gladly be received in our orchestras, walk the streets, and play the music of Rossini, Mozart, Beethoven, Meyerbeer, Weber, &c. beneath your windows. London is not as well arranged for this species of enjoyment as the towns of the Continent, for there are no courts in which the performers can get away from the clamour of the streets; but, about eight, the carriages cease, everybody being at dinner, and most of the more private places are quite silent. Since the weather has become mild, I have frequently paused in my evening walks, to listen to airs that have come from the harp, violin, and flageolet, and have almost fancied myself in Venice, or Naples, though surrounded by the dingy bricks of London. A party of French have found us out, and they come regularly twice a week, and play old

French airs beneath the windows; favours that are seldom conferred on private houses, the public hotels being their usual stopping places. The secret of this unusual feature in the town, is in the fact, that where an Italian, or a Frenchman, though filled with enthusiasm, would bestow a few sous, the Englishman, with immovable muscles, throws out half-a-crown. Walking to a dinner, the other evening, I heard a grand piano, on which some one was playing an overture of Rossini, accompanied by a flageolet, and, going a little out of my way to ascertain the cause, I found the artist in the street, seated before the open windows of a hotel. He trundled the machine about on a sort of wheelbarrow, and his execution was quite equal to what one usually hears in society.

English independence

THE ENGLISH ARE to be distinguished from the Americans by greater independence of personal habits. Not only the institutions, but the physical condition of our own country has a tendency to reduce us all to the same level of usages. The steam-boats, the overgrown taverns, the speculative character of the enterprises, and the consequent disposition to do all things in common, aid the tendency of the system in bringing about such a result. In England a man dines by himself, in a room filled with other hermits; he eats at his leisure, drinks his wine in silence, reads the paper by the hour, and, in all things, encourages his individuality and insists on his particular humours. The American is compelled to submit to a common rule; he eats when others eat, sleeps when others sleep, and he is lucky, indeed, if he can read the paper in a tavern without a stranger looking over each shoulder. The Englishman would stare at a proposal that should invade his habits under the pretence of a common wish, while the American would be very apt to yield tacitly, though this common wish should be more than an impudent assertion of some one who had contrived to effect his own purposes, under the popular plea. The Englishman is so much attached to his independence that he instinctively resists every effort to invade it, and nothing would be more likely to arouse him than to say the mass thinks differently from himself; whereas the American ever seems ready to resign his own opinion to that which is made to seem the opinion of the public. I say *seems* to be, for so manifest is the power of public opinion, that one of the commonest expedients of all American managers, is to create an impression that the public thinks in a particular way, in order to bring the common mind in subjection. One often renders himself ridiculous by a foolish obstinacy, and the other is as often contemptible by a weak compliance. A portion of what may be called the *community* of character and habits in America, is doubtless owing to the rustic nature of its society, for one more easily maintains his independence in a capital than in a village, but I think the chief reasons are to be found in the practice of referring everything to the common mind.

It is usual to ascribe the solitary and unsocial habits of English life to the natural dispositions of the people, but, I think, unjustly. The climate is made to bear the blame of no small portion of this peculiarity. Climate, probably, has an influence on us all, for we know that we are more elastic and more ready to be pleased in a clear bracing air, than in one that is close and *sciroccoish*; but, on the whole, I am led to think, the English owe their habits to their institutions, more than to any natural causes . . .

In most things that pertain to taste, the English have greatly the advantage of us, though *taste* is certainly not the strong side of English character. On this point, alone, one might write a book, but a very few remarks must now satisfy you. In nothing, however, is this superiority more apparent, than in their simplicity, and, particularly, in their simplicity of language. They call a spade a spade. I very well know, that neither men nor women, in America, who are properly educated, and who are accustomed to its really better tone, differ much, if any, from the English in this particular; but, in this case, as in most others, in which *national* peculiarities are sought, the better tone of America is overshadowed by its mediocrity. Although I deem the government of this country the very quintessence of hocus pocus, having scarcely a single practice that does not violate its theory, I believe that there is more honesty of public sentiment in England than in America. The defect at home, I ascribe, in common with the majority of our national failings, to the greater activity, and greater *unresisted* force of ignorance and cupidity, there, than here. High qualities are nowhere collected in a sufficient phalanx to present a front to the enemy, in America.

The besetting, the degrading vice of America, is the moral cowardice by which men are led to truckle to what is called public opinion; though this opinion is as inconstant as the winds—though, in all cases that enlist the feelings of factions, there are *two*, and sometimes twenty, each differing from all the others, and though, nine times in ten, these opinions are mere engines set in motion by the most corrupt and the least respectable portion of the community, for unworthy purposes. The English are a more respectable and constant nation than the Americans, as relates to this peculiarity; probably, because the condensed masses of intelligence and character enable the superior portion of the community to produce a greater impression on the inferior, by their collective force. In standing prejudices, they strike me as being worse than ourselves; but in passing impressions, greatly our superiors.

Leaving England

QUITTING ENGLAND IS, by no means, as easy a matter for a foreigner, as quitting almost any other European state. I was obliged to go first to the alien office, which is near Westminster Hall, and then proceed to the custom-house, a distance of several miles, in order to get the required permission. If all these forms are necessary, (and I shall not take it on myself to say they are not,) it would save trouble could everything be done in the same office, or, at least, in the same building.

My labours in obtaining the permit to embark, and in taking a passage, have taught me a secret in relation to the advantage we possess over the English in sailing ships. The excess of men causes all occupations to be crowded, and as each *employé* must have a livelihood out of his employment, he becomes a charge on the business. If an Englishman could live on a bit of garlic and a few chestnuts, this would not be of so much moment; but he is a beef-eating and a beer-drinking animal, and likes to be neat in his attire, and the trade is compelled to pay a pretty good price for his support. Thus, when I went on board the steamboat to take the necessary passage, I was compelled to return to the shore, and walk, at least, half a mile to an office to effect my purpose. The person to whom I was referred received me civilly, but after making his bow, he put his hands in his pockets, and ordered two or three clerks to receive my money, enter my name, and do the other necessary things. In America the captain would do all this himself, and would find no time to put his hands in his breeches pockets.

William Cullen Bryant

(1794–1878) was born at Cummington, Massachusetts, and trained for the law. He earned a reputation as a poet with affinities to Wordsworth and abandoned the law to become an editor of the New York *Evening Post*. Throughout his life, he was a champion of free speech, civil rights, abolition of slavery and the rights of labour. His death—after delivering a speech at the dedication of a statue of Mazzini in Central Park—seems characteristic of the man. His travel sketches, *Letters of a Traveller*, was published in 1850.

Railway travel in England

Manchester, May 30, 1845.

. . . YESTERDAY WE TOOK the railway for Manchester. The arrangements for railway travelling in this country are much more perfect than with us. The cars of the first class are fitted up in the most sumptuous manner, cushioned at the back and sides, with a resting-place for your elbows, so that you sit in what is equivalent to the most luxurious arm-chair. Some of the cars intended for night travelling are so contrived that the seat can be turned into a kind of bed. The arrangements of springs and other contrivances to prevent shocks, and to secure an equable motion, are admirable and perfectly effectual. In one hour we had passed over the thirty-one miles which separate Manchester from Liverpool; shooting rapidly over Chat Moss, a black blot in the green landscape, overgrown with heath, which, at this season of the year, has an almost sooty hue, crossing bridge after bridge of the most solid and elegant construction, and finally entered Manchester by a viaduct, built on massive arches, at a level with the roofs of the houses and churches. Huge chimneys surrounded us on every side, towering above the house-tops and the viaduct, and vomiting smoke like a hundred volcanoes.

The police—and the poor

London, June 24, 1845.

. . . I CALLED THE other day on a friend, an American, who told me that he had that morning spoken with his landlady about her carelessness in leaving the shutters of her lower rooms unclosed during the night. She answered that she never took the trouble to close them, that so secure was the city from ordinary burglaries, under the arrangements of the new police, that it was not worth the trouble. The windows of the parlour next to my sleeping-room open upon a rather low balcony over the street door, and they are unprovided with any fastenings, which in New York we should think a great piece of negligence. Indeed, I am told that these night robberies are no longer practiced, except when the thief is assisted by an accessary in the house. All classes of the people appear to be satisfied with the new police. The officers are men of respectable appearance and respectable manners. If I lose my way, or stand in need of any local information, I apply to a person in the uniform of a police officer. They are sometimes more stupid in regard to these matters than there is any occasion for, but it is one of their duties of their office to assist strangers with local information.

Begging is repressed by the new police regulations, and want skulks in holes and corners, and prefers its petitions where it can not be overheard by men armed with the authority of the law. 'There is a great deal of famine in London,' said a friend to me the other day, 'but the police regulations drive it out of sight.' I was going through Oxford-street lately, when I saw an elderly man of small stature, poorly dressed, with a mahogany complexion, walking slowly before me. As I passed him he said in my ear, with a hollow voice, 'I am starving to death with hunger', and these words and that hollow voice sounded in my ear all day.

Walking in Hampstead Heath a day or two since, with an English friend, we were accosted by two labourers, who were sitting on a bank, and who said that they had come to that neighbourhood in search of employment in hay-making, but had not been able to get either work or food. My friend appeared to distrust their story. But in the evening, as we were walking home, we passed a company of some four or five labourers in frocks, with bludgeons in their hands, who asked us for something to eat. 'You see how it is, gentlemen,' said one of them, 'we are hungry; we have come for work, and nobody will hire us; we have had nothing to eat all day.' Their tone was dissatisfied, almost menacing; and the Englishman who was with us, referred to it several times afterward, with an expression of anxiety and alarm.

I hear it often remarked here, that the difference of condition between the poorer and the richer classes becomes greater every day, and what the end will be the wisest pretend not to foresee.

Edinburgh

... ALL AROUND YOU are places the names of which are familiar names of history, poetry, and romance.

From this magnificence of nature and art, the transition was painful to what I saw of the poorer population. On Saturday evening I found myself at the market, which is then held in High-street and the Netherbow, just as you enter the Canon-gate, and where the old wooden effigy of John Knox, with staring black eyes, freshly painted every year, stands in its pulpit, and still seems preaching to the crowd. Hither a throng of sickly-looking, dirty people, bringing with them their unhealthy children, had crawled from the narrow wynds or alleys on each side of the street. We entered several of these wynds, and passed down one of them, between houses of vast height, storey piled upon storey, till we came to the deep hollow of the Cowgate. Children were swarming in the way, all of them, bred in that close and impure atmosphere, of a sickly appearance, and the aspect of premature age in some of them, which were carried in arms, was absolutely frightful. 'Here is misery', said a Scotch gentleman, who was my conductor. I asked him how large a proportion of the people of Edinburgh belonged to that wretched and squalid class which I saw before me. 'More than half', was his reply. I will not vouch for the accuracy of his statistics. Of course his estimate was but a conjecture.

In the midst of this population is a House of Refuge for the Destitute, established by charitable individuals for the relief of those who may be found in a state of absolute destitution of the necessaries of life. Here they are employed in menial services, lodged and fed until they can be sent to their friends, or employment found for them. We went over the building, a spacious structure, in the Canongate, of the plainest Puritan architecture, with wide low rooms, which, at the time of the union of Scotland with England, served as the mansion of the Duke of Queensbury. The accommodations of course are of the humblest kind. We were shown into the sewing-room, where we saw several healthy-looking young women at work, some of them barefooted. Such of the inmates as can afford it, pay for their board from three and sixpence to five shillings a week, besides their labour.

In this part of the city also are the Night Asylums for the Houseless.

Here, those who find themselves without shelter for the night, are received into an antechamber, provided with benches, where they first get a bowl of soup, and then are introduced into a bathing-room, where they are stripped and scoured. They are next furnished with clean garments and accommodated with a lodging on an inclined plane of planks, a little raised from the floor, and divided into proper compartments by strips of board. Their own clothes are, in the meantime, washed, and returned to them when they leave the place.

It was a very different spectacle from the crowd in the Saturday evening market, that met my eyes the next morning in the clean and beautiful streets of the new town; the throng of well-dressed churchgoers passing each other in all directions. The women, it appeared to me, were rather gaily dressed, and a large number of them prettier than I have seen in some of the more southern cities.

Bayard Taylor

born in Pennsylvania in 1825, was apprenticed to a printer but purchased his indentures and embarked on a walking-tour of Europe. The result was *Views Afoot*, published when he was 21. It was the beginning of a distinguished career as poet, journalist and indefatigable traveller, which culminated in his translation of Goethe's *Faust* and his appointment as U.S. Ambassador to Germany. He died in Berlin in 1878.

Unemployed miners

I WITNESSED A scene at Newcastle that cannot soon be forgotten; as it showed more plainly than I had before an opportunity of observing, the state to which the labouring classes of England are reduced. Hearing singing in the street, under my window, one morning, I looked out and saw a body of men, apparently of the lower class, but decent and sober looking, who were singing in a rude and plaintive strain some ballad, the purport of which I could not understand. On making inquiry, I discovered it was part of a body of miners, who, about eighteen weeks before, in consequence of not being able to support their families with the small pittance allowed them, had 'struck' for higher wages. This their employers refused to give them, and sent to Wales, where they obtained workmen at the former price. The houses these labourers had occupied were all taken from them, and for eighteen weeks they had no other means of subsistence than the casual charity given them for singing the story of their wrongs. It made my blood boil to hear those tones, wrung from the heart of poverty by the hand of tyranny. The ignorance, permitted by the government, causes an unheard amount of misery and degradation. We heard afterwards in the streets, another company who played on musical instruments. Beneath the proud swell of England's martial airs, there sounded to my ears a tone whose gathering murmur will make itself heard ere long by the dull ears of Power.

Crime in London

...IF LONDON IS unsurpassed in splendour, it has also its corresponding share of crime. Notwithstanding the large and efficient body of police, who do much towards the control of vice, one sees enough of degradation and brutality in a short time, to make his heart sick. Even the public thoroughfares are thronged at night with characters of the lowest description, and it is not expedient to go through many of the narrow bye-haunts of the old city in the day-time. The police, who are ever on the watch, immediately seize and carry off any offender, but from the statements of persons who have had an opportunity of observing, as well as from my own slight experience, I am convinced that there is an untold amount of misery and crime. London is one of the wonders of the world, but there is reason to believe it is one of the curses of the world also; though, in fact, nothing but an active and unceasing philanthropy can prevent any city from becoming so.

Greenwich Fair

A FEW DAYS ago, an American friend invited me to accompany him to Greenwich Fair. We took a penny steamer from Hungerford Market to London Bridge, and jumped into the cars, which go every five minutes. Twelve minutes' ride above the chimneys of London and the vegetable fields of Rotherhithe and Deptford brought us to Greenwich, and we followed the stream of people which was flowing from all parts of the city into the Park.

Here began the merriment. We heard on every side the noise of the 'scratchers', or, as the venders of these articles denominated them— 'the fun of the fair'. By this is meant a little notched wheel, with a piece of wood fastened to it, like a miniature watch-man's rattle. The 'fun' consists in drawing them down the back of any one you pass, when they make a sound precisely like that of ripping cloth. The women take a great delight in this, and as it is only deemed politeness to return the compliment, we soon had enough to do. Nobody seemed to take the diversion amiss, but it was so irresistibly droll to see a large crowd engaged in this singular amusement, that we both burst into hearty laughter.

As we began ascending Greenwich Hill, we were assailed with another kind of game. The ground was covered with smashed oranges, with which the people above and below were stoutly pelting each other. Half a dozen heavy ones whizzed uncomfortably near my head as I went up, and I saw several persons get the full benefit of a shot in their backs and breasts. The young country lads and lasses amused themselves by running at full speed down the steep side of a hill. This was, however, a feat attended with some risk; for I saw one luckless girl describe an arc of a circle, of which her feet was the centre and her body the radius. All was noise and nonsense. They ran to and fro under the long, hoary boughs of the venerable oaks that crest the summit, and clattered down the magnificent forest-avenues, whose budding foliage gave them little shelter from the passing April showers.

London fog

LONDON HAS THE advantage of one of the most gloomy atmospheres in the world. During this opening spring weather, no light and scarcely any warmth can penetrate the dull, yellowish-gray mist, which incessantly hangs over the city. Sometimes at noon we have for an hour or two a sickly gleam of sunshine, but it is soon swallowed up by the smoke and drizzling fog. The people carry umbrellas at all times, for the rain seems to drop spontaneously out of the very air, without waiting for the usual preparation of a gathering cloud... A few days ago we had a real fog—a specimen of November weather, as the people said. If November wears such a mantle, London, during that sober month, must furnish a good idea of the gloom of Hades. The streets were wrapped in a veil of dense mist, a dirty yellow color, as if the air had suddenly grown thick and mouldy. The houses on the opposite sides of the street were invisible, and the gas-lamps, lighted in the shops, burned with a white and ghastly flame. Carriages ran together in the streets, and I was kept constantly on the look-out, lest someone should come suddenly out of the cloud around me, and we should meet with a shock like that of the two knights at a tournament. As I stood in the centre of Trafalgar Square, with every object invisible around me, it reminded me, (hoping the comparison will not be accepted in every particular) of Satan resting in the middle of Chaos. The weather sometimes continues thus for whole days together.

Herman Melville

born in New York City in 1819, sailed as a cabin-boy to
Liverpool at the age of 18. His experiences, and his
impressions of Liverpool, are related in his fourth novel,
Redburn. Twelve years later, he visited England as a
professional writer, in order to find a publisher for his novel
of life in the U.S. Navy, *White Jacket*. He died in New York,
the greatest American imaginative writer of the century,
in 1891 almost entirely forgotten, and remained forgotten
for 30 years.

From Melville's Journal

Friday, November 9 (1849)
BREAKFASTED LATE, & went down to Queen's Hotel—saw McCurdy there & Mulligan. Parted from the Doctor & Adler near the Post Office, & went into Cheapside to see the 'Lord Mayor's Show' it being the day of the great civic feast and festivities. A most bloated pomp, to be sure. Went down to the bridges to see the people crowding there. Crossed by Westminster, through the Parks to the Edgware Road, & found the walk delightful—the sun coming out a little, & the air not cold. While on one of the Bridges, the thought struck me again that a fine thing might be written about a Blue Monday in November London—a city of Dis (Dante's)—clouds of smoke O the damned &c. —coal barges—coaly waters, cast-iron Duke &c.—its marks are left upon you, &c. &c. &c.

Stopped in at the Gallery of the Adelphi Theatre, Strand—horribly hot and crowded—good piece though—was in bed by ten o'clock.

Saturday, November 10
At breakfast received a note from Mr Bentley in reply to mine, saying he would come up from Brighton at any time convenient to me. Wrote him, 'Monday noon, in New Burlington St.'. After breakfast at a Coffee room, Adler went off to Hampton Court & the Dr to the Botanic Gardens, Regent's Park. For me, I lounged away the day —sauntering through the Temple courts & gardens, Lincoln's Inn, The New Hall, Gray's Inn, down Holborn Hill through Cock Lane (Dr Johnson's Ghost) to Smithfield (West). And so on to the Charter House, where I had a sociable chat with an old pensioner who guided me through some fine old cloisters, kitchens, chapels. Lord Ellenborough lies buried hard by the founder. They bury all their dead on their own premises. Duke of Norfolk was confined here in Elizabeth's time for treason. From the Charter House through the Goswell Street Road to Barbican towards London Wall. Asked an officer of the Fire Department where lay St Swithin's—He was very civil and polite & offered to show me the way in person. 'Perhaps you would like to see the way to the house where Whittington was born? Many Londoners

never saw it.' 'Lead on,' said I—& on we went—through squalid lanes, alleys & closes, till we got to a dirty blind lane; & there it was with a slab inserted in the wall. Thence, through the influence of the Fire Officer, I pushed my way through cellars and anti-lanes into the rear of Guildhall, with a crowd of beggars who were going to receive the broken meats and pies from yesterday's grand banquet (Lord Mayor's Day).—Within the hall, the scene was comical. Under the flaming banners and devices, were old broken tables set out with heaps of fowls, hams, &c. &c., pastry in profusion—cut in all directions—I could tell who had cut into this duck, or that goose. Some of the legs were gone —some of the wings, &c. (A good thing might be made of this.) Read the account of the banquet—the foreign ministers and many of the nobility were present. From the Guildhall, strolled through the Poultry to the Bank and New Exchange—thence, down King William Street to Fish Street Hill, & through Eastcheap to Tower Hill. Saw some fine Turkish armour (chain), every ring bearing a device. A superb cannon, cut and bored from one piece of brass—belonged to the Knights of Malta. The headman's block, upon which Kilmarnock & the Scotch lords were beheaded in the Pretender's time. The marks of the axe were very plain—like a butcher's board.—Lounged on by St Katherine's & London Docks and Ratcliffe's Highway, & within the dock walls to Wapping to the Tunnel. Crossed to Rotherhithe, & back by boat flinging a fourpenny piece to 'Poor Jack' in the mud. Took a steamer, & returned to the Temple landing & off to the Adelphi to dinner at five P.M.—dark. After dinner, Adler and I strolled over to Holborn & it being Saturday night, entertained ourselves by vagabonding through the courts and lanes, & looking in at the windows. Stopped in at a Penny Theatre—very comical—Adler afraid. To bed early.

William Hickling Prescott

member of a distinguished Massachusetts family, was born
in Salem, Massachusetts, in 1796 and died there in 1859.
He was educated at Harvard and despite being blind in one
eye and having gravely impaired vision in the other, the
result of an accident, settled down to become a historian.
At the age of 20 he went to Europe, partly for health reasons,
partly to prepare himself for his career as historian. His
History of the Conquest of Mexico was published in 1837, the
History of the Conquest of Peru ten years later.

English society and English gentlemen

FROM THESE PERSONAL courtesies I no doubt saw London society under a more favorable aspect than falls to most foreigners. And my impressions of it were certainly very agreeable. There is such a wonderful extent and variety in it. For all is drawn to this focus;—whatever talent there is in the country in letters and art, the splendours of fortune, the charms of beauty, and all that dazzles by rank, fashion and breeding, are collected at the dinners and in the saloons of London. There they are provided with all that can minister to *material* enjoyment, and subjected to those rules of a courtly society, that conventional code tacitly devised to enable persons of the most opposite habits and ways of thinking to meet together on familiar terms without jarring or jostling one another. The feature that most strikes one is the great number and variety of persons who are in the habit of interchanging these social courtesies in the same city. One may sail round and round in the vortex of fashion, and not meet the same face once a fortnight. There are so many concentric circles in the great whirlpool. Then, as all the celebrities and curiosities are sure to be drawn into the great emporium of wealth and fashion, one finds perpetual amusement in novelty. There is one thing that strikes a stranger, at least the republican stranger—that is, the great deference paid to caste—nowhere greater—not even in Spain in the days of the Philips. This causes a formality approaching to stiffness, which, combined with the natural shyness of the natives, raises sometimes a barrier to the free and easy intercourse which is the charm of society—especially to the stranger, who often finds one interview not long enough to thaw out the icy reserve of his neighbor. It almost always happens that this frosty covering wraps up a warm heart; and my belief is that once reach that heart it will not be likely soon to grow cold. I have never imagined anything like the devotion—spontaneous acts of kindness requiring contrivance and self-sacrifice, which these people show the stranger whom they do take cordially to their houses and their hearts. I shall be most ungrateful if I ever forget those shewn me by the Milmans, the Lyells, by Ford, Stirling, and every branch of the *famille* Howard—above all, my good friend, Lord Carlisle. It is to him and his family,

[68]

in its various branches, that I am indebted for the most attractive views I had of English life—life in the country.

Before quitting London, I must add that besides its social attractions, the stranger finds abundance of others in the new and rare objects of interest which an acquaintance with the right persons will readily open to him. I must not omit the clubs, among which I belonged to the Athenaeum, with its fine library of 20,000 volumes. After all, notwithstanding the great number and variety of interesting persons and things to be seen in this mammoth capital, and the splendor and gaiety of life in its higher circles, I do not think that a visit across the water to see London—alone—would pay—at least, as far as I am concerned. It was not so very different from what I had seen in my own land—more of it, to be sure—more variety, more splendor, more luxury, more of what is worth seeing and knowing of all. sorts—but still of the same general character. But English country life is quite another affair—altogether unique. It is only in the country that the Englishman finds the field for the full development for his energies, and his expansive, though in the town often hidden sympathies. One who has not seen English country life has not seen England. It is the predominance of the country and the country interests over the capital, overgrown as it is, that augurs well for the stability of English institutions. It is the preponderance of the capital over the country that furnished so bad an augury for those of their French neighbors...

On the whole, what I have seen raises my preconceived estimate of the English character. It is full of generous, true, and manly qualities, and I doubt if there ever was so high a standard of morality in an aristocracy which has such means for self-indulgence at its command, and which occupies a position that secures it so much deference. In general they do not seem to abuse their great advantages. Their respect for religion, at least for the forms of it, is universal; and there are few, I imagine, of the great proprietors who are not more or less occupied with improving their estates and with providing for the comforts of their tenantry—while many take a leading part in the great political movements of the time. There never was an aristocracy which combined so much practical knowledge and industry with the advantages of exalted rank.

The Englishman is seen to most advantage in his country-house. For he is constitutionally both domestic and rural in his habits. His fireside and his farm—these are the places in which one sees his simple and warm-hearted nature most freely unfolded. There is a shyness in an Englishman, a natural reserve which makes him cold to strangers, and difficult of approach. But once corner him in his own house, a frank and full expansion will be given to his feelings that we should look for in vain in the colder Yankee, and a depth not to be found in the light and superficial Frenchman—speaking of nationalities, not individuals.

The Englishman is the most truly rural in his tastes and habits of any people in the world. I am speaking of the higher classes. The aristocracy of other countries affect the camp and the city. But the English love their old castles and country seats with a patriotic love. They are fond of country sports. Every man shoots or hunts. No man is too old to be in the saddle some part of the day, and men of seventy years and more follow the hounds and take a five-barred gate at a leap. The women are good whips, are fond of horses and dogs, and other animals. Duchesses have their cows, their poultry, their pigs,—all watched over and provided with accommodation of Dutch-like neatness. All this is characteristic of the people. It may be thought to detract something from the feminine graces which in other lands make a woman so amicably dependent—as to be nearly imbecile. But it produces a healthy and blooming race of women, to match the hardy Englishman—the finest development of the physical and moral nature which the world has witnessed. For we are not to look on the English gentleman as a mere Nimrod. With all the relish for field sports and country usages, he has his house filled with collections of art and with extensive libraries. The tables of the drawing-rooms are covered with the latest works sent down by the London publisher. Every guest is provided with an apparatus for writing, and often a little library of books for his own amusement. The English country gentleman of the present day is anything but a Squire Western, though he does retain all his relish for field sports.

The character of the people, under this its most refined aspect, has some disagreeable points, which jar unpleasantly on the foreigner not accustomed to them. The consciousness of national superiority, combined with natural feelings of independence, gives him an air of arrogance—though it must be owned that this is never betrayed in his own house—I may almost say in his own country. But abroad, where he seems to institute a comparison between himself and the people he is thrown with, it becomes so obvious that he is the most unpopular, not to say odious person in the world. Even the open hand with which he dispenses his bounty will not atone for the violence he offers to national vanity.

There are other defects which are visible even in his most favored circumstances. Such is his bigotry, surpassing every thing in a quiet passive form that has been witnessed since the more active bigotry of the times of the Spanish Philips. Such, too, is the exclusive, limited range of his knowledge and conceptions on all political and social topics and relations. The Englishman, the cultivated Englishman, has no standard of excellence borrowed from mankind. His speculation never travels beyond his own little—great little island. That is the world to him. True he travels—shoots lions among the Hottentots, chases the grizzly bear over the Rocky Mountains, kills elephants in India and salmon on the coast of Labrador—comes home, and very likely makes a book. But the scope of his ideas does not seem to be enlarged by all this. The body travels, not the mind, and, however he may abuse his own land, he returns home as hearty a John Bull, with all his prejudices and national tastes, as rooted as before. The English— the men of fortune—all travel. Yet how little sympathy they show for other people or institutions, and how slight is the interest they take in them. They are islanders, cut off from the great world. But their island is indeed a great world of its own. With all their faults, never has the sun shone—if one may use the expression in reference to England— on a more noble race, or one that has done more for the great interests of humanity.

(From *The Literary Memoranda of William Hickling Prescott*, edited and with an introduction by C. Harvey Gardiner. Copyright 1961 by the University of Oklahoma Press.)

Francis Parkman

was born in Boston in 1824 of a wealthy and socially prominent Massachusetts family and educated at Harvard. When he was 20 he toured Europe. He returned to the United States to become, despite constant nervous illness and semi-blindness, the great historian of the explorations of the American interior. He died in 1893.

Impressions of London

WHEN I GOT to London, I thought I had been there before. There, in flesh and blood, was the whole host of characters that figure in *Pickwick*. Every species of cockney was abroad in the dark and dingy-looking streets, all walking with their heads stuck forwards, their noses turned up, their chin pointing down, their knee joints shaking, as they shuffled along with a gait perfectly ludicrous but indescribable. The hackney coachmen and cabmen, with their peculiar phraseology; the walking advertisements, in the shape of a boy completely hidden between two placards; and a hundred others seemed so many incarnations of Dickens' characters. A strange contrast to Paris. The cities are no more alike than the 'dining room' of London and the elegant restaurant of Paris—the one being a quiet, dingy establishment where each guest is put into a box, and supplied with porter, beef, potatoes, and plum-pudding. Red-faced old gentlemen of three hundred weight mix their 'brandy go' and read the *Times*. In Paris the tables are set in elegant galleries and saloons, and among the trees and flowers of a garden; and here resort coats cut by the first tailors and bonnets of the latest mode, whose occupants regale their delicate tastes on the lightest and most delicious viands. The waiters spring from table to table as noiselessly as shadows, prompt at the slightest sign; a lady, elegantly attired, sits within an arbor to preside over the whole. Dine at these places—then go to a London 'dining-room'—swill porter and devour roast beef!

The Haymarket Theatre—a little place, very plain and simple, and scarce larger than our departed Tremont. Not like the great theatres of Rome and Naples, or the still larger La Scala at Parma. Very unlike, too, the splendid opera house at Paris, where the richness of the decorations, the beauty of the architecture, and the excellence of the performances are only equalled by the extravagance of the prices. They gave us enough of it, certainly, at the Haymarket. The performance lasted from half past 7 till midnight. Such admirable acting I never saw before. Charles Matthews was the star; and appeared in a piece of his own, in which he took occasion to vent several sarcasms against American repudiation. But the drama is at its last gasp. The Hay-

[74]

market alone, among all its companions, preserves unaltered its ancient character—the rest are turned to opera houses.

I went immediately to Catlin's 'Indian Gallery'. It is in the Egyptian Hall, Piccadilly. There was a crowd around the door; servants in livery waiting; men with handbills of the exhibition for sale; cabmen, boys, and pickpockets. I was rejoicing in Mr Catlin's success, when the true point of attraction caught my eye in the shape of a full-length portrait of Major Tom Thumb, the celebrated American dwarf, who it seems occupies the 'Indian Gallery' for the present. I paid my shilling and went in. The little wretch was singing 'Yankee Doodle' with a voice like a smothered mouse, and prancing about on a table, à la Jeffrey Hudson, with a wooden sword in his hand. A great crowd of cockneys and gentlemen and ladies were contemplating his evolutions—but (as) for the 'Indian Gallery', its glory had departed; it had evidently ceased to be a lion. The portraits of the chiefs, dusty and faded, hung round the walls, and above were a few hunting shirts, and a bundle or two of arrows; but the rich and invaluable collection I had seen in Boston had disappeared, and no one thought of looking at the poor remains of that great collection that were hung about the walls. Catlin had done right. He would not suffer the fruits of his six years' labor and danger to rot in the dampness to gratify a few miserable cockneys—so has packed up the best part of his trophies.

St Paul's, which the English ridiculously compare to St Peter's, is without exception the dirtiest and gloomiest church I have been in yet. I went up to the ball at the top of the cupola, whence the prospect is certainly a most wonderful one. I have been on mountains whence nothing could be seen but unbroken forests stretching in every direction to the horizon, and I enjoyed the sight—but to look down from St Paul's and see the tiled roofs and steeples, half hid in smoke and mist —a filthy river covered with craft running through the midst; and to hear the incessant hum and to smell the coal smoke that pollutes the air—all this is very curious and amusing for a while, but I would scarce trouble myself to look again. All was dirty and foul; the air was chilly and charged with fog and sleet, though it is the genial month of May. The smoke, that you could see streaming in the wind from ten thousand earthen chimney-pots, mingled with the vapors and obscured the prospect like a veil. It was an indistinct but limitless panorama. The taller church-spires alone rose above the cloud into a comparatively clear atmosphere; and they could be seen faintly, far off on the horizon, to show how far this wilderness of houses reached. 'Now', thought I,

'I have under my eye the greatest collection of blockheads and rascals, the greatest horde of pimps, prostitutes, and bullies that the earth can show.' And straightway all the child's-book associations of London rose before me: the Lord Mayor's show 'all so grand', and the host of narrow, stupid, beef-eating civic functionaries, and the unmatched absurdities and self-conceit of cockneyism. 'Was there ever such a cursed hole?' I thought as I looked down on the smoky prospect.

You are shown a large stone vaulted room, covered with cobwebs and smoke-dust, where hang, already rotten and half dropping from their staffs, the flags that were borne at Nelson's funeral.

Walk out in the evening, and keep a yard or two behind some wretched clerk, who with nose elevated in the air, elbows stuck out at right angles, and the pewter knob of his cane playing upon his under lip, is straddling his bow legs over the sidewalk with a most majestic air. Get behind him, and you see his dignity greatly disturbed. First he glances over one of his narrow shoulders—then over the other—then he edges off to the other side of the walk, and turns his vacant lobster eyes full upon you—then he passes his hand over his coat-tail—and finally he draws forth from his pocket the object of all this solicitude in the shape of a venerable and ragged cotton handkerchief, which he holds in his hand to keep it out of harm's way. I have been thus taken for a pickpocket more than a dozen times tonight—not the less so for being respectably dressed, for these gentry are the most dashing men on the Strand.

There is an interesting mixture of vulgarity and helplessness in the swarm of ugly faces you see in the streets—meagre, feeble, ill-proportioned, or not proportioned at all, the blockheads must needs put on a game air and affect the 'man of the world' in their small way. I have not met one handsome woman since I have been here, and have kept my eyes open. To be sure, the weather has been raw and chill enough to keep beauty at home. Elsewhere Englishmen are tall, strong, and manly; here the crowd that swarms through the streets are like the outcasts of a hospital.

Ralph Waldo Emerson

In 1832 at the age of 29 Ralph Waldo Emerson resigned his
pastorate of the Second Unitarian Church of Boston, having
announced to his congregation: 'It is my desire, in the office
of a Christian minister, to do nothing which I cannot do
with all my heart. Having said this, I have said all. I have
no hostility to this institution; I am only stating my want
of sympathy with it.' Almost immediately afterwards, he
left for Europe and Britain, where he met his heroes
Wordsworth, Coleridge and Carlyle. Back in the States, he
bought his grandfather's house, the Old Manse, in Concord,
Massachusetts, and began his career as lecturer. It was
in that capacity, already famous, that he revisited Britain
in 1848. He died in 1882.

From Emerson's Journal

Liverpool, October 30 [1848]

EVERYTHING IN ENGLAND bespeaks an immense population. The buildings are on a scale of size and wealth out of all proportion to ours, the colossal masonry of the docks and of all the public to be accommodated by them, and to pay for them, so the manners of the people . . . The Englishman has thus a necessary talent of letting alone all that does not belong to him. They are physiognomically and constitutionally distinct from the Americans. They incline more to be large-bodied men; they are stocky, and especially the women seem to have that defect to their beauty; no tall slender girls of flowing shape, but stunted and stocky . . .

Englishman. A manly ability, a general sufficiency, is the genius of the English. They have not, I think, the special and acute fitness to their employment that Americans have, but a man is a man here,—a quite costly and respectable production, in his own, and in all other eyes.

The Englishman is cheerful, and his voice is.

Their nationality is intense.

Englishman is clean, methodical, veracious, proud, obstinate, comfort-loving, industrious, accumulative, nautical.

Englishman must have foothold. Security is in his face and manners, because he has solidity in his foundations and method in his procedure. The English secure the essentials, according to their light, and it falls, at present, on bodily good health and wealth. The Cyclops operative cannot subsist on food less solid than beef, and the masters cannot understand that there is any way to success but on capital and economy.

The Englishman is aboveboard and direct; he disdains, in fighting, to strike a foul blow, he disdains secret ballot. It is 'out of his nature to assassinate even property.' . . .

Woman is cheap and vile in England.

It rains at every tide at Manchester.

Only three or four per cent of this population is idle. Everybody works in England, said Mr Rawlins.

In Manchester they attribute the better character of this people for prudence and industry to the universal habit here of dining at one o'clock. If they are to go to business again in the afternoon, they say, we shall not eat so much. . . .

England   Among the local objects are horses and hounds *clothed all over*, and postilions in livery on every span of horses; and mourning coaches covered with nodding plumes; and gigs and carts with little horses of the Canadian (?) breed; and sedan-chairs; and men dressed in shawls; and they turn their horses to the left hand when they meet, and in Manchester lately there is an order for foot passengers to turn to the right; and escutcheons on the walls for one year after death.

All life moves here on machinery, 't is a various mill. . . .

Much of the differences between American and English, referable to dense population here, and will certainly be lost as America fills up.

What a misfortune to America that she has not original names on the land, but this whitewash of English names. Here every name is history.

December 23

Dined at Mr Swanwick's, Chesterfield, with George Stephenson. One quarter of a pound of coke will carry one ton one mile. . . .

No dissenter rides in his coach for three generations; he infallibly falls into the Establishment. . . .

In Leicester, the conversion of the letter h remarkable; an Act of Parliament is a Hact. . . .

The one rule to give to the traveller in England is, Do not sneak about diffidently, but make up your mind and carry your points.

The only girth or belt that can enable one to face these Patagonians of beef and beer, is an absorbing work of your own. Otherwise, with their excessive life they hustle you out of their world.

December 30

I went over Worcester Cathedral, part of which has stood nine hundred years (?). I saw the tomb of King John; of Prince Arthur, son of Henry VII; and especially, and with most delight, some old tombs of crusaders with their mailed legs crossed in marble, and the countenances, handsome and refined as the English gentleman of today, and with that uncorrupt youth in the face of manhood, which I often see here. From the tower I had the fine picture of the Severn for many a mile, and the Malvern Hills.

But the reason why any town in England does not grow is, that it is a cathedral town. If Birmingham had been a cathedral town, they say it would have been no larger than Worcester.

English aristocracy. It is curious to see the overflowings of aristocratic manners and culture in the inferior classes, especially in the coachmen, who see and hear so much from their superiors. My omnibus driver from Worcester, with his quotations from Shakespeare and his praise of his horses, and his condescending humor and his account of the visit of his relations to him with a little boy, were deserving of Dickens, or Ellery Channing.

January

I trace, then, the peculiarities of English manners to their working climate; their dense population; the presence of an aristocracy or model class for manners and speech; their diet, generously and orderly taken; and their force of constitution. Their manners betray real independence, and they are studiously inoffensive. They are castles compared with our men ... An American feels like some invalid in their company.

January 13

At York, I saw the skull of a Roman centurion. I saw the tree planted by George Fox; I saw the prisons, the pews in which the prisoners are locked up; the scales with which they can weigh their own food.

In the minster, I heard 'God save the King', of Handel, played by Dr Camidge on the grand organ. It was very great. I thought I had never heard anything so sublime. The music was made for the minster, and the minster for the music. . . .

The architects of York Minster are not known; yet what brains were those! It is beautiful beyond belief.

January

In Halifax (England) Mr Crossley employs in his carpet mills fifteen hundred operatives. Beautiful tapestry carpets at 7/6 per yard: saw the pattern sent to the Queen. Vista made by the looms resembled a church aisle. Mr Acroyd's stuff-mills employ five or six thousand operatives. In one hall I saw eight hundred looms. In many they were making ponchos. Here was a school spaciously built and well furnished for the children. In England, the manufacturers are not joint-stock companies, but individuals.

[80]

Near Leeds and Bradford, I observed the sheep were black, ... begrimed by the smoke ... The hopelessness of keeping clothes white
leads to a rather dowdy style of dress, I was told, among the ladies;
and yet they sometimes indemnify themselves; and Leeds in the ball-
room, I was assured, is a very different creature from Leeds in Briggate.

Mr Marshall's mill covers two acres of ground. The former owner,
James Marshall, presided in this immense hall at a dinner given to
O'Connell; and the Chartists having threatened an attack, Mr Marshall
had a water-pipe under his chair which was supplied by a steam-engine,
and which he was ready to direct on the mob, if they had ventured to
disturb him. ...

I hear it said that the sense which the manufacturers have of their
duties to the operatives, and the exertions they have made in establishing schools and 'Mechanics' Institutions' for them, is recent, and is,
in great part, owing to Carlyle. At Huddersfield, I was told that they
have over-educated the men in the working-class, so as to leave them
dissatisfied with their sweethearts and wives; and the good Schwann
and Kehls there were now busy in educating the women up to them. ...

At Rawdon, I inquired, how much the men earned who were breaking stone in the road, and was told twenty pence; but they can only
have work three days in the week, unless they are married; then they
have it four days.

The Chartists, if you treat them civilly, and show any good will to
their cause, suspect you, think you are going to *do* them.

Newcastle, February 9

At Newcastle, saw at Mr Crawshay's iron works the Nasmith
hammer, which will strike with a weight of six tons, yet so manageable
that Nasmith will put his hand under it if one of his own men directs
the strike. Crawshay put his new hat under it and received a slight
damage.

February 13

Glasgow the rapidest growth in Britain after Liverpool. As soon
as you cross the border at Berwick and enter Scotland, the face of
things changes, the grass is less green, the country has an iron-gray
look, it is cold and poor; no well-trained porters: you must carry your
own luggage; the ticket-master weighs your sovereign (it is a rare

piece) and finds it light: you can pay in copper now for what always cost silver in England. Nobody rides in first-class carriages: and the manners become gross and swainish in some observed particulars.

Glasgow has 320,000 people. Students in scarlet cloaks. Americans here, and a consul. Dr Hudson tells me some strange stories about the Foundation at Eton, and that the subscription made previous to entering declares that the signer is a beggar, yet is signed by noblemen. It confounds my understanding. Glasgow adds 1000 a month to its population. At Glasgow I spoke in a cavern called City Hall to two or three thousand persons.

The Scotch speech has a most unnecessary superfluous energy of elocution and of rolling the r. Great talkers, very fond of argument. Scotch are plainer drest, plainer mannered than the English, not so clean, and many of them look drunk when they are sober.

Scotch are intelligent reading and writing people, but Edinburgh is still but a provincial city; the tone of society is incurably provincial.

February 21

The Americans are sun-dried, the English are baked in the oven. The upper classes have only birth, people say here, and not thought. Yes, but they have manners, and 't is wonderful how much talent runs into manners. Nowhere and never so much as in England. And when they go into America and find that this gift has lost its power, the gold has become dry leaves, no wonder they are impatient to get away.

Every man in the carriage is a possible lord. Yet they look alike, and every man I meet in London I think I know . . .

Traits. In England the understanding rules, and materialistic truth; the becoming, the fit, the discreet, the brave, the advantageous; but they could not produce such a book as the *Bhagavat Geeta*. Dr Johnson is liked for his courage; 'a man who is afraid of anything is a scoundrel'.

Carlyle thought the clubs remarkable signs of the times; that union was no longer sought, but only the association of men who would not offend one another. There was nothing to do, but they could eat better.

He was very serious about the bad times. The Chartists were then preparing to go in a procession of two hundred thousand to carry their petition, embodying the six points of Chartism, to the House of

[82]

Commons, on the 10th April, 1848. He had seen this evil coming, but thought it would not come in his time. But now it is coming, and the only good he sees in it is the visible appearance of the Gods. He thinks it 'the only question for wise men—instead of art and fine fancies, and poetry, and such things as Tennyson plays with—to address themselves to the problem of society. This confusion is the inevitable end of such falsehood and nonsense as they have been embroiled with.'·

.... If such a person as Cromwell should come now it would be of no use; he could not get the ear of the House of Commons. You might as well go into Chelsea graveyard yonder, and say, *Shoulder arms!* and expect the old dead churchwardens to arise.

It is droll to hear this talker talking against talkers, and this writer writing against writers.

Jane Carlyle said that the rich people whom she knew had occasion for all the shillings they could find. The spending is, for a great part, in servants. Thirty-five servants in Lord Ashburton's house...

The people have wide range, but no ascending range in their speculation. An American, like a German, has many platforms of thought. But an Englishman requires to be humoured or treated with tenderness as an invalid, if you wish him to climb.

Let who will fail, England will not. She could not now build the old castles and abbeys, but the Nineteenth Century loves club-houses, railways, and docks and mills, and builds them fast enough....

Plural London. Immeasurable London, evidently the capital of the world, where men have lived ever since there were men. Yet it seems deliberately built. An aggregation of capitals.

There are several little nations here. A German quarter in Whitechapel, a French quarter where they still carry on a silk business in Spitalfields.

In London only could such a place as Kew Gardens be overlooked. Wealth of shops bursting into the streets; piles of plate breast-high on Ludgate Hill. In a London dock Mr Bates said he had seen nineteen miles of pipes of wine piled up to the ceiling.

Many of the characterizing features of London are new. Such as gas-light, the omnibuses, the steam ferries, the penny-post, and the building up the West End.

One goes from show to show, dines out, and lives in extremes. Electric sparks six feet long; light is polarized; Grisi sings; Rothschild is your banker; Owen and Faraday lecture; Macaulay talks; Soyer cooks. Is there not an economy in coming where thus all the dependence is on the first men of their kind?

Englishman has hard eyes. He is great by the back of the head.

In the new Parliament House, great poverty of ornament, the ball and crown repeated tediously all over the grand gate, near the Abbey, and *Vivat Regina* written incessantly all over the casements of the House of Lords. Houses of Parliament a magnificent document of English power and of their intention to make it last. The Irish harp and shamrock are carved with the rose and thistle over all the house. The houses cover some eight acres, and are built of Bolsover stone. Fault, that there is no single view commanding great lines; only, when it is finished, the Speaker of the House of Commons will be able with a telescope to see the Lord Chancellor in the Lords. But mankind can so rarely build a house covering eight acres that 't is a pity to deprive them of the joy of seeing a mass and grand and lofty lines.

In House of Commons, when a man makes his first speech, there is a cry of 'New member! new member!' and he is sure of attention. Afterwards, he must get it if he can. In a body of six hundred and forty-eight members every man is sure to have some who understand his views on whatever topic. Facts they will hear, and any measure proposed they will entertain, but no speculation, and no oratory. A sneer is the habitual expression of that body. Therefore Cobbett's maiden speech, 'I have heard a great deal of nonsense, since I have been sitting here,' was quite in their vein, and secured their ear.

Stand at the door of the House of Commons, and see the members go in and out, and you will say these men are all men of humanity, of good sense.

'Tis a long step from the cromlechs to York Minster.

Two seasons every night in which the House of Commons was ferocious, at the dinner hour by hunger and at two o'clock by sleep.

Englishman talks of politics and institutions, but the real thing which he values is his home, and that which belongs to it,—that

[84]

general culture and high polish which in his experience no man but the Englishman possesses, and which he naturally believes have some essential connection with his throne and laws. That is what he does not believe resides in America, and therefore his contempt for America only half concealed. This English tenacity in strong contrast with our facility. The facile American sheds his Puritanism when he leaves Cape Cod, runs into all English and French vices with great zest, and is neither Unitarian, nor Calvinist, nor Catholic, nor stands for any known thought or thing; which is very distasteful to English honour. It is a bad sign that I have met with many Americans who flattered themselves that they pass for English. Levity, levity. I do not wish to be mistaken for an Englishman, more than I wish Monadnock or Nahant or Nantucket to be mistaken for Wales or the Isle of Wight....

The Englishman is proud; yes, but he is admirable. He knows all things, has all things, can do all: how can he not be proud?

... If I stay here long, I shall lose all my patriotism and think that England has absorbed all excellences. My friend Alcott came here and brought away a couple of mystics and their shelf of books from Ham Common, and fancied that nothing was left in England; and I see that Kew Gardens and so many great men and things are obscure.

I look at the immense wealth and the solid power concentrated, and am quite faint: then I look in the street at the little girls running barefoot through the rain, with broom in hand, to beg a penny of the passenger at the crossing, and at so many Lascars, and pitifullest trades, and think of Saadi, who, barefooted, saw the man who had no legs, and bemoaned himself no more.

April 6

I fancied, when I heard that the times were anxious and political, that there is to be a Chartist revolution on Monday next, and an Irish revolution in the following week, that the right scholar would feel, now was the hour to test his genius. His kingdom is at once over and under these perturbed regions. Let him produce its Charter now, and try whether it cannot win a hearing, and make felt its infinite superiority today, as, in the arts, they make winter oil on the coldest, and spermaceti candles on the hottest, day of the year.

People here expect a revolution. There will be no revolution, none that deserves to be called so. There may be a scramble for money. But as all the people we see want the things we now have, and not better things, it is very certain that they will, under whatever change of forms, keep the old system. When I see changed men, I shall look for a changed world. Whoever is skilful in heaping money now will be skilful in heaping money again . . .

What wrong road have we taken that all the improvements of machinery have helped everybody but the operative? Him they have incurably hurt.

April

St Paul's is, as I remember it, a very handsome, noble architectural exploit, but singularly unaffecting. When I formerly came to it from the Italian cathedrals, I said, 'Well, here is New York.' It seems the best of show-buildings, a fine British vaunt, but there is no moral interest attached to it.

It is certain that more people speak English correctly in the United States than in Britain.

April 15

Among the trades of despair is the searching the filth of the sewers for rings, shillings, teaspoons, etc., which have been washed out of the sinks. These sewers are so large that you can go underground great distances. Mr Colman saw a man coming out of the ground with a bunch of candles. 'Pray, sir, where did you come from?' 'Oh, I've been seven miles,' the man replied. They say that Chadwick rode all under London on a little brown pony.

April 25

Dined with John Forster, Esq., at Lincoln's Inn Fields, and found Carlyle and Dickens, and young Pringle. Forster, who has an obstreperous cordiality, received Carlyle with loud salutation, 'My Prophet!' Forster called Carlyle's passion, 'musket-worship'. There were only gentlemen present and the conversation turned on the shameful lewdness of the London streets at night. 'I hear it,' he said, 'I hear whoredom in the House of Commons. Disraeli betrays whoredom, and the whole House of Commons universal incontinence, in every word they say.' I said that when I came to Liverpool, I inquired whether the prostitution was always as gross in that city as it then appeared, for to me it seemed to betoken a fatal rottenness in the state, and I saw not how any boy could grow up safe. But I was told it

[86]

was not better nor worse for years. Carlyle and Dickens replied that chastity in the male sex was as good as gone in our times; and in England was so rare that they could name all the exceptions. Carlyle evidently believed that the same things were true in America. He had heard this and that of New York, etc. I assured them that it was not so with us; that, for the most part, young men of good standing and good education, with us, go virgins to their nuptial bed, as truly as their brides. Dickens replied that incontinence is so much the rule in England that if his own son were particularly chaste, he should be alarmed on his account, as if he could not be in good health.

June 8

When I get into our first-class cars in the Fitchburg Road, and see sweltering men in their shirt-sleeves take their seats with some well-dressed men and women, and see really the very little difference of level that is between them all, and then imagine the astonishment that would strike the polished inmates of English first-class carriages if such masters should enter and sit beside them, I see that it is not fit to tell Englishmen that America is like England. No, this is the Paradise of the third class; here everything is cheap; here everything is for the poor. England is the Paradise of the first class; it is essentially aristo cratic, and the humbler classes have made up their minds to this, and do contentedly enter into the system. In England every man you meet is some man's son; in America, he may be some man's father.

June 27

Topics of conversation in England are Irish affairs; universal suffrage; pauperism; public education; right and duty of government to interefere with increase of population; taxes.

People eat the same dinner at every house in England. 1, soup; 2, fish; 3, beef, mutton, or hare; 4, birds; 5, pudding and pastry and jellies; 6, cheese; 7, grapes, nuts, and wine. During dinner, hock and champagne are offered you by the servant, and sherry stands at the corners of the table. Healths are not much drunk in fashionable houses. After the cloth is removed, three bottles, namely, port, sherry, and claret, invariably circulate. What rivers of wine are drunk in all England daily! One would say, every guest drinks six glasses.

The English youth has a narrow road to travel. Besides his horse and his gun, all he knows is the door to the House of Commons.

I stayed in London till I had become acquainted with all the styles of face in the street, and till I had found the suburbs and then straggling houses on each end of the city. Then I took a cab, left my farewell cards, and came home.

I saw Alison, Thackeray, Cobden, Tennyson, Bailey, Marston, Macaulay, Hallam, Disraeli, Milnes, Wilson, Jeffrey, Wordsworth, Carlyle, Dickens, Lockhart, Proctor, Montgomery, Collyer, Kenyson, Stephenson, Buckland, Sedgwick, Lyell, Edward Forbes, Richard Owen, Robert Owen, Cruikshank, Jenny Lind, Grisi, William Allingham, David Scott, William B. Scott, Kinglake, De Tocqueville, Lamartine, Leverrier, Rachel, Barbes, Eastlake, Spence, Wilkinson, Duke of Wellington, Brougham, Joanna Baillie, De Quincey, Sir C. Fellows, Sir Henry De La Beche, John Forster.

Harriet Beecher Stowe

born at Litchfield, Connecticut, in 1811, became internationally
famous in 1852 as the author of *Uncle Tom's Cabin*. A year later,
she toured England and Europe and obtained much innocent
gratification from the enthusiastic reception she had on all sides
from the great, the noble and the good. *Sunny Memories of
Foreign Lands* appeared in 1854. She died in 1896.

Why English ladies keep their beauty

A LADY ASKED me this evening what I thought of the beauty of the ladies of the English aristocracy: she was a Scotch lady, by-the-by; so the question was a fair one. I replied, that certainly report had not exaggerated their charms. Then came a home question—how the ladies of England compared with the ladies of America. 'Now for it, patriotism,' said I to myself; and, invoking to my aid certain fair saints of my own country, whose faces I distinctly remembered, I assured her that I had never seen more beautiful women than I had in America. Grieved was I to be obliged to add, 'But your ladies keep their beauty much later and longer.' This fact stares one in the face in every company; one meets ladies past fifty, glowing, radiant, and blooming, with a freshness of complexion and fulness of outline refreshing to contemplate. What can be the reason? Tell us, Muses and Graces, what can it be? Is it the conservative power of sea fogs and coal smoke—the same cause that keeps the turf green, and makes the holly and ivy flourish? How comes it that our married ladies dwindle, fade and grow thin—that their noses incline to sharpness, and their elbows to angularity, just at the time of life when their island sisters round out into a comfortable and becoming amplitude and fulness? If it is the fog and the sea-coal, why, then, I am afraid we never shall come up with them. But, perhaps, there may be other causes why a country which starts some of the most beautiful girls in the world produces so few beautiful women. Have not our close-heated stove-rooms something to do with it? Have not the immense amount of hot biscuits, hot corn cakes, and other compounds got up with the acrid poison of saleratus, something to do with it? Above all, has not our climate, with its alternate extremes of heat and cold, a tendency to induce habits of in-door indolence? Climate, certainly has a great deal to do with it; ours is evidently more trying and more exhausting: and because it is so, we should not pile upon its back errors of dress and diet which are avoided by our neighbours. They keep their beauty because they keep their health. It has been as remarkable as anything to me, since I have been here, that I do not constantly, as at home, hear one and another spoken of as in miserable health, as very delicate, &c. Health seems to be the rule, and not the exception. For my part, I must say, the most favourable omen that I know of for female beauty in America is, the multiplication of water-cure establishments, where our ladies, if they get nothing else, do gain some ideas as to the necessity of fresh air, regular exercise, simple diet, and the laws of hygiene in general.

There is one thing more which goes a long way towards the con-tinued health of these English ladies, and therefore towards their beauty; and that is, the quietude and perpetuity of their domestic institutions. They do not, like us, fade their cheeks lying awake at nights ruminating the awful question who shall do the washing next week, or who shall take the chambermaid's place, who is going to be married, or that of the cook, who has signified her intention of parting with the mistress. Their hospitality is never embarrassed by the con-sideration that their whole kitchen cabinet may desert at the moment that their guests arrive. They are not obliged to choose between washing their own dishes, or having their cut glass, silver, and china left to the mercy of a foreigner, who has never done anything but field-work. And last, not least, they are not possessed with that ambition to do the impossible in all branches, which, I believe, is the death of a third of the women in America. What is there ever read of in books, or described in foreign travel, as attained by people in possession of every means and appliance, which our women will not undertake, single-handed, in spite of every providential indication to the contrary? Who is not cognizant of dinner-parties invited, in which the lady of the house has figured successively as confectioner, cook, dining-room girl, and, lastly, rushed up stairs to bathe her glowing cheeks, smooth her hair, draw on satin dress and kid gloves, and appear in the drawing-room as if nothing were the matter? Certainly the undaunted bravery of our American females can never enough be admired. Other women can play gracefully the head of the establishment; but who, like them, could be head, hand, and foot, all at once?

Staying with the Duke of Argyll at Inveraray

THE COMMON ROUTINE of the day here is as follows: We rise about half past eight. About half past nine we all meet in the dining-hall, where the servants are standing in a line down one side, and a row of chairs for guests and visitors occupies the other. The duchess with her nine children, a perfectly beautiful little flock, sit together. The duke reads the Bible and a prayer, and pronounces the benediction. After that, breakfast is served—a very hearty, informal meal—and after that come walks, or drives, or fishing parties, till lunch time, and then more drives, or anything else: everybody, in short, doing what he likes till half past seven, which is the dinner hour. After that we have coffee and tea in the evening.

The first morning, the duke took me to see his mine of nickel silver. We had a long and beautiful drive, and talked about everything in literature, religion, morals and the temperance movement, about which last he is in some state of doubt and uncertainty, not inclining, I think, to have it pressed yet, though feeling there is need of doing something . . .

Every day I am more charmed with the duke and duchess; they are simple-hearted, frank, natural, full of feeling, of piety, and good sense. They certainly are, apart from any considerations of rank or position, most interesting and noble people. The duke laughed heartily at many things I told him of our Andover theological tactics, of your preaching, etc.; but I think he is a sincere, earnest Christian.

Nathaniel Hawthorne

was born in Salem, Massachusetts, in 1804, of a family that seemed to enshrine in itself, as *The Scarlet Letter* and the stories show, the essence of seventeenth-century New England. He was educated at Bowdoin College, Maine, where he was the friend of Franklin Pierce. Pierce ran for President in 1852 and Hawthorne wrote his campaign biography, for which he was rewarded on Pierce's election with the U.S. Consulate at Liverpool. He was Consul there and a critical observer of British life and manners for four years. He died in 1864.

The Liverpool poor

August 20th. 1853

THIS BEING SUNDAY, there commenced a throng of visitants to Rock Ferry. The boat, in which I came over, brought from the city a multitude of factory-people, male and female. They had bands of music, and banners inscribed with the Mills they belonged to, and other devices; pale-looking people, but not looking exactly as if they were underfed. They are brought on reduced terms by the railways and steamers, and come from considerable distances in the interior. These, I believe, were from Preston. I have not yet had an opportunity of observing how they amuse themselves during these excursions.

Almost every day, I take walks about Liverpool; preferring the darker and dingier streets, inhabited by the poorer classes. The scenes there are very picturesque in their way; at every two or three steps, a gin-shop; also filthy in clothes and person, ragged, pale, often afflicted with humors; women, nursing their babies at dirty bosoms; men haggard, drunken, care-worn, hopeless, but with a kind of patience, as if all this were the rule of their life; groups stand or sit talking together, around the door-steps, or in the descent of a cellar; often a quarrel is going on in one group, for which the next group cares little or nothing. Sometimes, a decent woman may be seen sewing or knitting at the entrance of her poor dwelling, a glance into which shows dismal poverty. I never walk through these streets without feeling as if I should catch some disease; but yet there is a strong interest in such walks; and moreover there is a bustle, a sense of being in the midst of life, and of having got hold of something real, which I do not find in the better streets of the city. Doubtless, this noon-day and open life of theirs is entirely the best aspect of their existence; and if I were to see them within doors, at their meals, or in bed, it would be unspeakably worse. They appear to wash their clothes occasionally; for I have seen them hanging out to dry in the street.

At the dock, the other day, the steamer from Rock Ferry with a countless multitude of female children in coarse blue-gowns, who, as they landed, formed in procession and walked up the dock. These girls had been taken from the work-houses, and educated at a charity-school, and would by-and-by be apprenticed as servants. I should not have conceived it possible that so many children could have been collected together, without a single trace of beauty, or scarcely of intelligence, in so much as one individual; such mean, coarse, vulgar features and figures, betraying unmistakeably a low origin, and ignorant and brutal parents. They did not appear wicked, but only stupid; animal and soulless. It must require many generations of better life to elicit a soul in them. All America could not show the like.

Liverpool street-scenes

August 25th. 1853

FURTHER ITEMS OF street-rambles:—little gray donkeys, dragging along disproportionately large carts; the anomalous aspect of cleanly dressed and healthy looking young women, whom one sometimes sees talking together in the street,—evidently residing in some contiguous house; the apparition, now and then, of a bright, intelligent, merry, child's face, with dark, knowing eyes, gleaming through the dirt like sunshine through a dusty window-pane; at provisions-shops, the little bits of meat, ready for poor customers, and little heaps of selvages and corners, snipt off from points and steaks;—the kindliness with which a little boy leads and lugs along his little sister;—a pale, hollow-cheeked, large-eyed girl of 12, or less, paying a sad, cheerless attention to an infant;—a milkwoman, with a wooden yoke over her shoulder, and a large pail on each side; in a more reputable street, respectably dressed women going into an ale and spirit-vault, evidently to drink there; the police-men loitering along, with observant eye, holding converse with none, and seldom having occasion to interfere with anybody;—the multitudinousness and continual motion of all this kind of life. The people are as numerous as maggots in cheese; you behold them, disgusting, and all moving about, as when you raise a plank or log that has long lain on the ground, and find many vivacious bugs and insects beneath it.

Peculiar behaviour of the English

October 20th. 1853

ONE SEES INCIDENTS in the streets, here, occasionally, which could not be seen in an American city. For instance, a week or two since, I was passing a quiet-looking elderly gentleman, when, all of a sudden, and without any apparent provocation, he uplifted his stick and struck a blackgowned boy a smart blow over the shoulders. The boy looked at him ruefully and resentfully, but said nothing, nor can I imagine why the thing was done. In Tithe Barn street, to-day, I saw a woman suddenly assault a man, clutch at his hair, and cuff him about the ears. The man, who was of decent aspect enough, immediately took to his heels, full speed, and the woman after him; and as far as I could discern the pair, the chase continued.

In the same street, I met two women, bearing on their backs bundles of large chips, absolutely bulkier than themselves. The burthens which women carry on their heads are absolutely marvellous; and they step along the crowded streets with the utmost freedom and security, without touching the loads with their hands. I meet many women barefoot, even at this advanced season.

An English beggar

Dec. 10th. 1853

I DON'T KNOW any place that brings all classes into contiguity, on equal ground, so completely as the waiting-room at Rock Ferry, on these frosty days. The room is not more than eight feet square, with walls of stone, and wooden benches ranged round them; and an open stove in one corner, generally well furnished with coal. It is almost always crowded; and I rather suspect that many persons, who have no fireside elsewhere, creep in here and spend the most comfortable part of their day.

This morning, when I looked into the room, there were one or two gentlemen and other respectable persons, male and female; but in the best place, close to the fire, and crouching almost into it, was an elderly beggar—with the raggedest of overcoats, two great rents on the shoulders, disclosing the dingy lining, all bepatched with various stuff, covered with dirt; and on his shoes and trowsers the mud of an interminable pilgrimage. Owing to the posture in which he sat, I could not see his face, but only the battered crown and rim of the very shabbiest hat that ever was. Regardless of the presence of women (which, indeed, Englishmen seldom do regard, when they wish to smoke) he was smoking a pipe of vile tobacco; but, after all, this was fortunate, because the man himself was not personally fragrant. He was terribly squalid—terribly—and when I had a glimpse at his face, it well befitted the rest of his development; grizzled, wrinkled, weather-beaten, yet sallow, down-looking with a watchful kind of eye, turning upon everybody and everything, meeting the eyes of other people rather boldly, yet soon shrinking away;—a long, thin nose, gray beard of a week's growth, hair not much mixed with gray, but rusty and lifeless. A miserable object; but it was curious to see how he was not ashamed of himself, but seemed to feel that he was one of the estates of the kingdom, and had as much right to live as other men. He did just as he pleased, took the best place by the fireside, nor would have cared though a nobleman were forced to stand aside for him. When the steamer's bell rang, he shouldered a large and heavy pack, and hobbled down the pier, leaning on a crook-staff, and looking like a pilgrim with his burden of sin, but certainly journeying to hell, instead of heaven. On board, he looked round for the best position, at first stationing himself near the boiler-pipe, but finding the deck damp under foot, went to the cabin-door, and took his stand on the stairs, protected from the wind, but very incommodiously to those who wished to pass. All this was done without any bravado or forced impudence, but in the most quiet way, merely because he was seeking his own comfort, and considered that he had a right to seek it. It was an Englishman's spirit; but, in our country, I imagine, a beggar considers himself a kind of outlaw, and would hardly assume the privileges of a man, in any place of public resort. Here, beggary is a system, and beggars are a numerous class, and make themselves, in a certain way, respected as such. Nobody evinced the slightest disapprobation of this man's proceedings. In America, I think, we should have seen many aristocratic airs, on such provocation; and probably the ferry-people would have rudely thrust the beggar-man aside;—giving him a shilling, however—which no Englishman would ever think of doing. There would also have been a great deal of fun made of this squalid and ragged figure; whereas, nobody smiled at him, this morning, nor in any way evinced the slightest disrespect. This is good; but it is the result of a state of things by no means good.

Letters to the Editor

Jan. 6th. 1854

... EVERY ENGLISHMAN RUNS to 'The Times' with his little grievance, as a child runs to his mother.

Fruit and sunshine

July 6th. 1854

MR CECIL, THE other day, was saying that England could produce as fine peaches as any other country. I asked what was the particular excellence of a peach, and he answered, its 'cooling and refreshing quality, like that of a melon'. Just think of this idea of the richest, lusciousest of all fruits. But the untravelled Englishman has no more real idea of what fruit is, than of what sunshine is; he thinks that he has tasted the first, and felt the last;—but they are both watery alike. I heard a lady in Lord-street talking about the 'broiling sun' (with a breadth and emphasis that sounded like bacon in a frying-pan) when I was almost in a shiver. They keep up their animal-heat by means of ale and wine; else they could not bear this climate.

In a Law-court

August 21st. 1854

IN THE CROWN-COURT, on Saturday, sitting in the Sheriff's seat. The Judge, Baron Platt, an old gentleman of upwards sixty, with very large, long features; his wig helped him to look like some strange kind of animal—very queer, but yet with a sagacious and, on the whole, benefi-cent aspect. During the session, some mischievous young barrister occupied himself with sketching the Judge in pencil; and being handed about, it found its way to me. It was very like, and very laughable, but hardly caricatured. The judicial wig is an exceedingly odd affair; and as it covers both ears, it would seem intended to prevent his lordship (and Justice in his person) from hearing anything of the case on either side—that thereby he may decide the better. It is like the old idea of blind-folding the statue of Justice.

It seems to me there is less formality—less distance between the Judge, jury witnesses, and bar—in the English courts than in our own. The Judge takes a very active part in the trial—constantly putting a question to the witness on the stand—making remarks on the conduct of the trial—putting in his word on all occasions—and letting his own sense of the matter in hand be pretty plainly seen; so that, before the trial is over, and long before his own charge is delivered, he must have exercised a very powerful influence over the minds of the jury. All this seems to be done, not without dignity, yet in a familiar kind of way: it is a sort of paternal supervision of the whole matter, quite unlike the cold awfulness of an American Judge. But all this may be owing partly to the personal characteristics of Baron Platt. It appeared to me, however, that from this closer relation of all parties, truth was likely to be arrived at, and justice to be done. As an innocent man, I should not be much afraid to be tried by Baron Platt.

At the Mayor of Liverpool's soirée

September 26th. 1854

ON SATURDAY EVENING, my wife and I went to a soirée, given by the Mayor and Mrs Lloyd at the Town Hall. It was quite brilliant; the public rooms being really magnificent; and adorned for the occasion with a large collection of pictures, belonging to Mr Naylor. They were mostly (I believe entirely) of modern artists, comprising some of Turner, Wilkie, Landseer, and others of the best English painters. Turner's seemed too airy to have been done by mortal hands.

The British scientific association being now in session here, many distinguished strangers were present. What chiefly struck me, however, was the lack of beauty in the women, and the horrible ugliness of not a few of them. I have heard a good deal of the tenacity with which English women retain their personal charms to a late period of life; but my experience is, that an English lady of forty or fifty is apt to become the most hideous animal that ever pretended to human shape. No caricature could do justice to some of their figures and features; so puffed out, so huge, so without limit, with such hanging dewlaps, and all manner of fleshly abomination—dressed, too, in a way to show all these points to the worst advantage, and walking about with entire self-satisfaction, unconscious of the wrong they are doing to one's idea of womanhood. They are gross, gross, gross. Who would not shrink from such a mother! Who would not abhor such a wife! I really pitied the respectable elderly gentlemen whom I saw walking about with such atrocities on their arms—the grim, red-faced monsters! Surely, a man would be justified in murdering them—in taking a sharp knife and cutting away their mountainous flesh, until he had brought them into reasonable shape, as a sculptor seeks for the beautiful form of woman in a shapeless block of marble. The husband must feel that something alien has grown over and incrusted the slender creature whom he married, and that he is horribly wronged by having all this flabby flesh imposed upon him as his wife. 'Flesh of his flesh', indeed! And this ugliness surely need not be, at least to such a dreadful extent; it must be, in great part, the penalty of a life of gross feeding—of much ale-guzzling and beef-eating. Nor is it possible to conceive of any delicacy and grace of soul existing within; or if there be such, the creatures ought to be killed, in order to release the spirit so vilely imprisoned.

I really and truly believe that the entire body of American washerwomen would present more grace than the entire body of English ladies, were both to be shown up together. American women, of all ranks, when past their prime, generally look thin, worn, care-begone, as if they may have led a life of much trouble and few enjoyments; but English women look as if they had fed upon the fat of meat, and made themselves gross and earthy in all sorts of ways. As a point of taste, I prefer my own countrywomen; though it is a pity that we must choose between a greasy animal and an anxious skeleton.

The Englishman's contemptuous jealousy of America

October 6th. 1854

THE PEOPLE, FOR several days, have been in the utmost anxiety, and latterly in the highest exultation, about Sebastopol; and all England, and Europe to boot, has been fooled by the belief that it has fallen. This, however, turns out to be incorrect; and the public visage is somewhat grim, in consequence. I am glad of it. In spite of his natural sympathies, it is impossible for a true American to be otherwise than glad. Success makes an Englishman intolerable; and, already, on the mistaken idea that the way was open to a prosperous conclusion of this war, The Times had begun to throw out menaces against America. I shall never love England till she sues to us for help; and, in the meantime, the fewer triumphs she obtains, the better for all parties. An Englishman in adversity is a very respectable character; he does not lose his dignity, but merely comes to a proper conceit of himself and is thereby a great deal less ridiculous than he generally is. It is rather touching, to a mere observer like myself, to see how much the universal heart is in this matter;—to see the merchants gathering round the telegraphic messages, posted on the pillars of the Exchange newsroom —the people in the streets, who cannot afford to buy a paper, clustering round the windows of the news-offices, where a copy is pinned up;—the groups of corporals and sergeants at the recruiting rendezvous, with a newspaper in the midst of them;—and all earnest and sombre, and feeling like one man together, whatever their rank. I seem to myself like a spy or a traitor, when I meet their eyes, and am conscious that I neither hope nor fear in sympathy with them, although (unless they detect me for an American by my aspect) they look at me in full confidence of sympathy. Their heart 'knoweth its own bitterness'; and as for me, being a stranger and an alien, I 'inter-meddle not with their joy'. There is an account to settle between us and them for the contemptuous jealousy with which (since it has ceased to be unmitigated contempt) they regard us; and if they do not make us amends by coming humbly to ask our assistance, they must do it by fairly acknowledging us as their masters.

Time telescoped

October 9th. 1854

MY ANCESTOR LEFT England in 1635. I return in 1853. I sometimes feel as if I myself had been absent these two hundred and eighteen years—leaving England just emerging from the feudal system, and finding it on the verge of Republicanism. It brings the two far separated points of time very closely together, to view the matter thus.

Meekness of the unemployed

February 21st. 1855

YESTERDAY, TWO COMPANIES of work-people came to our house at Rock Park, asking assistance—being out of work, and with no resources other than charity. There were a dozen or more in each party. Their deportment was quiet, and altogether unexceptionable—no rudeness, no gruffness, nothing of menace. Indeed, such demonstrations would not have been safe, as they were followed by two policemen; but they really seem to take their distress as their own misfortune and God's will, and impute it to nobody as a fault. This meekness is very touching, and makes one question the more whether they have all their rights. There have been disturbances, within a day or two, in Liverpool, and shops have been broken open and robbed of bread and money; but this is said to have been done by idle vagabonds, not by the really hungry work-people. These last submit to starvation meekly and patiently, as if it were an every day matter with them, or, at least, nothing but what lay fairly within their horoscope. I suppose, in fact, their stomachs have the physical habit that makes hunger not intolerable, because customary. If they had been used to a full flesh-diet, their hunger would be fierce, like that of ravenous beasts;—but now, like the eels, they are 'used to it'.

English restraint breaks down

Septr. 11th. Tuesday. 1855

. . . EMERGING FROM THE Temple, I stopt to smoke a cigar at a tavern in the Strand, the waiter of which observed to me—'they say Sebastopol is taken, Sir!' It was only such an interesting event that could have induced an English waiter to make a remark to a stranger, not called for in the way of business.

London street-scenes

Septr. 14th. Friday. 1855

. . . TUMBLERS, HAND-ORGANISTS, puppet-showmen, musicians, Highland bag-pipers, and all such vagrant mirthmakers, are very numerous in the streets of London. The other day, passing through Fleet-street, I saw a crowd filling up a narrow court, and high above their heads, a tumbler, standing on his head on the top of a pole that reached as high as the third story of the neighbouring houses. Sliding down the pole, headforemost, he disappeared out of my sight. A multitude of Punches go the rounds continually. Two have passed through our street, this morning. The first asked two shillings for his performance; so we sent him away. The second demanded, in the first place, half-a-crown, but finally consented to take a shilling, and gave us the show at that price, though much maimed of its proportions. Besides the spectators in our windows, he had a little crowd on the sidewalk, to whom he went round for contributions, but I did not observe that anybody gave him so much as a half-penny. It is strange to see how many people are aiming at the small change in your pocket; in every square, a beggar-woman meets you, and turns back to follow your steps with her miserable murmur; at the street-crossings, there are old men or little girls with their brooms; urchins propose to brush your boots; if you get into a cab, a man runs to open the door for you, and touches his hat for a fee, as he closes it again.

Christmas in England

December 26th. Wednesday. 1855

ON CHRISTMAS EVE, and yesterday, there were little branches of mistletoe hanging in several parts of our house, in the kitchen, the entries, the parlor, and the smoking room–suspended from the gas-fittings. The maids of the house did their utmost to entrap the gentlemen-boarders, old and young, under these privileged places, and there to kiss them, after which they were expected to pay a shilling. It is very queer, being customarily so respectful, that they should assume this license now, absolutely trying to pull the gentlemen into the kitchen by main force, and kissing the harder and more abundantly, the more they were resisted. A little rosy-cheeked Scotch lass—at other times very modest—was the most active in this business. I doubt whether any gentleman but myself escaped. I heard old Mr Smith parleying with the maids last evening, and pleading his age; but he seems to have met with no mercy; for there was a sound of prodigious smacking, immediately afterwards. Julian was assaulted, and fought most vigorously, but was outrageously kissed—receiving some scratches, moreover, in the conflict. The mistletoe has white, wax-looking berries, and dull green leaves, with a parasitical stem.

Early in the morning of Christmas Day, long before daylight, I heard music in the street, and a woman's voice, powerful and melodious, singing a Christmas hymn. Before bedtime, I presume one half of England, at a moderate calculation, was the worse for liquor. They are still a nation of beastly eaters and beastly drinkers; this tendency manifests itself at holiday time, though, for the rest of the year, it may be decently repressed. Their market-houses, at this season, show the national taste for heavy feeding; carcases of prize oxen, immensely fat and bulky, fat sheep, with their woolly heads and tails still on, and stars and other devices ingeniously wrought on the quarters; fat pigs, adorned with flowers, like corpses of virgins; hares, wild fowl, geese, ducks, turkeys; and green boughs and banners suspended about the stalls—and a great deal of dirt and griminess on the stone-floor of the market-house, and on the persons of the crowd.

There are some Englishmen whom I like—one or two for whom, I might almost say, I have an affection;—but still there is not the same union between us, as if they were Americans. A cold, thin medium intervenes betwixt our most intimate approaches. It puts me in mind of Alnaschar, when he went to bed with a princess, but placed the cold steel of his scimitar between. Perhaps, if I were at home, I might feel differently; but, in this foreign land, I can never forget the distinction between English and American.

Dung-collectors

January 1st. 1856. Tuesday

... I SEE NOTHING more disgusting than the women and the girls here in Liverpool, who pick up horsedung in the streets—rushing upon the treasure, the moment it is dropt, taking it by the handsfull and putting it in their baskets. Some are old women; some marriageable girls, and not uncomely girls, were they well dressed and clean. What a business is this!

In the House of Commons

April 13th. Sunday. 1856

... FROM DOWNING-STREET, we crossed over and entered Westminster Hall and passed through it, and up the flights of steps at its further end, and along the avenue of statues into the vestibule of the House of Commons. It was now somewhat past five; and we stood at the inner entrance of the House to see the members pass in, Bennoch pointing out to me the distinguished ones. I was not much impressed with the appearance of the members generally; they seemed to me rather shabbier than English gentlemen generally, and I saw, or fancied, in many of them, a certain self-importance, as they passed into the interior, betokening them to be very full of their dignity. Some of them looked more American—more like American politicians—than most Englishmen do. There was now and then a gray-headed country-gentleman, the very type of stupidity; and two or three city-members came up and spoke to Bennoch, and showed themselves quite as dull, in their aldermanic way, as the country squires. I suppose there are not ten men in the entire six hundred, who would be missed. Bennoch pointed out Lord John Russell; a little, very short, elderly gentleman, in a brown coat, and so large a hat—not large of brim, but large like a peck measure—that I saw really no face beneath it. By and by, came a rather tall, slender person, in a black frock, buttoned up, and black pantaloons, taking long steps, but, I thought, rather feebly or listlessly. His shoulders were round; or else he had a habitual stoop in them. He had a prominent nose, a thin face, and a sallow, very sallow, complexion, and was a very unwholesome looking person; and had I seen him in America, I should have taken him for a hard-worked editor of a newspaper, weary and worn with night-work and want of exercise; shrivelled, and withered, before his time. It was Disraeli, and I never saw any other Englishman look in the least like him; though, in America, his appearance would not attract notice, as being unusual. I do not remember any other noteworthy person whom we saw enter; in fact, the house had already been some time in session, and most of the members were in their places.

We were to dine in the refectory of the house, with Mr Ingram, the new member for Boston; and, meanwhile, Bennoch obtained admittance for us into the speaker's gallery, whence we had a view of the members, and could hear what was going on. A Mr Muntz was speaking on the Income Tax, and he was followed by Sir George Cornewall Lewis, and others; but it was all very interesting, without the slightest animation, or attempt at oratory—which indeed would have been quite out of place. We saw Lord Palmerston, but at too great a distance to distinguish anything but a gray head. The House had daylight in it when we entered, and for some time afterwards; but, by and by the roof, which I had taken to be a solid and opaque ceiling, suddenly brightened, and showed itself to be transparent; a vast expanse of tinted and figured glass, through which came down a great, mild radiance upon the members below. The character of the debate, however, did not grow more luminous or vivacious; so we went down into the vestibule, and there waited for Mr Ingram, who soon came and led us into the refectory. It was very much like the coffee-room of a club. The strict rule forbids the entrance of any members of parliament; but it seems to be winked at, although there is another room, opening beyond this, where the law of exclusion is strictly enforced.

Mr Ingram's dinner was good—not remarkably so, but good enough —a soup, some turbot or salmon, some cutlets, and I know not what else; and a bottle of claret, a bottle of sherry, and a bottle of port; for, as he said, he did not wish to be stingy. Mr Ingram is a self-made man, and a strong instance of the difference between the Englishman and the American, when self-made, and without early education. He is no more a gentleman now, than when he began life, not a whit more refined, either outwardly or inwardly; while the American would have been, after the same experience, in no whit distinguishable, outwardly, and perhaps as refined within, as nine-tenths of the gentlemen born, in the House of Commons. And, besides, an American comes naturally to any distinction to which his success in life may bring him; he takes them as if they were his proper inheritance, and in no wise to be wondered at. Mr Ingram, on the other hand, took evidently a childish delight in his position, and felt a childish wonder in having arrived at it; nor did it seem real to him, after all. He made his first fortunes, I believe, by inventing a quack-pill, and he established the Illustrated News, as a medium of advertising this pill. The pill succeeded marvellously, and the Illustrated News had likewise an independent success of its own; so that he had recently been offered eighty-thousand pounds for it. Mr Ingram is a man of liberal politics, of a kindly nature, of the homeliest personal appearance and manners. He will have no shadow of influence in the House of Commons, beyond his own vote; and, to say the truth, I was a little ashamed of being entertained by such a very vulgar man, especially as I was recognized by Mr Bramley-Moore, and some other Liverpool people. This was really snobbish of me.

While we were drinking our wine, we again saw Disraeli, another adventurer, who has risen from the people by modes perhaps as quackish as those of Mr Ingram. He came, and stood near our table, looking at the bill of fare, and then sat down on the opposite side of the room, with another gentleman, and ate his dinner. He didn't look as if he had a healthy appetite. Bennoch says that he makes himself up with great care, and spends a long time plucking the white hairs from among his sable locks. He is said to be poor; and though he had property with his wife, it is all gone. The story of his marriage (which Bennoch told me, but which I do not remember well enough to record it) does him much credit; and, indeed, I am inclined to like Disraeli, as a man who has made his own place good among a hostile aristocracy, and leads instead of following them.

Reflections on Hampton Court

Septr. 9th. Tuesday. 1856

... ON THE SATURDAY, after our return to Blackheath, Sophia and I, with Julian, went to Hampton Court, about which, as I have already recorded a visit to it, I need say little here. But I was again impressed with the stately grandeur of Wolsey's Great Hall, with its great window at each end, and one side-window descending almost to the floor, and a row of windows, on each side, high towards the roof, and throwing down their many-colored light on the stone-pavement, and on the Gobelin tapestry, which must have been so gorgeously rich, when the walls were first clothed with it. I fancied, then, that no modern architect could produce so fine a room; but, oddly enough, in the great entrance-hall of Euston Railway Station, yesterday, I could not see how this last fell very much short of Wolsey's Hall, in grandeur. I was quite wearied, and Sophia was altogether over-wrought, in passing through the endless suites of rooms, in Hampton Court, and gazing at the thousands of pictures; it is too much for one day—almost enough for one life, in such measure as life can be bestowed on pictures. It would have refreshed us had we spent half the time in wandering about the grounds, which, as we glimpsed at them from the windows of the palace, seem very beautiful, though laid out with antique formality of straight lines, and broad, gravelled paths. Before the central window, there is a beautiful sheet of water, and a fountain up-shooting itself and plashing into it, with a continuous and pleasant sound. How beautiful the royal robe of a monarchy is embroidered! Palaces, pictures, parks! They do enrich life; and kings and aristocracies cannot keep these things to themselves—they merely take care of them for others. Even a king, with all the glory that can be shed around him, is but a liveried and bedizened footman of his people, and the toy of their delight. I am very glad that I came to this country while the English are still playing with such a toy.

Reputation of Americans in England

... A SHORT TIME ago, in the evening, in a street of Liverpool, I saw a decent man, of the lower orders, taken much aback by being roughly brushed against by a rowdy fellow. He looked after him and exclaimed indignantly—'Is that a Yankee?' It shows the kind of character we have here.

In Manchester Cathedral

April 14th. Wednesday, 1857, at Southport
... IN THE MORNING, we went out and visited Manchester Cathedral, a particularly black and grimy old ediface, containing some genuinely old wood carvings within the choir. We staid a good while, in order to see some people married. One couple, with their groomsman and bridesmaid were sitting within the choir; but when the clergyman was robed and ready, there entered five other couples, each attended by groomsman and bridesmaid. They all seemed to be of the lower orders; one or two respectably dressed, but most of them poverty-stricken; the men in their ordinary loafer's or laborer's attire; the women with their poor, shabby shawls drawn closely about them; faded untimely, wrinkled with penury and care; nothing fresh, virginlike, or hopeful about them; joining themselves to their mates, with the idea of making their own misery less intolerable by adding another's to it. All the six couples stood up in a row before the altar, with the groomsmen and bridesmaids in a row behind them; and the clergyman proceeded to marry them in such a way that it almost seemed to make every man and woman the husband and wife of every other. However, there were some small portions of the service directed towards each separate couple; and they appeared to assort themselves in their own fashion afterwards, each man saluting his bride with a kiss. The clergyman, the sexton, and the clerk, all seemed to find something funny in this affair; and the woman, who admitted us into the church, smiled too, when she told us that a wedding-party was waiting to be married.

But I think it was the saddest thing we have seen since leaving home; though funny enough, if one likes to look at it from the ludicrous point of view.

Leamington

October 10th. Lansdowne Circus, Leamington. 1857 I RETURNED HITHER from Liverpool on Wednesday evening of last week, and have spent the time here idly, since then, reposing myself after the four years of unnatural restraint in the Consulate. Being already pretty much acquainted with the neighbourhood of Leamington, I have little or nothing to record about this prettiest, cheerfullest, cleanest of English towns, with its beautiful elms, its lazy river, its villas, its brilliant shops —its whole smartness and gentility in the midst of green, sylvan scenery and hedgerows, and in the neighbourhood of old thatched and moss-grown villages clustering each about the little, square battlemented tower of a church; villages such as Leamington itself was before Dr Jephson transformed it into a fashionable watering-place fifty years ago. Our immediate abode is a small, neat house, in a circle of just such houses, so exactly alike that it is difficult to find one's own peculiar domicile; each with its little ornamented plot of grass and flowers, with a bit of iron fence in front, and an intersecting hedge between its grass plot and that of its neighbor; and in the center of the Circus a little paddock of shrubbery and trees, box, yew, and much other variety of foliage, now tinged autumnally. I have seldom seen, and never before lived in, such a quiet, cozy, comfortable, social seclusion and snuggery. Nothing disturbs us; it being an eddy quite aside from the stream of life. Once or twice a day, perhaps, a cab or private carriage drives round the Circus and stops at one or another of the doors; twice a day comes the red-coated postman, delivering letters from door to door; in the evening, he rings a handbell as he goes his round, a signal that he is ready to take letters for the post; in other respects, we are quite apart from the stir of the world. Our neighbours (as I learn from the list of visitors and residents in a weekly newspaper) are half-pay officers with their families, and other such quiet and respectable people, who have no great figure to make or particular business to do in life. I do not wonder at their coming here to live; there cannot be a better place for people of moderate means, who have done with hope and effort, and only want to be comfortable.

York Minster

July 14th. Tuesday, Southport. 1857

... AFTER BREAKFAST, WE all went to the Cathedral; and no sooner were we within it, than we found how much our eyes had recently been educated, by the power of appreciating this magnificent interior; for it impressed both my wife and me with a joy that we never felt before. Julian felt it too, and insisted that the Cathedral must have been altered and improved, since we were last here. But it is only that we have seen much splendid architecture, since then, and have so grown in some degree fitted to enjoy it. York Cathedral (I say it now, for it is my present feeling) is the most wonderful work that ever came from the hands of man. Indeed, it seems like a 'house not made with hands', but rather to have come down from above, bringing an awful majesty and sweetness with it; and it is so light and aspiring, with all its vast columns and pointed arches, that one would hardly wonder if it should ascend back to heaven again, by its mere spirituality. Positively, the pillars and arches of the choir are so very beautiful that they give the impression of being exquisitely polished, though such is not the fact; but their beauty throws a gleam around them. I thank God that I saw this Cathedral again, and thank Him that he inspired the builder to make it, and that mankind has so long enjoyed it.

In the British Museum

Gt. Russell St., Dec. 7th. Monday. 1857

... IN ALL THE rooms, I saw people of the poorer classes, some of whom seemed to view the objects intelligently and to take a genuine interest in them. A poor man in London has great opportunities of cultivating himself, if he will only make the best of them; and such an institution as the British Museum can hardly fail to attract, as the magnet does steel, the minds that are likeliest to be benefitted by it in its various departments. I saw many children there, and some ragged boys.

It deserves to be noticed, that some figures of Indian Thugs, represented as engaged in their profession and handiwork of cajoling and strangling travellers, have been removed from the place which they formerly occupied in the part of the Museum shown to the general public. They are now in the more private room; and the reason of their withdrawal is, that, according to the Chaplain of Newgate, the practice of garrotting was suggested to the English thieves by this representation of Indian Thugs. It is edifying, after what I have written in the preceding paragraph, to find that the only lesson known to have been inculcated here, is that of a new mode of outrage.

Henry Brooks Adams

great-grandson of the second President of the United States
and grandson of the sixth, was born in Boston in 1838 and
educated at Harvard. When his father, Charles Francis Adams,
was appointed U.S. Minister to England in 1861 he accompanied
him as his secretary. His conclusions about his British experiences
are set down in his autobiography, *The Education of Henry Adams.*
He died in Washington in 1919.

Arriving in England

THE OCEAN, THE *Persia*, Captain Judkins, and Mr G. P. R. James, the most distinguished passenger, vanished one Sunday morning in a furious gale in the Mersey, to make place for the drearier picture of a Liverpool street as seen from the Adelphi coffee-room in November murk, followed instantly by the passionate delights of Chester and the romance of red-sandstone architecture. Millions of Americans have felt this succession of emotions. Possibly very young and ingenuous tourists feel them still, but in the days before tourists, when the romance was a reality, not a picture, they were overwhelming. When the boys went out to Eaton Hall, they were awed, as Thackeray or Dickens would have felt in the presence of a Duke. The very name of Grosvenor struck a note of grandeur. The long suite of lofty, gilded rooms with their gilded furniture; the portraits; the terraces; the gardens, the landscape; the sense of superiority in the England of the fifties, actually set the rich nobleman apart, above Americans and shopkeepers. Aristocracy was real. So was the England of Dickens. Oliver Twist and Little Nell lurked in every church-yard shadow, not as shadow but alive. Even Charles the First was not very shadowy, standing on the tower to see his army defeated. Nothing thereabouts had very much changed since he lost his battle and his head. An eighteenth-century American boy fresh from Boston naturally took it all for education, and was amused at this sort of lesson. At least he thought he felt it.

Then came the journey up to London through Birmingham and the Black District, another lesson, which needed much more to be rightly felt. The plunge into darkness lurid with flames; the sense of unknown horror in this weird gloom which then existed nowhere else, and never had existed before, except in volcanic craters; the violent contrast between this dense, smoky, impenetrable darkness, and the soft green charm that one glided into, as one emerged—the revelation of an unknown society of the pit—made a boy uncomfortable, though he had no idea that Karl Marx was standing there waiting for him, and that sooner or later the process of education would have to deal with Karl Marx much more than with Professor Bowen of Harvard College or his Satanic free-trade majesty John Stuart Mill. The Black District was a practical education, but it was infinitely far in the distance. The boy ran away from it, as he ran away from everything he disliked.

Had he known enough to know where to begin he would have seen something to study, more vital than the Civil Law, in the long, muddy, dirty, sordid, gas-let dreariness of Oxford Street as his dingy four-wheeler dragged its weary way to Charing Cross. He did notice one peculiarity about it worth remembering. London was still London. A certain style dignified its grime; heavy, clumsy, arrogant, purse-proud, but not cheap; insular but large; barely tolerant of an out-side world, and absolutely self-confident. The boys in the streets made such free comments on the American clothes and figures, that the travellers hurried to put on tall hats and long overcoats to escape criti-cism. No stranger had rights even in the Strand. The eighteenth century held its own. History muttered down Fleet Street, like Dr Johnson, in Adams's ear; Vanity Fair was alive on Piccadilly in yellow chariots with coachmen in wigs, on hammer-cloths; footmen with canes, on the footboard, and a shrivelled old woman inside; half the great houses, black with London smoke, bore large funereal hatch-ments; every one seemed insolent, and the most insolent structures in the world were the Royal Exchange and the Bank of England. In November, 1858, London was still vast, but it was the London of the eighteenth century that an American felt and hated.

London society

To Charles Francis Adams, Jr.

.   .   .   .   .   London, June 10, 1861.

THE EXPERIENCES IN this city are enormous and if the Ambassador's private income fails we must cut our establishment down to a very low figure, as one can do little here with less than forty thousand, and occasionally live on less, but if so, they must have assistance from the public charities. The scale of living and the prices are curious examples of the beauties of a high civilization.

As for myself, I have only the same old story to sing which I have chanted many times, especially in my letters to you. I have done nothing whatever in the way of entering society, nor do I mean to take the plunge until after my presentation on the 19th. Getting into society is a repulsive piece of work here. Supposing you are invited to a ball. You arrive at eleven o'clock. A footman in powder asks your name and announces you. The lady or ladies of the house receive you and shake hands. You pass on and there you are. You know not a soul. No one offers to introduce you. No one even looks at you with curiosity. London society is so vast that the oldest habitués know only their own sets, and never trouble themselves even to look at anyone else. No one knows that you're a stranger. You see numbers of men and women just as silent and just as strange as yourself. You may go from house to house and from route to route and never see a face twice. You may labor for weeks at making acquaintances and yet go again and again to balls where you can't discover a face you ever saw before. And supposing you are in society, what does it amount to? The state dinners are dull, heavy, lifeless affairs. The balls are solemn stupid crushes without a scintilla of the gayety of our balls. No one enjoys them so far as I can hear. They are matters of necessity, of position. People have to entertain. They were born to it and it is one of the duties of life. My own wish is quietly to slide into the literary set and leave the heavy society, which without dancing is a frightful and irredeemable bore to me, all on one side . . .

The American Civil War and the English

To Charles Francis Adams, Jr.

London, 20 March, 1863.

. . . . .

WE ARE IN a shocking bad way here. I don't know what we are ever going to do with this damned old country. Some day it will wake up and find itself at war with us, and then what a squealing there'll be. By the Lord, I would almost be willing to submit to our sufferings, just to have the pleasure of seeing our privateers make ducks and drakes of their commerce. I'll tell you what I mean to do . . .

But meanwhile, as I say, we are in a worse mess here than we have known since the *Trent* affair, and the devil of it is that I am in despair of our getting any military success that would at all counter-

[116]

balance our weight. When our armies try to do anything they are invariably beaten, and now they seem to be tired of trying. I'll bet a sovereign to a southern shin-plaster that we don't take Charleston; either that we don't try or are beaten. I'll bet five golden pounds to a diminutive greenback that we don't clear the Mississippi, and that we don't hurt Richmond. My only consolation is that the Southerners are suffering dreadfully under the tension we keep them at, and as I prefer this to having fresh disasters of our own, I am in no hurry to see anyone move. But meanwhile we are in a tangle with England that can only be cleared with our excellent good navy cannon. If I weren't so brutally seasick, I would go into the navy and have a lick at these fat English turkey-buzzards.

At the same time, individually, I haven't at all the same dislike to the English. They are very like ourselves and are very pleasant people. And then they are quite as ready to blackguard themselves as anyone could wish, if they're let alone. There are all the elements of a great, reforming, liberal party at work here, and a few years will lay in peace that old vindictive rogue who now rules England and weighs like an incubus on all advance. Then you will see the new generation, with which it is my only satisfaction here to have some acquaintance, take up the march again and press the country into shape.

The marriage of the Prince of Wales

To Charles Francis Adams, Jr.

London, 6 March, 1863.

.   .   .   .   .   .

SUCH A BOTHER and fuss as all the world keeps up about this unhappy Prince of Wales, who would give his best pair of new breeches to be a very humble private individual for the next week. He is quite popular here, for he is thoughtful of others and kind, and hates ceremony. So it seems as though a temporary bee has lodged in the bonnet of this good people, who have set to work with a sort of determined, ponderous and massive hilarity, to do him honour. I suppose you will get from first hand a correct account of the events of last Saturday at Court. Also you will receive a photograph of our sister as she appeared. She is now fairly launched. Pretty, attractive, sympathetic and well-informed;

but the time and contact with the world will have to do much to develop her. To my mind, London fashionable society (routs, receptions, dances, I mean) is intolerably stupid. I've not the genius to find anything in it worthy of tasting, to one who has drunk the hot draughts of our flirtatious style of youthful amusement. If she can learn to prefer the heavy patronage of stupid elder sons, to a gayer style of thing, she will learn, no doubt, to have a good time.

As to public affairs I have nothing to tell you, as we are going on excellently well. We have done our work in England, and if you military heroes would only give us a little encouragement, we should be cocks of the walk in England. But diplomacy has certainly had no aid from the sword to help a solution of its difficulties. Couldn't some of you give us just one leetle sugar-plum? We are shocking dry.

Of course, there is plenty to do. I am busy writing, recording, filing and collating letters and documents four or five hours every day, and my books and files for the last two years are beginning to assume a portentous size. Still it is very easy and mechanical work and doesn't prevent me from another sort of application which is more on my own account in these times, when the chances are indefinitely against one's ever succeeding in bringing the results into action.

Tomorrow is to be the entrance of the Princess Alexandra, and all the world is going to see it. Next Tuesday is the wedding and an illumination. Ye Gods! what an infernal row it is! . . .

In the Hebrides

To Charles Francis Adams, Jr.

Lowood Hotel,
Windermere,
Thursday, 3 Sept., 1863.

. . . . . .

FROM BANAVIE, WHERE we slept, our road lay for several miles along the head of Loch Eil. Then it rose among the mountains, wild and desolate scenery, where hardly even a miserable cabin is to be seen for miles together. At intervals it rained, and at times we caught a little sunshine, which had a wonderful effect in lighting up a scene so sad and dark without it that even our spirits could only counteract the impression by attempts to learn Gaelic phrases from our driver, a *divertissement* which kept us roaring for miles. At length, after some twelve miles of this work, we suddenly came upon a marshy plain at the head of a long loch (Shiel), where a solitary stone column rose in a way that impressed me curiously with the dreary nature of the place. Of all things in the world a monument of that size seemed to be the thing one least expected there. I asked the driver what it was, and he told me it commemorated the spot where Prince Charles the Pretender was killed. I could not conceive what the blockhead meant, being aware that the Pretender had not gratified his enemies by getting himself put an end to. But as the dogcart came to a halt for an hour to rest, a short distance further on, Brooks and I walked back, and after much wading and jumping and wetting, we reached the spot and found a long inscription in English, Latin and Gaelic, stating that it was here Prince Charles raised his standard in 1745. A more desolate, repelling spot I have seldom seen, and I appreciated for the first time the courage of that young fellow, who could drag himself from Paris and sunlight, in order to lead a desperate venture of filthy barbarians and plant his standard on a spot like this.

In long reaches of Scotch mist, diversified by gleams of gray sunshine, we climbed mountain after mountain, all barren as your saddle, except for heath and waterfalls, and all stamped with the same character of stern and melancholy savageness. The roads however are excellent and as there is never much snow or great cold, they keep in good order. We changed our horses some ten miles further on, and then began descending towards the sea. As our miserable horse, urged on by steady and vigorous chastisement, slowly worried forwards, the weather began to improve, and to my surprise, the country began to take on a civilized aspect. When at last we reached the seashore, we found a lovely landscape—wide woods, and green pastures, cattle and even deer, a mild air and a pleasant sun beaming upon us, as though there had never been a Scotch mist (a phrase which means a heavy rain). This is the peninsula of Arisaig; a sort of Wood's Hole, deserted in the afternoon sun, and at the inn, the only one, we descended and dismissed our vehicle. Two cares oppressed my mind. The first was to order some dinner, for it was five o'clock. The second to procure a boat to take us over to Skye. The first was soon eased. We had our dinner, if a dish of burnt steaks and potatoes deserves that honoured title. The second was also relieved, but as it takes every Highlander two hours to do what should occupy fifteen minutes, and as our men had to be summoned from the plough and the anvil, it was seven o'clock before we were on board. Three men made our crew, and a boat like a man of war, and in this form, in consideration of the sum of five dollars, we were to be conveyed to the nearest public house in Skye, a distance of ten or twelve miles.

The evening was calm, hardly a breath of air helping us, but it was fine. A gentle roll swelled against our quarter, and yielding to its influence, I lay down on the seat across the boat, and watched our course. . . . The long mountainous coast of Scotland, lighted by the sunset and twilight, looked very grand in the distance, and on our left were the mountains of Skye covered with heavy folds of mist. For three hours or more we went on in this manner, the men relieving each other at the oars, for they had to pull the whole way. I enjoyed immensely this evening sail on the Hebridean seas. Civil wars, disgust and egoism, social fuss and worry, responsibility and worry, were as far at least as the moon. They left me free on the Sound of Sleat. I felt as peaceful and as quiet as a giant, and saw the evening shades darken into night, and phosphorus waves of light swell in the air and under the boat, with a joyful sense of caring not a penny when I had my breakfast.

Arrive we did at last, though Brooks thought we never should, but this part was rather embarrassing. The little hamlet near Armadale Castle boasts a landing place only at high tide, whereas the tide was now low. We had therefore to land on the rocks and paddle in the dark over the bogs to firm land. As we stepped along, our shoes, crushing the wet seaweed, called out at every moment bright, flashing phosphoric flames, so that we seemed to be walking on liquid fire. Pretty thoroughly wet, we did at last reach a road and made our way to a wayside inn, from which much merriment and singing proceeded. The maid who appeared at our call, was innocent of the tongue of Shakespeare and Milton. She owned allegiance only to her native Gaelic. A man, however, was at length produced, who seemed mortified to have no better to offer us, but the nearest town was fifteen miles and more, and there were no vehicles. If there had been, we shouldn't have used them. There we were and there we meant to sleep, so we took possession of two rooms, which were new and therefore reasonably clean. Our sheets were clean but ragged, and the other bed-clothes! Well they were rough! After nearly being assaulted by one of the band of minstrels, who were salmon fishers, drinking and howling a monotonous song, which they accompanied by stamping their feet, I got some supper, tea, toast, boiled eggs, etc., and Brooks and I having sleepily supped, and waited long for the salmon fishers' drunken dirge to cease, turned in towards midnight and so slept in peace.

The sun was bright on our first morning in the Hebrides. I looked out at nine o'clock, shuddered at the sight of my resting-place, and dressed with a cheerfulness and a light heart. Poor Brooks, however, came into my room, looking very fishy, and complained of a sick headache. We had breakfast, and I swallowed much porridge, a dish that is in itself neither savory nor rich, but which is far superior to tough ham drowned in bowls of oil, or even to hard boiled eggs. I then desired a conveyance to the next town, seventeen miles, but to my alarm (on Brooks' account) learned that no conveyance was to be had except one, which I proceeded to examine and which proved to be a heavy farm cart, which might have been drawn by oxen, but which in fact was conducted by a horse. *Que faire!* Seventeen miles in an ox cart with a sick headache! Still, our baggage must go and my mind resigned itself. The sluggish cart was drawn before the door, and my pipe being lighted, I sounded boot and saddle. Before we departed, however, the Gaelic damsel persuaded me through an interpreter to buy a pair of woollen socks knit by her fair hands, which I may send to you, and in case their proportions be too elephantine, you can make them over to some deserving foot.

I can't tell you how I enjoyed this morning. England boasts of few days in her year. For ten miles I walked along the shore of the Sound, and a more splendid scene I couldn't put my finger on. The west coast of Scotland is rugged and wild, with deep scorings or indentations that form salt water lochs. Towards this shore I was looking, across a sound some five miles broad, which gradually was lost in the lands towards the north. Mountains were all around, but they were so softened by the sun that again I fancied myself in Italy. This corner of Skye is quite civilized too. There are trees, hedges and green pastures towards the sea-shore, and it was only as I advanced and at length turned away from the east, that we reached a desolate region, where heather and peat-bogs are the sole articles of production. I shall always remember my morning between Armadale and Broadford as a day *comme il y en a peu* . . .

If the morning's walk from Armadale was lovely and made me think of Italy, the afternoon's drive to Sligachan was enormous and belonged to no country on God's earth except Skye alone. Between smooth conical mountains, whose sides were tinged with a doubtful green where the gaunt skeleton did not break out, and the blue sea, our road drove on, round silent lochs and through a howling wilderness strewn with the débris of ancient glaciers, and offering not one blade of grass or grain, except on a narrow strip along the sea-shore. The mountains of Skye are peculiar, but more of that hereafter. Not only was our ride delightful on account of the beauty of the scenery, the exquisite evening and all that, but Brooks showed signs of returning peckishness, and from the rapid fire of questions which he, à la Charles Kuhn, began to open on the driver, I knew he felt better. Several miles of the distance we walked, and when we rounded the last headland and had but two miles more, I sent them ahead, and in a solitude and deadly silence walked up the long loch at the head of which stands the solitary inn of Glen Sligachan, where I arrived just as the purple mountain tops were changing to a dark, cold, and solemn gray. It reminded me of my voyage with Ben Crowninshield up the Furca Pass in Switzerland. Solitude of utter barrenness on every side.

A supper of broiled salmon made up for our dinner, and Brooks had at last found his appetite. The inn was not a paradise, being like all highland inns, of an ugly and throat-cutting appearance. But you will have no great sympathy for me on this reckoning.

The next morning was cloudy, and I felt that a storm was brewing. As I have no fancy for early rising, and am quite ready to leave to you the benefits of that habit, I ordered breakfast at our usual hour of nine o'clock and ponies for ten. As Brooks and I were seating ourselves at breakfast, contemplating the broil with pleasure, in comes a new arrival, seats himself at the table and coolly asks me to help him to some of the salmon; *my* salmon, by the Lord, and he poached it as coolly as though he were proprietor of fish in general. The man is a sucker, thought I to myself, and we will avoid him. Consequently, when we mounted our ponies and I saw that the person had also ordered a pony and joined himself to us and our guide, I was very short and sharp, and ignored him entirely, treating with silence his mild hints as to the route. So our caravan of three ponies and a guide moved slowly off, up Glen Sligachan.

Quietly and between ourselves, I am no admirer of the Scotch mountain scenery. It is too uniform in its repulsive bareness. I like another sort of thing. Grand mountain peaks covered with glistening snow, whose base descends towards Italian plains and is green with olive trees and vineyards; that is my ideal of the sublime and beautiful. Yet certain it is that the scenery of Loch Coruisk made an impression on me that few things can, and like all great masterpieces, the more I think of it, the more extraordinary it seems to be. Evidently it was formerly the bed of an enormous glacier. A vast volume of ice, creeping down year after year, to the sea, carried with it every trace of soil, and scored and polished the rocks over which it passed. When the glacier yielded to some unexplained change of temperature, it left behind it nothing but this lake among the rocks close to the sea, and in a semi-circle around it, a series of sharp mountain peaks, jagged and excoriated, whose summits seem to have raised a barrier against the outside world. I might give you a good-sized volume of epithets without conveying the least idea of the really awful isolation and silence of this spot. There is as yet nothing human within miles of it, nor any trace of man's action. Even in Switzerland I recollect nothing like it, nor can there ever be, unless the ocean is brought to the foot of the Alps. Should you ever come to England, by all means go and see Coruisk. I would like to have a chance to go with you, and even to pitch my tent there and pass a few days in examining this melancholy district . . .

My original idea had been to go on to Portree and the extremity of the island, but as I found there was little or nothing to see there, and as the weather was so unpromising, I concluded to turn back and make my way to civilized land. So the next morning we set out on our return. The salmon poacher asked to join us in a carriage, and we departed in an open wagon. Before we had gone five miles, the rain descended and the flood came. Tremendous gusts of wind from the mountains drove down regular waves of water on us, and coats and umbrellas were wet through like sieves. The fifteen miles were long as the road to Heaven, and the scenery was, ah! *quantum mutatis ab illo!* When we arrived at Broadford I determined to go no further, and incontinently ordered a lunch of broiled herrings, which were indeed savory.

The storm, which was furious, showed no signs of slackening that evening, and the next day, which was Sunday, it continued with the same violence. As the passage to the mainland was an unknown road to me, and as there are no inns near the ferry, I did not venture to leave my quarters. It was not gay. Brooks tried going to church, but having entered in the middle of service at about one o'clock, and listened some time to the Gaelic parson, he asked his neighbor how long it would last and on hearing that it would be over at five, he precipitately fled. I made no such venture. The only satisfactory thing I did was to have a long talk with a man who had some reason to be acquainted with the island, as to the people. You must know that I have been greatly disgusted with the appearance of the brave high-landers. They strike me as stupid, dirty, ignorant and barbarous. Their mode of life is not different from that of African negroes. Their huts are floorless except for earth; they live all together in them like pigs; there are no chimneys, hardly a window; no conveniences of life of any sort. Dirty, ragged, starved and imbruted, they struggle to cultivate patches of rocky ground where nothing can mature, and in wretched superstition and prejudice they are as deep sunk as their ancestors ever were. One of the best things in Scott's novel of the *Pirate*, which indeed apart from its absurd story, I rate higher than most men do, is a character of the people of Zetland put into the mouth of Triptolemus Yellowley. It would do tolerably well for the Hebrides as well. The character of such out-of-the-way people must always be narrow and ungenerous. Everything tends to crystallize and remain stationary. They are envious, jealous and prejudiced. Any population is too much for such barren regions, and the numbers of the people always tend to undue increase, for they pup like rabbits. Hence a continual struggle for existence, and eternal misery and degradation.

Monday morning, it did not rain. We had some difficulty in getting away, and had to share a dog-cart with a lunatic-inspector as far as Kyle Rhea ferry. As the lunatic was slow, we walked ahead, intending to be caught about five miles out. When we had gone the five miles, it began to rain again, and as no lunatic made his appearance we trudged on the whole eleven miles, to the wretched inn at the ferry. Here we waited and ate oatmeal porridge, Brooks amusing himself by feeding a small dog with it, till, as he expressed it, he 'burst'; that is, became very ill. At last the lunatic appeared and we got across the strait, which is here hardly a mile wide, to Glenelg, where after much highland delay we had to take a carriage and went on, cold and wet to Shiel Inn, where we got a dog-cart and pressed forward ten miles more to Clunie Inn. Imagination had painted here a luxurious supper and snowy beds. Reality showed squalidity and starvation. Unable to stomach it, we took another dog-cart and drove on another ten miles across the mountains to Tomdown Inn. From its neat appearance we imagined wealth and plenty, as we came to it at ten o'clock at night, but our supper consisted of broiled ham and two eggs, all they had, which we ate ferociously.

The next day our family picked our baggage up as they passed from Mr Ellice's to Invergarry, and Brooks and I walked the eleven miles, and went to stay several days with Mr Peabody and Mr Lampson . . .

Elihu Burritt

'the learned blacksmith', was born in Connecticut in 1810. One
of the most formidable autodidacts of his time, he mastered many
languages while still working at the forge. Among other things, he
translated Longfellow's poems into Sanskrit. He became a journalist
and a leading advocate of pacifism. He wrote *Walks in the
Black Country and Its Green Border-lands* while U.S. Consul in
Birmingham, where his identification with the nonconformist
traditions of the town made him a notably popular figure. He died
in 1879.

Farm wagons and farm-labourers' boots

WE OVERTOOK, HALF-WAY up a long hill, one of the great farm wagons of this country, loaded heavily with clay and drawn by three splendid gray horses, each with a hoof that would not go into a peck measure. The whole turn-out looked as if it belonged to a first-class farmer; wagon, horses, and harnesses were of the highest order of perfection. But I was peculiarly struck with that strange economy of forces which distinguishes English farmers, by such marked contrasts, from those of America. Of course it is natural, and perhaps inevitable, that the farmers of all countries should be the most conservative as to traditional habits; that they should cling with the most tenacious adhesion to systems for which they can give no better and no other reason than that their fathers and ancestors did the same before them. Although English farmers are so stoutly conservative in this respect, they show the greatest leaning towards the masses; and they seemingly endeavour to make the masses as solid and as heavy as possible. They have the best roads and the heaviest wagons in the world. You may frequently see in New England a two-story frame house drawn up and down hills on four wheels, not a whit more heavy and solid than those of the average one-horse carts of the English farmer. As for one of the great four-wheeled wagons used here, thilled instead of poled, an American farmer would hardly think of dragging it up a hill with a single horse. But it is not so much in the solidity and weight of their carts and wagons that this peculiar economy of tractor forces, inherited and perpetuated here, may be seen most strikingly illustrated. It is in their application to the masses to be moved. Here before us was an example of the system. I asked the driver to let his three magnificent gray horses straighten their trace chains. I then paced the distance from the collar of the leader to the forward axle of the wagon, and found it a little over *two rods*! Nearly half the length of one horse was lost in the connexion between them. Indeed, as nearly as I could measure it with my walking-stick, it was full six feet between a perpendicular line from the hip of one horse to the collar ring of the one behind him

[126]

to which he was attached. And still the owner of that noble team must have been a farmer of the first-class—doubtless a man of general intelligence, but who had not yet learned to give a reason to himself or others for this strange use of horse-power. You seldom ever see farm-horses used in England in any other way. Whether on plough, cart, or wagon they are nearly always strung together in 'Indian file', with spaces from four to six feet between each couple. I do not now recollect ever having seen a four-wheeled farm-wagon in England with a pole to it. However long and large, it is fitted with a pair of shafts, into which the thill-horse is put. Then frequently, perhaps, even if not generally, you will see the traces of the forward horse hooked into the same ring of the one behind instead of into his drawing chain. This makes another waste, for a great deal of drawing force is lost in the uneven sway and movement of the hindermost horse, and a considerable portion of his weight has to be added to the loaded cart, to make it more *solid* and heavy. It would be almost amusing to an American teamster to watch the manure-wagons climbing over the hills from Birmingham. He would sometimes see a long procession of horses mounting the crown of the eminence seemingly detached from any load. On looking again he would see a huge long wagon looming up so far behind the leader that one would hardly fancy there was any connexion between the two. Sometimes this economy is varied in a unique way. The stoutest horse is put into the shafts, and two spans are attached to him, with not only the long, wasting space between him and them and between each other longitudinally, but laterally; so that if the two horses thus spanned walk evenly abreast, they frequently walk four feet apart, or nearly enough asunder to admit a passing phaeton between them. In travelling through different parts of England I have noticed with much attention this remarkable characteristic—this hereditary and voluntary service and adhesion to *solidity*. And I think any careful observer will come to the conclusion which I have formed, that the farmers of England waste full one-third of their horse-power; or one-sixth in the superfluous weight of their wagons, carts, and ploughs, and one-sixth in its application to them or to the load to be drawn. Often while watching one of these long, straggling string of horses drawing a wagon up a hill, with the leader a full three rods from the forward axle, I have wished that the owner were obliged to take a few rudimental lessons in dynamics, that he might learn to be more merciful to his beasts. I hope it was not wrong to wish him such an exercise for example as this: to undertake to draw a fifty-six pound weight up a hill at the end of a string forty feet long. Having tried this little experiment in tractorial forces two or three times, he would be quite likely to hitch his horses nearer to the load thereafter. Apparently no modern improvements have impaired this homage and tribute to solidity. I doubt if the road-wagons of English farmers of today weigh a single pound less than they did before Macadam was born, or when the highways of the country were made of its own clay or sand.

But not only horseflesh is so burdened and wasted by this 'terrible tractoration', but human bone, blood, and muscle are fearfully sacrificed to this the most exacting of *Penates Anglicani*. From the cradle to the grave the English agricultural labourer bears the heavy burden of this homage. Should this book go to another edition, I intend it shall present, among its illustrations, not only English and American wagons, carts, ploughs, scythes, rakes, and axes, but also the farm-labourers' shoes of the two countries, in comparison. Those worn by the majority of the agricultural labourers here are verifiable clogs to locomotion, in weight half leather and half iron. Indeed the latter must often preponderate. When on my walk from London to Land's End, I stepped into a blacksmith's shop to see the smith shoe a donkey. Near the anvil was a pair of leather shoes brought in to be shod. The number and size of the nails driven into the soles and heels were perfectly wonderful. I am sure they would weigh as much as the four iron shoes the smith was nailing to the donkey's hoofs. The effect of wearing such heavy shoes from youth up is as perceptible in the labourer's gait as the wearing of heavy iron armour must have been in the walk and carriage of the knights of old. In the first place, there is no spring or elasticity to a pair of shoes thus bottomed with iron. They do not shed mud by the motion of the foot. Then, being so thick and broad soled, they inevitably *interfere* with each other if lifted perpendicularly. So the wearer at every step describes the segment of a circle with his foot. This motion brings his knees together, like the joints of a pair of compasses. And the habit becomes a second nature to him, and he wears it all his life long. You will not see one English farm-labourer in ten lift his foot and set it down perpendicularly, or in a direct line with his knee. So you may always recognize him, though walking many rods before you, by this peculiar swinging gait. Adding to such shoes the heavy agricultural implements he wields, he has to run the race of labour with our American farming-men so heavily weighted that it is a wonder he can accomplish as much as he does.

Joaquin Miller

'the Byron of Oregon', was born in Liberty, Indiana, in 1841 and, according to his own account, went West in a covered wagon and was horse-thief, pony-express messenger and Indian fighter before turning poet. It was in London in 1870 and 1871 that he published his *Pacific Poems* and *Songs of the Sierras*, works that impressed the English as those of a frontier poet. He seems to have been less successful in the United States. He died in 1913.

Living in the slums

London, November 2, 1870. Am at last in the central city of this earth. I was afraid to come here, and so it was I almost went quite around this boundless spread of houses before I entered it: saw all these islands and nearly all the continent first. But I feel at home almost, even now, and have only been here three days. Tired though, so tired! And then my leg bothers me badly. There is a bit of lead in there about as big as the end of my thumb. But ever since that night in Melrose Abbey it has felt as big as a cannon-ball. And then I have been rather active of late. Active! The Oregonians ought to have seen me running away from the French, the Germans—both at once. But you see they took my pistols away from me before I had a chance to protest or even suspected what they were going to do. Ah well! I am safe out of it all now, and shall, since I am too crippled to get about, sit still and write in this town. When I came in on the rail from Dover, I left my bag at the station; paid two pence—great big coppers, big as five of America's—and took a ticket for it, and so set out to walk about the city. And how delightfully different from New York!

Now, I want to note something strange. I walked straight to Westminster Abbey—straight as the crooked streets would let me; and I did not ask anyone the way, nor did I have the remotest idea where it was. As for a guide-book, I never had one in my life. But my heart was in that Abbey, going out to the great spirits, the immortal dust gathered there, and I walked straight to where my heart was. . . . And this encourages me very much. . . . As if by some possible turn of fortune or favor of the gods I—I may really get there, or at least set out upon the road that these silent giants have journeyed on. . . .

> The Abbey broods beside the turbid Thames;
> Her mother heart is fill'd with memories;
> Her every niche is stored with storied names;
> They move before me like a mist of seas.

After keeping on my feet till hardly able to stand, I left the Abbey and walked up Whitehall, up Regent Street, down Oxford Street towards St Paul's. Then I broke down, and wanted to find a place to stop. But I must have looked too tired and wretched as I dragged myself along. I told a woman finally, who had rooms to let, that I was ill and must stop. She shut the door in my face after forcing me out of the hall. New cities, cities new to me, of course, have new ways. If one does not know their ways one frightens the honest folk, and can't get on with them at all.

A public-house here is not a tavern or an inn. I tried to get to stop at two or three of these reeking gin-mills. They stared at me, but went on jerking beer behind the counter, and did not answer. At one place I asked for water. All stopped and looked at me—women with great mugs of beer half way to their brutal big red mouths; a woman with a baby in one arm, wrapped tightly in a shawl along with herself, and a jug of beer in the other, came up and put her face in mine curiously; then the men all roared. And then one good-natured Briton paid for a pewter mug full of beer for me. But as I have never tasted beer, and could not bear the smell of it, I was obliged to refuse it. I was too tired to explain, and so backed out into the street again and hobbled on. I did not get the water. I now learn that one must not ask for water here. No one drinks water here. No public-house keeps it. Well, to one from Oregon, the land of pure water, where God pours it down from the snowy clouds out of the hollow of His hand—the high-born, beautiful great white rain, this seems strange. . . .

All drinking-shops here—or rather 'doggeries', as we call them in Oregon—are called 'publics'. And a man who keeps one of these places is called a publican. Now I see the sense and meaning of the Bible phrase, 'publicans and sinners'.

When I reached Aldersgate Street that first day, I saw the name 'Little Britain' to my left, and knowing that Washington Irving had dwelt there, I turned aside to follow where he had been, in the leaves of the Sketch Book. But I could go but a little way. Seeing the sign of the Young Men's Christian Association close at hand, I climbed up the long crooked stairs, and soon was made quite at home and well refreshed by a cup of coffee and a roll at three half-pence; also a great deal of civility and first-class kindness for nothing at all. I had bed and breakfast at the same reasonable rate; and the next morning, leaving my watch and money here, I went to Mile End by 'bus, to see where Mr Bayard Taylor had lived when here.

I lost my way in one of the by-streets, and asked how to get out. People were kind and good-natured, but they spoke with such queer accent that I could not understand. At last a little girl of a dozen years, very bright and very beautiful, proposed to show me the way to the main street. She was a ray of sunlight after a whole month of storms. . . . She was making neckties, she said, and getting sixpence a day;

five pence she paid to a Mrs Brady, who lived at 52 New Street, and this left her a penny a day to dress and enjoy life upon!

'And can I live with Mrs Brady for five pence a day?'

'Maybe so. Mrs Brady has a room; maybe you can get it. Let us go and see.'

We came, we saw, and settled! I give Lizzie a shilling a day to run errands, for my leg is awful. She went to the station and got my bag, and she keeps my few things in perfect shape. I think she has some doubts about my sanity. She watches me closely, and I have seen her shake her head at this constant writing of mine. But she gets her shilling regularly, and oh! she is so happy—and so rich! Mrs Brady is about six feet high, and very slim and bony. She has but one eye, and she hammers her husband, who drives a wagon for a brewery, most cruelly. He is short and stout as one of his beer-barrels, and a good-hearted soul he is too. He loves his old telegraph-pole of a wife, however, and refuses to pound her back when she pounds him, although he assured me yesterday, in confidence, that he was certain he could lick her if he tried.

November 8. Mrs Brady must be very old or a very great liar. Last night she assured me that her father used to shoe Dick Turpin's horses. She went into detail to show how he would set the shoes on hind side before to look as if he was going away from London, when, in fact, he was coming this way. As if I did not know anything about horses, and how that all this was impossible. I expect she will next develop that she had some intimate relations with Jack Sheppard, or, most likely, some of his descendants. . . .

November 20. Lizzie is a treasure, but she will lie like sixty. Yet she is honest. She goes out and brings me my coffee every morning. Mrs Brady acts as a sort of mother, and is very careful of her in her coarse, hard way. I must find out who she is, and get her to school if I get on. She tells me her people live over on the 'Surrey side', wherever that is. But I have already found that, like Mrs Brady, she does not like to tell the truth about herself if she can get round to it. How odd that poor people will lie so! Truth, the best and chiefest thing on this earth, is about the only luxury that costs nothing; and they ought to be persuaded to indulge in it oftener. New Street! It is the oldest street, I should say, in this part of London. This house we are in is cracked, and has been condemned. The reliable Mrs Brady says it has only a few months more to stand; that the underground railroad or something runs under it. So I must get out, I guess.

James Russell Lowell

poet and literary critic, was born in Cambridge, Massachusetts,
in 1819, educated at Harvard, where he was class poet, and
succeeded Longfellow as Professor of French and Spanish at Harvard
in 1855. A pillar of the Republican Party, he was appointed U.S.
Minister to Spain in 1877 and to England in 1880. He died in 1891.

The advantages of a great capital

To C. E. Norton.

10, Lowndes Sq., S. W. April 22, 1883.
. . . I LIKE LONDON, and have learned to see as I never saw before the advantages of a great capital. It establishes one set of weights and measures, moral and intellectual, for the whole country. It is, I think, a great drawback for us that we have as many as we have States. The flow of life in the streets, too—sublimer, it seems to me often, than the tides of the sea—gives me a kind of stimulus that I find agreeable even if it prompt to nothing. For I am growing old, dear Charles, and haven't the go in me I once had. Then I have only to walk a hundred yards from my door to be in Hyde Park, where, and in Kensington Gardens, I can tread on green turf and hear the thrushes sing all winter. I often think of what you said to me about the birds here. There *are* a great many more and they sing more perennially than ours. As for the climate, it suits me better than any I have ever lived in, and for the inward weather, I have never seen civilization at so high a level in some respects as here. In plain living and high thinking I fancy we have, or used to have, the advantage, and I have never seen society, on the whole, so good as I used to meet at our Saturday Club.

The Lord Mayor's Show

To Mrs W. K. Clifford.

31, Lowndes Square, S.W. Nov. 9, 1884.
. . . No, THE LORD Mayor's Show was pure circus and poor circus at that. It was cheap, and the other adjective that begins with n. 'Twas an attempt to make poetry out of commonplace by contract. 'Twas antiquity as conceived by Mr Sanger. Why, I saw the bottoms of a Norman knight's trousers where they had been hitched up into a tell-tale welt round the ankle by his chain armour! There was no pretence at illusion; nay, every elephant, every camel, every chariot was laden

[134]

with disillusion. It was worth seeing once, to learn how dreary prose
can contrive to be when it has full swing.

The attractions of fog

To Miss Sedgwick.

2, Radnor Place, Oct. 3, 1888.

... WE ARE IN the beginning of our foggy season, and today are having
a yellow fog, and that always enlivens me, it has such a knack of trans-
figuring things. It flatters one's self-esteem, too, in a recondite way,
promoting one for the moment to that exclusive class which can afford
to wrap itself in a golden seclusion. It is very picturesque also. Even the
cabs are rimmed with a halo, and people across the way have all
that possibility of suggestion which piques the fancy so in the figures
of fading frescoes. Even the gray, even the black fogs make a new and
unexplored world not unpleasing to one who is getting palled with
familiar landscapes ...

Oliver Wendell Holmes

like Lowell a Boston 'Brahmin', was born at Cambridge,
Massachusetts, in 1809. Poet and wit, he was also a physician,
Professor of Anatomy at Harvard and later Dean of the Harvard
Medical School. At 77 he toured Europe with his daughter, his
One Hundred Days in Europe appearing in 1887. He died in
Boston in 1894.

Some first impressions

HERE ARE SOME of my first impressions of England as seen from the carriage and from the cars. How very English! I recall Birket Foster's Pictures of English Landscape, a beautiful, poetical series of views, but hardly more poetical than the reality. How thoroughly England *is groomed!* Our New England out-of-doors landscape often looks as if it had just got out of bed, and had not finished its toilet. The glowing green of everything strikes me: green hedges in place of our rail-fences, always ugly, and our rude stone-walls, which are not wanting in a certain look of fitness approaching to comeliness, and are really picturesque when lichen-coated, but poor features of landscape as compared with these universal hedges. I am disappointed in the trees so far; I have not seen one large tree as yet. Most of those I see are of very moderate dimensions, feathered all the way up their long slender trunks with a lopsided mop of leaves at the top, like a wig which has slipped awry. I trust that I am not finding every-thing *couleur de rose*; but I certainly do find the cheeks of children and young persons of such brilliant rosy hue as I do not remember that I have ever seen before. I am almost ready to think this and that child's face has been colored from a pink saucer. If the Saxon youth exposed for sale at Rome, in the days of Pope Gregory the Great, had complexions like these children, no wonder that the pontiff exclaimed, Not *Angli*, but *angeli!* All this may sound a little extrava-gant, but I am giving my impressions without any intentional exagger-ation. How far these first impressions may be modified by after-experiences there will be time enough to find out and to tell. It is better to set them down at once just as they are. A first impression is one never to be repeated; the second look will see much that was not noticed before, but it will not reproduce the sharp lines of the *first proof*, which is always interesting, no matter what the eye or the mind fixes upon. 'I see men as trees walking.' That first experience could not be mended. When Dickens landed at Boston, he was struck with the brightness of all objects he saw,—buildings, signs, and so forth. When I landed in Liverpool, everything looked very dark, very dingy, very massive, in the streets I drove through. So in London, but in a week it all seemed natural enough.

Waiting for the carriage

THE MOST FORMIDABLE thing about a London party is getting away from it. 'C'est le *dernier* pas qui coute.' A crowd of anxious persons in retreat is hanging about the windy door, and the breezy stairway, and the airy hall.

A stentorian voice, hard as that of Rhadamanthus, exclaims—

'Lady Vere de Vere's carriage stops the way!'

If my Lady Vere de Vere is not on hand, and that pretty quickly, off goes her carriage and the stern voice bawls again,—

'Mrs Smith's carriage stops the way!'

Mrs Smith's particular Smith may be worth his millions and live in his marble palace; but if Mrs Smith thinks her coachman is going to stand with his horses at that door until she appears, she is mistaken, for she is a minute late, and now the coach moves on, and Rhadamanthus calls aloud—

'Mrs Brown's carriage stops the way!'

Half the lung fevers that carry off the great people are got waiting for their carriages.

A party at the Rothschilds'

WE WERE TO go to a fine musical party at Lady Rothschild's on the evening of the 30th of May. It happened that the day was Sunday, and if we had been as punctilious as some New England Sabbatarians, we might have felt compelled to decline the tempting invitation. But the party was given by a daughter of Abraham, and in every Hebrew household the true Sabbath was over. We were content for that evening to shelter ourselves under the old dispensation.

The party, or concert, was a very brilliant affair, Patti sang to us, and a tenor, and a violinist played for us. How we two Americans came to be in so favored a position I do not know; all I know is that we were shown to our places, and found them very agreeable ones. In the same row of seats was the Prince of Wales, two chairs off from A —'s seat. Directly in front of A — was the Princess of Wales, 'in ruby velvet,

[139]

with six rows of pearls encircling her throat, and two more strings falling quite low'; and next her, in front of me, the startling presence of Lady de Grey, formerly Lady Lonsdale, and before that Gladys Herbert. On the other side of the Princess sat the Grand Duke Michael of Russia.

As we were among the grandest of the grandees, I must enliven my sober account with an extract from my companion's diary:—

'There were several great beauties there, Lady Claude Hamilton, a queenly blonde, being one. Minnie Stevens Paget had with her the pretty Miss Langdon, of New York. Royalty had one room for supper, with its attendant lords and ladies. Lord Rothschild took me down to a long table for a sit-down supper,—there were some thirty of us. The most superb pink orchids were on the table. The (Thane) of—sat next to me, and how he stared before he was introduced!... This has been the finest party we have been to, sitting comfortably in such a beautiful ball-room, gazing at royalty in the flesh, and at the shades of departed beauties on the wall, by Sir Joshua and Gainsborough. It was a new experience to find that the royal lions fed upstairs, and mixed animals below!'

Windsor Castle

WINDSOR CASTLE, WHICH everybody knows, or can easily learn all about, is one of the largest of those huge caverns in which the descendants of the orginal cave men, when they have reached the height of human grandeur, delight to shelter themselves. It seems as if such a great hollow quarry of rock would strike a chill through every tenant, but modern improvements reach even the palaces of kings and queens, and the regulation temperature of the castle, or of its inhabited portions, is fixed at sixty-five degrees of Fahrenheit. The royal standard was not floating from the tower of the castle, and everything was quiet and lonely. We saw all we wanted to,—pictures, furniture, and the rest. My namesake, the Queen's librarian, was not there to greet us, or I should have had a pleasant half-hour in the library with that very polite gentleman, whom I had afterwards the pleasure of meeting in London.

After going through all the apartments in the castle that we cared to see, or our conductress cared to show us, we drove in the park, along the 'three-mile walk', and in the by-roads leading from it. The beautiful avenue, the open spaces with scattered trees here and there, made this a most delightful excursion. I saw many fine oaks, one about sixteen feet of honest girth, but no one which was very remarkable. I wished I could have compared the handsomest of them with one in Beverly, which I never look at without taking my hat off. This is a young tree, with a future before it, if barbarians do not meddle with it, more conspicuous for its spread than its circumference, stretching not very far from a hundred feet from bough-end to bough-end. I do not think I saw a specimen of the British *Quercus robur* of such consummate beauty. But I know from Evelyn and Strutt what England has to boast of, and I will not challenge the British oak.

Two sensations I had in Windsor park, or forest, for I am not quite sure of the boundary which separates them. The first was the lovely sight of the *hawthorn* in full bloom. I had always thought of the hawthorn as a pretty shrub, growing in hedges; as big as a currant bush or a barberry bush, or some humble plant of that character. I was surprised to see it as a tree, standing by itself, and making the most delicious roof a pair of young lovers could imagine to sit under. It looked at a little distance like a young apple-tree covered with a new-fallen snow. I shall never see the word hawthorn in poetry again without the image of the snowy but far from chilling canopy rising before me. It is the very bower of young love, and must have done more than any growth of the forest to soften the doom brought upon man by the fruit of the forbidden tree.

Presently I heard a sound to which I had never listened before, and which I had never heard since:

Cuvvo—cuuoo!

Nature had sent one cuckoo from her aviary to sing his double note for me, that I might not pass away from her pleasing show without once hearing the call so dear to poets. It was the last day of spring. A few more days, and the solitary voice might have been often heard; for the bird becomes so common as to furnish Shakespeare an image to fit 'the skipping king':

> 'He was but as the cuckoo is in June,
> Heard, not regarded.'

. . . Only one hint of the prosaic troubled my emotional delight: I could not help thinking how capitally the little rogue imitated the cuckoo clock, with the sound of which I was pretty well acquainted.

[141]

In the Abbey

ON THE WHOLE, the Abbey produces a distinct sense of being over-crowded. It appears too much like a lapidary's store-room. Look up at the lofty roof, which we willingly pardon for shutting out the heaven above us,—at least in an average London day; look down at the floor, and think of what precious relics it covers; but do not look around you with the hope of getting any clear, concentrated satisfying effect from this great museum of gigantic funereal bricabrac. . . . Amidst all the imposing recollections of the ancient edifice, one impressed me in the inverse ratio of its importance. The Archdeacon pointed out the little holes in the stones, in one place, where the boys of the choir used to play marbles, before America was discovered, probably,—centuries before, it may be. It is a strangely impressive glimpse of a living past, like the *graffiti* of Pompeii.

Afternoon tea

. . . THE AFTERNOON TEA is almost a necessity in London life. It is con-sidered useful as 'a pick me up', and it serves an admirable purpose in the social system. It costs the household hardly any trouble or expense. It brings people together in the easiest possible way, for ten minutes or an hour, just as their engagements or fancies may settle it. A cup of tea at the right moment does for the virtuous reveller all that Falstaff claims for a good sherris-sack, or at least the first half of its 'twofold operation': 'It ascends me into the brain; dries me there all the foolish and dull and crudy vapors which environ it; makes it apprehensive, quick, forgetive, full of nimble, fiery and delectable shapes, which delivered over to the voice, the tongue, which is the birth, becomes excellent wit.'

But it must have the right brain to work upon, and I doubt if there is any brain to which it is so congenial and from which it brings so much as that of a first-rate London old lady. I came away from the great city with the feeling that this most complex product of civilization was nowhere else developed to such perfection. The octogenarian

Londoness has been in society,—let us say the highest society,—all her days. She is as tough as an old macaw, or she would not have lasted so long. She has seen and talked with all the celebrities of three generations, all the beauties of at least half a dozen decades. Her wits have been kept bright by constant use, and as she is free of speech it requires some courage to face her. Yet nobody can be more agreeable, even to young persons, than one of these precious old dowagers. A great beauty is almost certainly thinking how she looks while one is talking with her; an authoress is waiting to have one praise her book; but a grand old lady, who loves London society, who lives in it, who understands young people and all sorts of people, with her high-colored recollections of the past and her grand-maternal interests in the new generation, is the best of companions, especially over a cup of tea just strong enough to stir up her talking ganglions.

Bond Street and Oxford Street

I DID NOT do a great deal of shopping myself while in London, being contented to have it done for me. But in the way of looking in at shop windows I did a very large business. Certain windows attracted me by a variety in unity which surpasses anything I have been accustomed to. Thus one window showed every conceivable convenience that could be shaped in ivory, and nothing else. One shop had such a display of magnificent dressing-cases that I should have thought a whole royal family was setting out on its travels. I see the cost of one of them is two hundred and seventy guineas. Thirteen hundred and fifty dollars seems a good deal to pay for a dressing-case.

On the other hand, some of the first-class tradesmen and workmen make no show whatever. The tailor to whom I had credentials, and who proved highly satisfactory to me, as he had proved to some of my country-men and to Englishmen of high estate, had only one small sign, which was placed in one of his windows, and received his customers in a small room that would have made a closet for one of our stylish merchant tailors. The bootmaker to whom I went on good recommendation had hardly anything about his premises to remind one of his calling. He came into his studio, took my measure very carefully, and made me a pair of what we call Congress boots, which fitted well once on my feet, but which cost more trouble to get into and to get out of than I could express my feelings about without dangerously enlarging my limited vocabulary.

Bond Street, Old and New, offered the most inviting windows, and I indulged almost to profligacy in the prolonged inspection of their contents. Stretching my walk along New Bond Street till I came to a great intersecting thoroughfare, I found myself in Oxford Street. Here the character of the shop windows changed at once. Utility and convenience took the place of show and splendour. Here I found various articles of use in a household, some of which were new to me. It is very likely that I could have found most of them in our own Boston Cornhill, but one often overlooks things at home which at once arrest his attention when he sees them in a strange place. I saw great numbers of illuminating contrivances, some of which pleased me by their arrangement of reflectors. Bryant and May's safety matches seemed to be used everywhere. I procured some in Boston with these names on the box, but the label said they were made in Sweden, and they diffused vapors that were enough to produce asphyxia. I greatly admired some of Dr Dresser's water-cans and other contrivances, modelled more or less after the antique, but I found an abundant assortment of them here in Boston, and I have one I obtained here more original in design and more serviceable in daily use than any I saw in London. I should have regarded Wolverhampton, as we glided through it, with more interest, if I had known at that time that the inventive Dr Dresser had his headquarters in that busy-looking town ...

One beauty of the Old World shops is that if a visitor comes back to the place where he left them fifty years before, he finds them, or has a great chance of finding them, just where they stood at his former visit. In driving down to the old city, to the place of business of the Barings, I found many little streets changed. Temple Bar was gone, and the much-abused griffin stood in its place. There was a shop close to Temple Bar, where, in 1834, I had bought some brushes. I did not ask the young man who served me how the old shopkeeper who attended to my wants on the earlier occasion was at this time. But I thought what a different color the locks these brushes smooth show from those that knew their predecessors in the earlier decade!

England's chief product

... WE MUST ALL beware of hasty conclusions. If a foreigner of limited intelligence were whirled through England on the railways, he would naturally come to the conclusion that the chief product of that country is *mustard*, and that its most celebrated people are Mr Keen and Mr Colman, whose great advertising boards, yellow letters on a black ground, and black letters on a yellow ground, stare the traveller in the face at every station.

William James

older than his brother Henry by a year, took his medical degree at Harvard and for a time taught physiology there. Then he moved on to psychology and philosophy, writing among other works *Principles of Psychology*, *The Varieties of Religious Experience* and *Pragmatism*. A frequent visitor to Europe. he died in 1910.

On the bus to Hampton Court

July 29. 1889

TOWARDS FOUR O'CLOCK (the weather fine) I mounted the top of a bus and went (with thousands of others similarly enthroned) to Hampton Court, through Kew, Richmond, Bushey Park, etc., about 30 miles there and back, all for 4s. 6d. I strolled for an hour or more in the Hampton Court Gardens, and overlooked the Thames all *bigarrée* with row-boats and male and female rowers, and got back, *perdu dans la foule*, at 10 p.m.—a most delightful and interesting six hours, with but the usual drawback, that *you* were not along. How you would have enjoyed every bit of it, especially the glimpses, between Richmond and Hampton, over the high brick walls and between the bars of the iron gates, of these extraordinary English gardens and larger grounds, all black with their tufted vegetation. More different things can grow in a square foot here, if they're taken care of, than I've ever seen elsewhere, and one of these high ivy-walled gardens is something the *like* of which is altogether unknown to us. Like all human things (except wives) they grow banal enough, if one stays long in their company, but the first acquaintance between Alice Gibbens and them is something which I would fain see. The crowd was immense and the picturesqueness of everything quite medieval, as were also the good manners and the tendency to a certain hearty sociability, shown in the chaffing from vehicle to vehicle along the road. I'm glad I had this sight of the greatness of the English people, and glad I had no social duties to perform. . . .

Henry James

was born in New York City in 1843 and educated partly in
Europe before going on to Harvard. In 1872 he decided to
settle in Europe and went to live in Paris. Four years later he
moved to London, then in 1898 to Rye, Sussex, which was to be his
home for the rest of his life. A few months before his death
in 1916 he was naturalized a British subject; it was his way of
identifying himself with England in the dark days of the
first world war. But in essential respects he was always the
observer looking at England from the outside, and though he
was among other things one of the great London novelists, his
London was a stranger's London, a city experienced and
appreciated by a writer who could compare it with many cities
of very different cultures. The passages that follow are from
English Hours.

London during the Season

... I HAVE NOTED that the London-lover loves everything in the place, but I have not cut myself off from saying his sympathy has degrees, or from remarking that the sentiment of the author of these pages has never gone all the way with the dense movement of the British carnival. That is really the word for the period from Easter to midsummer; it is a fine, decorous, expensive, Protestant carnival, in which the masks are not of velvet or of silk, but of wonderful deceptive flesh and blood, the material of the most beautiful complexions in the world. Holding that the great interest of London is the sense the place gives us of multitudinous life, it is doubtless an inconsequence not to care most for the phase of greatest intensity. But there is life and life, and the rush and crush of these weeks of fashion is after all but a tolerably mechanical expression of human forces. Nobody would deny that it is a more universal, brilliant, spectacular one than can be seen anywhere else; and it is not a defect that these forces often take the form of women extremely beautiful. I risk the declaration that the London season brings together year by year an unequalled collection of handsome persons. I say nothing of the ugly ones; beauty has at the best been allotted to a small minority, and it is never, at the most, anywhere, but a question of the number by which that minority is least insignificant.

There are moments when one can almost forgive the follies of June for the sake of the smile which the sceptical old city puts on for the time and which, as I noted in an earlier passage of this disquisition, fairly breaks into laughter where she is tickled by the vortex of Hyde Park Corner. Most perhaps does she seem to smile at the end of the summer days, when the light lingers and lingers, though the shadows lengthen and the mists redden and the belated riders, with dinners to dress for, hurry away from the trampled arena of the Park. The population at that hour surges mainly westward and sees the dusts of the day's long racket turned into a dull golden haze. There is something that has doubtless often, at this particular moment, touched the fancy even of the bored and the *blasés* in such an emanation of hospitality, of waiting dinners, of the festal idea, of the whole spectacle of the West End preparing herself for an evening six parties deep. The scale on

[150]

which she entertains is stupendous, and her invitations and 'reminders' are as thick as the leaves of the forest.

For half an hour, from eight to nine, every pair of wheels presents the portrait of a diner-out. To consider only the rattling hansoms, the white neckties and 'dressed' heads which greet you from over the apron in a quick, interminable succession, conveys the overwhelming impression of a complicated world. Who are they all, and where are they all going, and whence have they come, and what smoking kitchens and gaping portals and marshalled flunkeys are prepared to receive them, from the southernmost limits of a loosely interpreted, an almost transpontine Belgravia, to the hyperborean confines of St John's Wood? There are broughams standing at every door, and carpets laid down for the footfall of the issuing if not the entering reveller. The pavements are empty now, in the fading light, in the big sallow squares and the stuccoed streets of gentility, save for the groups of small children holding others that are smaller—Amelia-Ann intrusted with Sarah Jane— who collect, wherever the strip of carpet lies, to see the fine ladies pass from the carriage or the house. The West End is dotted with these pathetic little gazing groups; it is the party of the poor—*their* Season and way of dining out, and a happy illustration of 'the sympathy that prevails between classes'. The watchers, I should add, are by no means all children, but the lean mature also, and I am sure these wayside joys are one of the reasons of an inconvenience much deplored—the tendency of the country poor to flock to London. They who dine only occasionally or never at all have plenty of time to contemplate those with whom the custom has more amplitude. However, it was not my intention to conclude these remarks in a melancholy strain, and goodness knows that the diners are a prodigious company. It is as moralistic as I shall venture to be if I drop a very soft sigh on the paper as I confirm that truth. Are they all illuminated spirits and is their conversation the ripest in the world? This is not to be expected, nor should I ever suppose it to be desired that an agreeable society should fail to offer opportunity for intellectual rest. Such a shortcoming is not one of the sins of the London world in general, nor would it be just to complain of that world, on any side, on grounds of deficiency. It is not what London fails to do that strikes the observer, but the general fact that she does everything in excess. Excess is her highest reproach, and it is her incurable misfortune that there is really too much of her. She overwhelms you by quantity and number—she ends by making human life, by making civilization, appear cheap to you. Wherever you go, to parties, exhibitions, concerts, 'private views', meetings, solitudes, there are many more people than enough on the field. How it makes you understand the high walls with which so much of English life is surrounded, and the priceless blessing of a park in the country, where there is nothing animated but rabbits and pheasants and, for the worst, the importunate nightingales! And as the monster grows and grows for ever, she departs more and more—it must be acknowledged—from the ideal of a convenient society, a society in which intimacy is possible, in which the associated meet often and sound and measure and inspire each other, and relations and combinations have time to form themselves. The substitute for this in London, is the momentary conclusion of a million of atoms. It is the difference between seeing a great deal of a few and seeing a little of everyone. 'When did you come—are you "going on"?' and it is over; there is no time even for the answer. This may seem a perfidious arraignment, and I should not make it were I not prepared, or rather were I not eager, to add two qualifications. One of these is that, cumbrously vast as the place may be, I would not have had it smaller by a hair's-breadth, or have missed one of the fine and fruitful impatiences with which it inspires you and which are at bottom a heartier tribute, I think, than any great city receives. The other is that out of its richness and its inexhaustible good humour it belies the next hour any generalization you may have been so simple as to make about it.

James at the Derby

... EVERY ONE ASSURED me that this was the great festival of the English people and that one didn't really know them unless one had seen them at it. So much, since it had to do with horse-flesh, I could readily believe. Had not the newspapers been filled for weeks with recurrent dissertations upon the animals concerned in the ceremony? and was not the event, to the nation at large, only imperceptibly less momentous than the other great question of the day—the fate of empires and the reapportionment of the East? The space allotted to sporting intelligence in a compact, eclectic, 'intellectual' journal like the *Pall Mall Gazette*, had seemed for some time past a measure of the hold of such questions upon the native mind. These things, however, are very natural in a country in which in 'society' you are liable to make the acquaintance of some such syllogism as the following. You are seated at dinner next a foreign lady who has on her other hand a communicative gentleman through whom she is under instruction in the art of the right point-of-view for English life. I profit by their conversation and I learn that this point-of-view is apparently the saddle. 'You see, English life,' says the gentleman, 'is really English country life. It's the country that is the basis of English society. And you see, country life is—well, it's the *hunting*. It's the hunting that is at the bottom of it all.' In other words 'the hunting' is the basis of English society. Duly impressed with this explanation, the American observer is prepared for the huge proportions of the annual pilgrimage to Epsom. This pilgrimage, however, I was assured, though still well worth taking part in, is by no means so characteristic as in former days. It is now performed in a large measure by rail, and the spectacle on the road has lost many of its earlier and most of its finer features. The road has been given up more and more to the populace and the strangers and has ceased to be graced by the presence of ladies. Nevertheless, as a man and a stranger, I was strongly recommended to take it, for the return from the Derby is still, with all its abatements, a classic show.

I mounted upon a four-horse coach, a charming coach with a yellow body and handsome, clean-flanked leaders; placing myself beside the coachman, as I had been told this was the point of vantage. The coach was one of the vehicles of the new fashion—the fashion of public conveyances driven, for the entertainment of themselves and of the public, by gentlemen of leisure. On the Derby day all the coaches that start from the classic headquarters—'The White Horse' in Piccadilly—and stretch away from London towards a dozen different and well-selected goals, had been dedicated to the Epsom road. The body of the vehicle is empty, as no one thinks of occupying any but one of the thirteen places on the top. On the Derby day, however, a properly laden coach carries a company of hampers and champagne-baskets in its inside places. I must add that on this occasion my companion was by exception a professional whip, who proved a friendly and amusing cicerone. Other companions there were, perched in the twelve places behind me, whose special quality I made less of a point of testing—though in the course of the expedition their various characteristics, under the influence of champagne, expanded so freely as greatly to facilitate the process. We were a society of exotics—Spaniards, Frenchmen, Germans. There were only two Britons, and these, according to my theory, were

[153]

Australians—an antipodal bride and groom on a centripetal wedding-tour.

The drive to Epsom, when you get well out of London, is sufficiently pretty; but the part of it which most took my fancy was a district pre-eminently suburban—the classic community of Clapham. The vision of Clapham had been a part of the furniture of one's milder historic consciousness—the vision of its respectable common, its evangelical society, its rich drab humanity, its goodly brick mansions of the Georgian era. I now seemed really to focus these elements for the first time, and I thought them very charming. This epithet indeed scarcely applies to the evangelical society, which naturally, on the morning of the Derby day and during the desecrating progress of the Epsom revellers, was not much in the foreground. But all around the verdant if cockneyfied common are ranged commodious houses of a sober red complexion, from under whose neo-classic pediments you expect to see a mild-faced lady emerge—a lady in a cottage-bonnet and mittens, distributing tracts from a green silk satchel. It would take, however, the very ardour of the missionary among cannibals to stem the current of heterogeneous vehicles which at about this point takes up its metropolitan affluents and bears them in its rumbling, rattling tide. The concourse of wheeled conveyances of every possible order here becomes dense, and the spectacle from the top of the coach proportionately absorbing. You begin to perceive that the brilliancy of the road has in truth departed, and that a sustained high tone of appearance is not the note of the conditions. But when once you have grasped this fact your entertainment is continuous. You perceive that you are 'in' for the vulgar on an unsurpassable scale, something blatantly, unimaginably, heroically shocking to timid 'taste'; all that is necessary is to accept this situation and look out for illustrations. Beside you, before you, behind you, is the mighty London populace taking its ébats. You get for the first time a notion of the London population at large. It has piled itself into carts, into omnibuses, into every possible and impossible species of 'trap'. A large proportion of it is of course on foot, trudging along the perilous margin of the middle way in such comfort as may be gathered from fifteen miles' dodging of broken shins. The smaller the vehicle, the more rat-like the animal that drags it, the more numerous and ponderous its human freight; and as everyone is nursing in his lap a parcel of provender as big as himself, wrapped in ragged newspaper, it is not surprising that roadside halts are frequent and that the taverns all the way to Epsom (it is wonderful how many there are) are en-

[154]

compassed by dense groups of dusty pilgrims, indulging liberally in refreshment for man and beast. And when I say man I must by no means be understood to exclude woman. The female contingent on the Derby day is not the least remarkable part of the London outpouring. Everyone is prepared for 'larks', but the women are even more brilliantly and resolutely prepared than the men; there is no better chance to follow the range of type—not that it is to be called large—of the British female of the lower orders. The lady in question is usually not ornamental. She is useful, robust, prolific, excellently fitted to play the somewhat arduous part allotted to her in the great scheme of English civilization, but she has not the graces which enable her to lend herself easily to the decorations of life. On smaller holidays—or on simple working-days—in London crowds, I have often thought she had points to contribute to the primary fine drawing, as to head and shoulders, of the Briton of the two sexes as the race at large sketches them. But at Epsom she is too stout, too hot, too red, too thirsty, too boisterous, too strangely accoutred. And yet I wish to do her justice; so I must add that if there is something to which an American cannot refuse a tribute of admiration in the gross plebeian jollity of the Derby day, it is not evident why these dowdy Bacchantes should not get part of the credit of it. The striking thing, the interesting thing, both on the outward drive and on the return, was that the holiday was so frankly, heartily, good-humouredly taken. The people that of all people is habitually the most governed by decencies, proprieties, rigidities of conduct, was for one happy day unbuttoning its respectable straitjacket and affirming its large and simple sense of the joy of life. In such a spectacle there was inevitably much that was unlucky and unprofitable; these things came uppermost chiefly on the return, when demoralization was supreme, when the temperament of the people had begun really to take the air. For the rest, to be dressed with a kind of brutal gaudiness, to be very thirsty and violently flushed, to laugh perpetually at everything and at nothing, thoroughly to enjoy, in short, a momentous occasion—all this is not, in simple persons of the more susceptible sex, an unpardonable crime.

The course at Epsom is in itself very pretty, and disposed by nature herself in sympathetic prevision of the sporting passion. It is something like the crater of a volcano without the mountain. The outer rim is the course proper; the space within it is a vast, shallow, grassy concavity in which vehicles are drawn up and beasts tethered and in which the greater part of the multitude—the mountebanks, the betting-men and the myriad hangers-on of the scene—are congregated. The outer margin of the uplifted rim in question is occupied by the grand stand, the small stands, the paddock. The day was exceptionally beautiful; the charming sky was spotted over with little idle-looking, loafing, irresponsible clouds; the Epsom Downs went swelling away as greenly as in a coloured sporting-print, and the wooded uplands, in the middle distance, looked as innocent and pastoral as if they had never seen a policeman or a rowdy. The crowd that spread itself over this immense expanse was as rich a representation of human life off its guard as one need see. One's first fate after arriving, if one is perched upon a coach, is to see the coach guided, by means best known to the coachman himself, through the tremendous press of vehicles and pedestrians, introduced into a precinct roped off and guarded from intrusion save under payment of a fee, and then drawn up alongside of the course, as nearly as possible opposite the grand stand and the winning post. Here you have only to stand up in your place—on tiptoe, it is true, and with a good deal of stretching—to see the race fairly well. But I hasten to add that seeing the race is indifferent entertainment. In the first place you *don't* see it, and in the second—to be Irish on the occasion of a frolic—you perceive it to be not much worth the seeing. It may be fine in quality, but in quantity it is inappreciable. The horses and their jockeys first go dangling and cantering along the course to the starting-point, looking as insubstantial as sifted sunbeams. Then there is a long wait, during which, of the sixty thousand people present (my figures are imaginary), thirty thousand declare positively that they have started, and thirty thousand as positively deny it. Then the whole sixty thousand are suddenly resolved into unanimity by the sight of a dozen small jockey-heads whizzing along a very distant sky-line. In a shorter space of time than it takes me to write it, the whole thing is before you, and for the instant it is anything but beautiful. A dozen furiously revolving arms—pink, green, orange, scarlet, white—whacking the flanks of as many straining steeds; a glimpse of this, and the spectacle is over. The spectacle, however, is of course an infinitesimally small part of the purpose of Epsom and the interest of the Derby. The finer vibration resides presumably in having money on the affair.

When the Derby Stakes had been carried off by a horse of which I confess I am barbarous enough to have forgotten the name, I turned my back to the running, for all the world as if I too were largely 'interested', and sought entertainment in looking at the crowd. The crowd was very animated; that is the most succinct description I can give of it.

The horses of course had been removed from the vehicles, so that the pedestrians were free to surge against the wheels and even to a certain extent to scale and overrun the carriages. This tendency became most pronounced when, as the mid-period of the day was reached, the process of lunching began to unfold itself and every coach-top to become the scene of a picnic. From this moment, at the Derby, demoralization begins. I was in a position to observe it, all around me, in the most characteristic forms. The whole affair, as regards the conventional rigidities I spoke of a while since, becomes a real *dégringolade*. The shabbier pedestrians bustle about the vehicles, staring up at the luckier mortals who are perched in a kind of tormentingly near empyrean—a region in which dishes of lobster-salad are passed about and champagne-corks cleave the air like celestial meteors. There are nigger-minstrels and beggars and mountebanks and spangled persons on stilts and gipsy matrons, as genuine as possible, with glowing Oriental eyes and dropping their *h*'s; these last offer you for sixpence the promise of everything genteel in life except the aspirate. On a coach drawn up beside the one on which I had a place, a party of opulent young men were passing from stage to stage of the higher beatitude with a zeal which excited my admiration. They were accompanied by two or three young ladies of the kind that usually shares the choicest pleasures of youthful British opulence—young ladies in whom nothing has been neglected that can make a complexion superlative. The whole party had been drinking deep, and one of the young men, a pretty lad of twenty, had in an indiscreet moment staggered down as best he could to the ground. Here his cups proved too many for him, and he collapsed and rolled over. In plain English he was beastly drunk. It was the scene that followed that arrested my observation. His companions on the top of the coach called down to the people herding under the wheels to pick him up and put him away inside. These people were the grimiest of the rabble, and a couple of men who looked like coal-heavers out of work undertook to handle this hapless youth. But their task was difficult; it was impossible to imagine a young man more drunk. He was a mere bag of liquor—at once too ponderous and too flaccid to be lifted. He lay in a helpless heap under the feet of the crowd —the best intoxicated young man in England. His extemporized chamberlains took him first in one way and then in another; but he was like water in a seive. The crowd hustled over him; every one wanted to see; he was pulled and shoved and fumbled. The spectacle had a grotesque side, and this it was that seemed to strike the fancy of the young man's comrades. They had not done lunching, so they were unable to bestow upon the incident the whole of that consideration which its high comicality deserved. But they did what they could. They looked down very often, glass in hand during the half-hour that it went on, and they stinted neither their generous, joyous laughter nor their appreciative comments. Women are said to have no sense of humour; but the young ladies with the complexions did liberal justice to the pleasantry of the scene. Toward the last indeed their attention rather flagged; for even the best joke suffers by reiteration, and when you have seen a stupefied young man, infinitely bedusted, slip out of the embrace of a couple of clumsy roughs for the twentieth time, you may very properly suppose that you have arrived at the furthest limits of the ludicrous.

After the great race had been run I quitted my perch and spent the rest of the afternoon in wandering about the grassy concave I have mentioned. It was amusing and picturesque; it was just a huge Bohemian encampment. Here also a great number of carriages were stationed, freighted in like manner with free-handed youths and young ladies with gilded hair. These young ladies were almost the only representatives of their sex with pretensions to elegance; they were often pretty and always exhilarated. Gentlemen in pairs, mounted on stools, habited in fantastic sporting garments and offering bets to whomsoever listed, were a conspicuous feature of the scene. It was equally striking that they were not preaching in the desert and that they found plenty of patrons among the baser sort. I returned to my place in time to assist at the rather complicated operation of starting for the drive back to London. Putting in horses and getting vehicles into line seemed in the midst of the general crush and entanglement a process not to be facilitated even by the most liberal swearing on the part of those engaged in it. But little by little we came to the end of it; and as by this time a kind of mellow cheerfulness pervaded the upper atmosphere—the region of the perpendicular whip—even those interruptions most trying to patience were somehow made to minister to jollity. It was for people below not to get trampled to death or crunched between opposing wheel-hubs, but it was all for *them* to manage it. Above, the carnival of 'chaff' had set in, and it deepened as the lock of vehicles grew denser. As they were all locked together (with a comfortable padding of pedestrians at points of acutest contact), they contrived somehow to move together; so that we gradually got away and into the road. The four or five hours consumed on the road were simply an exchange of

[158]

repartee, the profuse good-humoured savour of which, on the whole, was certainly striking. The chaff was not brilliant nor subtle nor especially graceful; and here and there it was quite too tipsy to be even articulate. But as an expression of that unbuttoning of the popular strait-jacket of which I spoke a while since, it had its wholesome and even innocent side. It took indeed frequently an importunate physical form; it sought emphasis in the use of pea-shooters and water-squirts. At its best too, it was extremely low and rowdyish. But a stranger even of the most refined tastes might be glad to have a glimpse of this popular revel, for it would make him feel that he was learning something more about the English people. It would give a meaning to the old description of England as merry. It would remind him that the natives of that country are subject to some of the lighter of the human impulses, and that the decent, dusky vistas of the London residential streets—those discreet creations of which Thackeray's Baker Street is the type—are not a complete symbol of the complicated race that erected them.

Britons in America

William Cobbett

one of the greatest of English radical journalists, was born at
Farnham, Surrey, in 1762, the son of a small farmer. He served
in the British Army in Nova Scotia and New Brunswick,
rising to the rank of sergeant-major, but had to flee to the
United States in 1792 to escape prosecution for his exposures
of army frauds. As Peter Porcupine, he established himself as
a vigorous crusading journalist, but an infringement of the
libel laws compelled him to return to England in 1800, where
he became a considerable political force on the radical side.
In 1817, in order to escape possible imprisonment without
trial under the 'Gagging Acts', he returned to the United States
and farmed on Long Island. The *Journal of a Year's Residence
in the United States* was the fruit of that experience. He came
back to England in 1819 and at the time of his death in 1835
was M.P. for Oldham.

Long Island

THE *dwellings and gardens, and little out-houses of labourers*, which form so striking a feature of beauty in England, and especially in Kent, Sussex, Surrey, and Hampshire, and which constitute a sort of fairy-land, when compared with those of the labourers in France, are what I, for my part, most feel the want of seeing upon Long Island. Instead of the neat and warm little cottage, the yard, cow-stable, pig-sty, hen-house, all in miniature, and the garden, nicely laid out and the paths bordered with flowers, while the cottage door is crowned with a garland of roses or honey-suckle; instead of these, we here see the labourer content with a shell of boards, while all around him is as barren as the sea-beach; though the natural earth would send melons, the finest in the world, creeping round his door, and though there is no English shrub, or flower, which will not grow and flourish here. This want of attention in such cases is hereditary from the first settlers. They found land so plenty, that they treated small spots with contempt. Besides, the *example* of neatness was wanting. There were no gentlemen's gardens, kept as clean as drawing-rooms, with grass as even as a carpet. From endeavouring to imitate perfection men arrive at mediocrity; and, those who have never seen, or heard of perfection, in these matters, will naturally be slovens.

Yet, notwithstanding these *blots*, as I deem them, the face of the country, in summer, is very fine. From December *to May*, there is not a *speck of green*. No green-grass and turnips, and wheat, and rye, and rape, as in England. The frost comes and sweeps all vegetation and verdant existence from the face of the earth. The wheat and rye *live*; but they lose all their verdure, yet the state of things *in June*, is, as to crops, and fruits, much about what it is in England; for, when things do begin to grow, they grow indeed; and the general harvest for *grain* (what we call *corn*) is a full month *earlier* than in the *South* of England!

Lancaster, Pennsylvania

... LANCASTER IS A pretty place. No *fine* buildings; but no *mean* ones. Nothing *splendid* and nothing *beggarly*. The people of the town seem to have had the prayer of HAGAR granted them: 'Give me, O Lord, neither *poverty* nor *riches*.' Here are none of those poor, wretched habitations, which sicken the sight at the *out-skirts* of cities and towns in England; those abodes of the poor creatures, who have been reduced to beggary by the cruel extortions of the rich and powerful. And, this remark applies to *all* the towns of America that I have ever seen. This is a fine part of America. *Big barns*, and modest dwelling houses. Barns of *stone* a *hundred feet* long and *forty wide*, with two floors, and raised roads to go into them, so that the wagons go into the *first floor up-stairs*. Below are stables, stalls, pens, and all sorts of conveniences. Up-stairs are rooms for threshed corn and grain; for tackle, for meal, for all sorts of things. In the front (South) of the barn is the cattle yard. These are very fine buildings. And, then, all about them looks so comfortable, and gives such manifest proofs of ease, plenty, and happiness! Such is the country of WILLIAM PENN'S settling! It is a curious thing to observe the *farm-houses* in this country. They consist, almost without exception, of a considerably large and a very neat house, with sash windows, and of a *small house*, which seems to have been *tacked on* to the large one; and, the proportion they bear to each other, in point of dimensions, is, as nearly as possible, the proportion of size between a *cow* and *her calf*, the latter a month old. But, as to the *cause*, the process has been the opposite of this instance of the works of nature, for it is *the large house which has grown out of the small one*. The father, or grandfather, while he was toiling for his children, lived in the small house, constructed chiefly by himself, and consisting of rude materials. The means, accumulated in the small house, enabled a son to rear the large one; and, though, when *pride* enters the door, the small house is sometimes demolished, few sons in America have the folly or want of feeling to commit such acts of filial ingratitude, and of real self-abasement. For, what inheritance so valuable and so honourable can a son enjoy as the proofs of his father's industry and virtue? The progress of wealth and ease and enjoyment, evinced by this regular increase of the size of the farmer's dwellings, is a spectacle, at once pleasing, in a very high degree, in itself, and, in the same degree, it speaks the praise of the system of government, under which it has taken place. What a contrast with the farm-houses in England! There the *little* farm-houses are falling into ruins, or, are actually become cattle-sheds, or, at best, *cottages*, as they are called, to contain a miserable labourer, who ought to have been a farmer, as his grandfather was.

Absence of bird song and wild flowers

THERE ARE *two things*, which I have not yet mentioned, and which are almost wholly wanting here, while they are so amply enjoyed in England. The *singing-birds* and the *flowers*. Here are many birds in summer, and some of very beautiful plumage. There are some wild flowers, and some English flowers in the best gardens. But, generally speaking, they are birds without song, and flowers without smell. The *linnet* (more than a thousand of which I have heard warbling upon one scrubbed oak on the sand-hills in Surrey), the *sky-lark*, the *gold-finch*, the *wood-lark*, the *nightingale*, the *bullfinch*, the *black-bird*, the *thrush*, and all the rest of the singing tribe are wanting in these beautiful woods and orchards of garlands. When these latter have dropped their bloom, all is gone in a flowery way. No *shepherd's rose*, no *honey-suckle*, none of that endless variety of beauties that decorate the hedges and the meadows in England. No *daisies*, no *primroses*, no *cowslips*, no *blue-bells*, no *daffodils*, which, as if it were not enough for them to charm the sight and the smell, must have names, too, to delight the ear. All these are wanting in America. Here are, indeed, birds, which bear the *name* of robin, blackbird, thrush, and gold-finch; but, alas! the thing at Westminster has, in like manner, the *name* of parliament, and speaks the voice of the people whom it pretends to represent, in much about the same degree that the black-bird here speaks the voice of its namesake in England.

Versatility and independence of American workers

BESIDES THE GREAT quantity of work performed by the American labourer, his *skill*, the *versatility* of his talent, is a great thing. Every man can use an *axe*, a *saw*, and a *hammer*. Scarcely one who cannot do any job at rough carpentering, and mend a plough or a wagon. Very few indeed, who cannot kill and dress pigs and sheep, and many of them oxen and calves. Every farmer is a *neat* butcher; a butcher for *market*; and of course, 'the boys' must learn. This is a great convenience. It makes you so independent as to a main part of the means of house-keeping. All are *plough-men*. In short, a good labourer here can do *any thing* that is to be done upon a farm . . .

An American labourer is not regulated, as to time, by *clocks* and *watches*. The *sun*, who seldom hides his face, tells him when to begin in the morning and when to leave off at night. He has a dollar, a *whole dollar* for his work; but then it is the work of a *whole day*. Here is no dispute about *hours*. 'Hours were made for slaves,' is an old saying; and, really, they seem here to act upon it as a practical maxim. This is a *great thing* in agricultural affairs. It prevents so many disputes. It re-moves so great a cause of disagreement. The American labourers, like the tavern keepers, are never *servile*, but always *civil*. Neither *boobish-ness* nor *meanness* mark their character. They never *creep* and *fawn*, and are never *rude*. Employed about your house as day-labourers, they never come to interlope for victuals or drink. They have no idea of such a thing: their pride would restrain them if their plenty did not; and, thus would it be with all labourers, in all countries, were they left to enjoy the fair produce of their labour. Full pocket or empty pocket, these American labourers are always the *same men*: no saucy cunning in the one case, and no base crawling in the other. This, too, arises from the free institutions of government. A man has a voice *because he is a man*, and not because he is the *possessor of money*.

Basil Hall, Captain R.N.

was born in 1788. He was one of the first Englishmen to visit
Korea, on which he wrote a book. He visited the United States
in 1827–28 and wrote *Travels in North America* as a result.
It was not a book that pleased Americans. He died in 1844.

New York: first impressions

As WE PASSED along, many things recalled the seaports of England to my thoughts, although abundant indications of another country lay on all hands. The signs over the shop doors were written in English; but the language we heard spoken was different in tone from what we had been accustomed to. Still it was English. Yet there was more or less of a foreign air in all we saw, especially about the dress and gait of the men. Negroes and negresses also were seen in abundance on the wharfs. The form of most of the wheeled carriages was novel; and we encountered several covered vehicles, on which was written in large characters, ICE. I was amused by observing over one of the stores, as the shops are called, a great, staring, well-wigged figure painted on the sign, under which was written, LORD ELDON. A skinny row of white law books explained the mystery. The whole seemed at times, more like a dream than a sober reality. For there was so much about it that looked like England, that we half fancied ourselves back again; and yet there was quite enough to show in the next instant, that it was a very different country. This indistinct, dreamy kind of feeling, lasted for several days . . .

American self-praise

At THIS STAGE of the journey, I find from my notes that the most striking circumstance in the American character, which had come under our notice, was the constant habit of praising themselves, their institutions, and their country, either in downright terms, or by some would-be indirect allusions, which were still more tormenting. I make use of this sharp-edged word, because it really was exceedingly teasing, when we were quite willing and ready to praise all that was good, and also to see every thing, whether good or bad, in the fairest light, to be called upon so frequently to admit the justice of such exaggerations. It is considered, I believe, all over the world, as bad manners for a man to praise himself or his family. Now, to praise one's country appears, to say the least of it, in the next degree of bad taste.

It was curious to see with what vigilant adroitness the Americans availed themselves of every little circumstance to give effect to this self laudatory practice. I happened one day to mention to a lady, that I had been amused by observing how much more the drivers of the stages managed their horses by word of mouth, than by touch of the whip. Upon which she replied, 'Oh yes, sir, the circumstance you relate is very interesting, as it shows both intelligence in the men, and sagacity in the animals.' This was pretty well; but I merely smiled and said nothing, being somewhat tickled by this amiable interchange of human wisdom and brute sagacity. The lady's suspicions however instantly took fire on seeing the expression of my countenance, and she answered my smile by saying, 'Nay, sir, do you not think the people in America, upon the whole, particularly intelligent?'

Thus it ever was, in great things as well as in small, on grave or ludicrous occasions; they were eternally on the defensive, and gave us to understand that they suspected us of a design to find fault, at times when nothing on earth was farther from our thoughts. Whenever any thing favourable happened, by chance or otherwise, to be stated with respect to England, there was straightway a fidget, till the said circumstance was counterbalanced by something equally good, or much better, in America. To such an extent was this jealous fever carried, that I hardly recollect above half-a-dozen occasions during the whole journey, when England was mentioned, that the slightest interest of an agreeable kind was manifested on the part of the audience; or that a brisk cross fire was not instantly opened on all hands, to depreciate what had been said; or which was still more frequent, to build up something finer, or taller, or larger, in America to overmatch it. It always occurred to me, that they paid themselves and their institutions the very poorest description of compliment by this course of proceeding; and it would be quite easy to show why.

American restlessness

THIS PASSION FOR turning up new soils, and clearing the wilderness, heretofore untouched by the hand of man, is said to increase with years.

Under such constant changes of place, there can be very little individual regard felt or professed for particular spots. I might almost say, that as far as I could see or learn, there is nothing in any part of America similar to what we call local attachments. There is a strong love of country, it is true; but this is quite a different affair, as it seems to be entirely unconnected with any permanent fondness for one spot more than another.

A large and handsome farm-house, near Canandaigua, was pointed out to me one day, the owner of which had come to that part of the country between twenty and thirty years before, at which period it was pretty nearly an unbroken forest. He commenced with very slender means; but persevered in clearing away the woods, and ploughing up the ground, till he came at last to accumulate a considerable fortune. He then built a large brick house, married, brought up sons and daughters, and having retained his health and spirits entire to the age of sixty, had the prospect of a quiet, hearty, green old age before him.

Nothing, however, was farther from his thoughts, or more repugnant to his habits, than quiet. He missed the ardent excitement of his past life, and sighed to be once again in the heart of the thicket. Instead of finding agreeable companionship in the population which was crowding round him, he considered each fresh settler as an intruder on his freedom of action; a sort of spy on his proceedings. At length, after struggling for a while with the privations and inconveniences of civilization, he declared he could stand it no longer. So he made over his farm to his children, and carrying with him only his axe and his wife, a few dollars, a team of oxen, and a waggon and horses, set off for the territory of Michigan, the Lord knows how far off in the North-West. There he is now chopping down wood, and labouring in a sort of wild happiness from morning till night, to bring new lands into cultivation; which, in the course of time, if he live, he will dispose of to newer settlers, and again decamp to the westward.

Rochester, N.Y.

ON THE 26TH of June 1827, we strolled through the village of Rochester, under the guidance of a most obliging and intelligent friend, a native of this part of the country. Every thing in this bustling place appeared to be in motion. The very streets seemed to be starting up of their own accord, ready-made, and looking as fresh and new, as if they had been turned out of the workmen's hands but an hour before—or that a great boxful of new houses had been sent by steam from New York, and tumbled out on the half-cleared land. The canal banks were at some places still unturfed; the lime seemed hardly dry in the masonry of the aqueduct, in the bridges, and in the numberless great saw-mills and manufactories. In many of these buildings the people were at work below stairs, while at top the carpenters were busy nailing on the planks of the roof.

Some dwellings were half-painted, while the foundations of others, within five yards' distance, were only beginning. I cannot say how many churches, court-houses, jails, and hotels I counted, all in motion, creeping upwards. Several streets were nearly finished, but had not yet received their names; and many others were in the reverse predicament, being named, but not commenced,—their local habitation being merely signified by lines of stakes. Here and there we saw great warehouses, without window sashes, but half filled with goods, and furnished with hoisting cranes, ready to fish up the huge pyramids of flour barrels, bales, and boxes lying in the streets. In the centre of the town the spire of a Presbyterian church rose to a great height, and on each side of the supporting tower was to be seen the dial-plate of a clock, of which the machinery, in the hurry-skurry, had been left at New York. I need not say that these half-finished, whole-finished, and embryo streets were crowded with people, carts, stages, cattle, pigs, far beyond the reach of numbers;—and as all these were lifting up their voices together, in keeping with the clatter of hammers, the ringing of axes, and the creaking of machinery, there was a fine concert, I assure you!

But it struck us that the interest of the town, for it seems idle to call it a village, was subordinate to that of the suburbs. A few years ago the whole of that part of the country was covered with a dark silent forest, and even as it was, we could not proceed a mile in any direction except that of the highroad, without coming full-butt against the woods of time immemorial. When land is cleared for the purposes of cultivation, the stumps are left standing for many years, from its being easier, as well as more profitable in other respects, to plough round them, than to waste time and labour in rooting them out, or burning them, or blowing them up with gunpowder. But when a forest is levelled with a view to building a town in its place, a different system must of course be adopted. The trees must then be removed sooner or later, according to the means of the proprietor, or the necessities of the case. Thus one man possessed of capital will clear his lot of the wood, and erect houses, or even streets, across it; while on his neighbour's land the trees may still be growing. And it actually occurred to us, several times, within the immediate limits of the inhabited town itself, in streets, too, where shops were opened, and all sorts of business actually going up, that we had to drive first on one side, and then on the other, to avoid the stumps of an oak, or a hemlock, or a pine-tree, staring us full in the face.

On driving a little beyond the streets towards the woods, we came to a space, about an acre in size, roughly enclosed, on the summit of a gentle swell in the ground.

'What can this place be for?'

'Oh,' said my companion, 'that is the grave yard.'

'Grave yard—what is that?' said I: for I was quite adrift.

'Why, surely,' said he, 'you know what a grave yard is? It is a burying ground. All the inhabitants of the place are buried there, whatever be their persuasion. We don't use churchyards in America.'

After we had gone about a mile from town the forest thickened, we lost sight of every trace of a human dwelling, or of human interference with nature in any shape. We stood considering what we should do next, when a loud crash of a falling tree met our ears. Our friendly guide was showing off the curiosities of the place, and was quite glad, he said, to have this opportunity of exhibiting the very first step in the process of town-making. After a zig-zag scramble amongst the trees, which had been allowed to grow up and decay century after century, we came to a spot where three or four men were employed in clearing out a street, as they declared, though any thing more unlike a street could not well be conceived. Nevertheless, the ground in question certainly formed part of the plan of the town. It had been chalked out by surveyors' stakes, and some speculators having taken up the lots for immediate building, of course found it necessary to open a street through the woods, to afford a line of communication with the rest of the village.

Frances Trollope

mother of Anthony, was born in 1780 and emigrated in 1827
to Cincinnati in order to open a fancy-goods bazaar that she
hoped would restore the family fortunes. It did not, but the
book that came out of it, *Domestic Manners of the Americans*,
was a *succès de scandale* that very largely did. Back in England,
she became a prolific writer of novels and travel books.
She died in Florence in 1863.

American spitting

I HARDLY KNOW any annoyance so deeply repugnant to English feelings, as the incessant, remorseless spitting of Americans. I feel that I owe my readers an apology for the repeated use of this, and several other odious words; but I cannot avoid them, without suffering the fidelity of description to escape me. It is possible that in this phrase, 'Americans', I may be too general. The United States form a continent of almost distinct nations, and I must now, and always, be understood to speak only of that portion of them which I have seen. In conversing with Americans I have constantly found that if I alluded to any thing which they thought I considered as uncouth, they would assure me it was local, and not national; the accidental peculiarity of a very small part, and by no means a specimen of the whole. 'That is because you know so little of America', is a phrase I have listened to a thousand times, and in nearly as many different places. *It may be so*—and having made this concession, I protest against the charge of injustice in relating what I have seen.

On a Mississippi steamboat

THE GENTLEMEN IN the cabin (we had no ladies) would certainly, neither from their language, manners, nor appearance, have received that designation in Europe; but we soon found their claim to it rested on more substantial ground, for we heard them nearly all addressed by the titles of general, colonel, and major. On mentioning these military dignitaries to an English friend some time afterwards, he told me that he too had made the voyage with the same description of company, but remarking that there was not a single captain among them; he made the observation to a fellow-passenger, and asked how he accounted for it. 'Oh, sir, the captains are all on deck,' was the reply.

Our honours, however, were not all military, for we had a judge among us. I know it is equally easy and invidious to ridicule the peculiarities of appearance and manner in people of a different nation from ourselves; we may, too, at the same moment, be undergoing the same ordeal in their estimation; and, moreover, I am by no means disposed to consider whatever is new to me as therefore objectionable; but, nevertheless, it was impossible not to feel repugnance to many of the novelties that now surrounded me.

The total want of all the usual courtesies of the table, the voracious rapidity with which the viands were seized and devoured, the strange uncouth phrases and pronunciation; the loathsome spitting, from the contamination of which it was absolutely impossible to protect our dresses; the frightful manner of feeding with their knives, till the whole blade seemed to enter into the mouth; and the still more frightful manner of cleaning the teeth afterwards with a pocket knife, soon forced us to feel that we were not surrounded by the generals, colonels, and majors of the old world; and that the dinner hour was to be any thing rather than an hour of enjoyment.

The little conversation that went forward while we remained in the room, was entirely political, and the respective claims of Adams and Jackson to the presidency were argued with more oaths and more vehemence than it had ever been my lot to hear. Once a colonel appeared on the verge of assaulting a major, when a huge seven-foot Kentuckian gentleman horse-dealer, asked of the heavens to confound them both, and bade them sit still and be d — d. We too thought we should share this sentence; at least, sitting still in the cabin seemed very nearly to include the rest of it, and we never tarried there a moment longer than was absolutely necessary to eat.

Refuse-disposal in Cincinnati

WE WERE SOON settled in our new dwelling, which looked neat and comfortable enough, but we speedily found that it was devoid of nearly all the accommodation that Europeans conceive necessary to decency and comfort. No pump, no cistern, no drain of any kind, no dustman's cart, or any other visible means of getting rid of rubbish, which vanishes with such celerity in London, that one has no time to think of its existence; but which accumulated so rapidly at Cincinnati, that I sent for my landlord to know in what manner refuse of all kinds was to be disposed of.

'Your Help will just have to fix them all into the middle of the street, but you must mind, old woman, that it is the middle. I expect you don't know as we have got a law what forbids throwing such things at the sides of the streets; they must just all be cast right into the middle, and the pigs soon takes them off.'

In truth the pigs are constantly seen doing Herculean service in this way through every quarter of the city; and though it is not very agreeable to live surrounded by herds of these unsavoury animals, it is well they are so numerous, and so active in their capacity of scavengers, for without them the streets would soon be choked up with all sorts of substances, in every stage of decomposition.

A frontier farm in Ohio

WE VISITED ONE farm which interested us particularly from its wild and lonely situation, and from the entire dependence of the inhabitants upon their own resources. It was a partial clearing in the very heart of the forest. The house was built on the side of a hill, so steep that a high ladder was necessary to enter the front door, while the back one opened against the hill side; at the foot of this sudden eminence ran a clear stream, whose bed had been deepened into a little reservoir, just opposite the house. A noble field of Indian-corn stretched away into the forest on one side, and a few half-cleared acres, with a shed or two upon them, occupied the other, giving accommodation to cows, horses, pigs, and chickens innumerable. Immediately before the house was a small potato garden, with a few peach and apple trees. The house was built of logs, and consisted of two rooms, besides a little shanty or lean-to, that was used as a kitchen. Both rooms were comfortably furnished with good beds, drawers, &c. The farmer's wife, and a young woman who looked like her sister, were spinning, and three little children were playing about. The woman told me that they spun and wove all the cotton and woollen garments of the family, and knit all the stockings; her husband, though not a shoe-maker by trade, made all the shoes. She manufactured all the soap and candles they used, and prepared her sugar from the sugar-trees on their farm. All she wanted with money, she said, was to buy coffee, tea, and whiskey, and she could 'get enough any day by sending a batch of butter and chicken to market'. They used no wheat, nor sold any of their corn, which, though it appeared a very large quantity, was not more than they required to make their bread and cakes of various kinds, and to feed all their live stock during the winter. She did not look in health, and said they had all had ague in 'the fall'; but she seemed contented, and proud of her independence; though it was in somewhat a mournful accent that she said, ''Tis strange to us to see company: I expect the sun may rise and set a hundred times before I shall see another *human* that does not belong to the family'.

I have been minute in the description of this forest farm, as I think the best specimen I saw of the back-wood's independence, of which so much is said in America. These people were indeed independent, Robinson Crusoe was hardly more so, and they eat and drink abundantly; but yet it seemed to me that there was something awful and almost unnatural in their loneliness. No village bell ever summoned them to prayer, where they might meet the friendly greeting of their fellow men. When they die, no spot sacred by ancient reverence will receive their bones—Religion will not breathe her sweet and solemn farewell upon their grave; the husband or the father will dig the pit that is to hold them, beneath the nearest tree; he will himself deposit them within it, and the wind that whispers through the boughs will be their only requiem. But then they pay neither taxes nor tythes, are never expected to puff off a hat or to make a curtsey, and will live and die without hearing or uttering the dreadful words, 'God save the king'.

Southern attitudes to slaves

I OBSERVED EVERYWHERE throughout the slave States that all articles which can be taken and consumed are constantly locked up, and in large families, where the extent of the establishment multiplies the number of the keys, these are deposited in a basket, and consigned to the care of a little negress, who is constantly seen following her mistress's steps with this basket on her arm, and this, not only that the keys may be always at hand, but because, should they be out of sight one moment, that moment would infallibly be employed for the purposes of plunder. It seemed to me in this instance, as in many others, that the close personal attendance of these sable shadows, must be very annoying; but whenever I mentioned it, I was assured that no such feeling existed, and that use rendered them almost unconscious of their presence.

I had, indeed, frequent opportunities of observing this habitual indifference to the presence of their slaves. They talk of them, of their condition, of their conduct, exactly as if they were incapable of hearing. I once saw a young lady, who, when seated at table between a male and a female, was induced by her modesty to intrude on the chair of her female neighbour to avoid the indelicacy of touching the elbow of *a man*. I once saw this very young lady lacing her stays with the most perfect composure before a negro footman. A Virginian gentleman told me that ever since he had married, he had been accustomed to have a negro girl sleep in the same chamber with himself and his wife. I asked for what purpose this nocturnal attendance was necessary? 'Good heaven!' was the reply, 'if I wanted a glass of water during the night, what would become of me?'

Cooking, parties and women's dress

IN RELATING ALL I know of America, I surely must not omit so important a feature as the cooking. There are sundry anomalies in the mode of serving even a first-rate table; but as these are altogether matters of custom, they by no means indicate either indifference or neglect in this important business; and whether castors are placed on the table or on the side-board; whether soup, fish, patties, and salad be eaten in orthodox order or not, signifies but little. I am hardly capable, I fear, of giving a very erudite critique on the subject; general observations therefore must suffice. The ordinary mode of living is abundant, but not delicate. They consume an extraordinary quantity of bacon. Ham and beef-steaks appear morning, noon and night. In eating, they mix things together with the strangest incongruity imaginable. I have seen eggs and oysters eaten together; the sempiternal ham with apple-sauce; beef-steak with stewed peaches; and salt fish with onions. The bread is everywhere excellent, but they rarely enjoy it themselves, as they insist upon eating horrible half-baked hot rolls both morning and evening. The butter is tolerable; but they have seldom such cream as every little dairy produces in England; in fact, the cows are very roughly kept, compared with ours. Common vegetables are abundant and very fine. I never saw sea-cale or cauliflowers, and either from the want of summer rain, or the want of care, the harvest of green vegetables is much sooner over than with us. They eat the Indian corn in a great variety of forms; sometimes it is dressed green, and eaten like peas; sometimes it is broken to pieces when dry, boiled plain, and brought to table like rice; this dish is called hominy. The flour of it is made into at least a dozen different sorts of cakes; but in my opinion all bad. This flour, mixed in the proportion of one-third with fine wheat, makes by far the best bread I have ever tasted.

I never saw turbot, salmon, or fresh cod; but the rock and shad are excellent. There is a great want of skill in the composition of sauces; not only with fish, but with everything. They use very few made dishes, and I never saw any that would be approved by our savants. They have an excellent wild duck, called the Canvass Back, which, if delicately served, would surpass the black cock; but the game is very inferior to ours; they have no hares, and I never saw a pheasant. They seldom indulge in second courses, with all their ingenious temptations to the eating a second dinner; but almost every table has its dessert, (invariably pronounced desart) which is placed on the table before the cloth is removed, and consists of pastry, preserved fruits, and creams. They are 'extravagantly fond', to use their own phrase, of puddings, pies, and all kinds of 'sweets', particularly the ladies; but are by no means such connoisseurs in soups and ragoûts as the gastronomes of Europe. Almost every one drinks water at table, and by a strange contradiction, in the country where hard drinking is more prevalent than in any other, there is less wine taken at dinner; ladies rarely exceed one glass, and the great majority of females never take any. In fact, the hard drinking, so universally acknowledged, does not take place at jovial dinners, but, to speak in plain English, in solitary dram-drinking. Coffee is not served immediately after dinner, but makes part of the serious matter of tea-drinking, which comes some hours later. Mixed dinner parties of ladies and gentlemen are very rare, and unless foreigners are present, but little conversation passes at table. It certainly does not, in my opinion, add to the well ordering a dinner table, to set gentlemen at one end of it, and the ladies at the other; but it is very rarely that you find it otherwise.

Their large evening parties are supremely dull; the men sometimes play cards by themselves, but if a lady plays, it must not be for money; no ecarté, no chess; very little music, and that little lamentably bad. Among the blacks, I heard some good voices, singing in tune; but I scarcely ever heard a white American, male or female, go through an air without being out of tune before the end of it; nor did I ever meet any trace of science in the singing I heard in society. To eat inconceivable quantities of cake, ice, and pickled oysters—and to show half their revenue in silks and satins, seem to be the chief object they have in these parties.

The most agreeable meetings, I was assured by all young people, were those to which no married women are admitted; of the truth of this statement I have not the least doubt. These exclusive meetings occur frequently, and often last to a late hour; on these occasions, I believe, they generally dance. At regular balls, married ladies are admitted, but seldom take much part in the amusement. The refreshments are always profuse and costly, but taken in a most uncomfortable manner. I have known many private balls, where everything was on the most liberal scale of expense, where the gentlemen sat down to supper in one room, while the ladies took theirs, standing, in another.

What we call pic-nics are very rare, and when attempted, do not often succeed well. The two sexes can hardly mix for the greater part of a day without great restraint and ennui; it is quite contrary to their general habits; the favourite indulgences of the gentlemen (smoking cigars and drinking spirits), can neither be indulged in with decency, nor resigned with complacency.

The ladies have strange ways of adding to their charms. They powder themselves immoderately, face, neck, and arms, with pulverised starch; the effect is indescribably disagreeable by day-light, and not very favourable at any time. They are also unhappily partial to false hair, which they wear in surprising quantities; this is the more lamented, as they generally have very fine hair of their own. I suspect this fashion to arise from an indolent mode of making their toilet, and from accomplished ladies' maids not being very abundant; it is less trouble to append a bunch of waving curls here, there, and everywhere, than to keep their native tresses in perfect order.

Though the expense of the ladies' dress greatly exceeds, in proportion to their general style of living, that of the ladies of Europe, it is very far (excepting Philadelphia) from being in good taste. They do not consult the seasons in the colours or in the style of their costume; I have often shivered at seeing a young beauty picking her way through the snow with a pale rose-coloured bonnet, set on the very top of her head: I knew one young lady whose pretty little ear was actually frost-bitten from being thus exposed. They never wear muffs or boots, and appear extremely shocked at the sight of comfortable walking shoes and cotton stockings, even when they have to step to their sleighs over ice and snow. They walk in the middle of winter with their poor little toes pinched into a miniature slipper, incapable of excluding as much moisture as might bedew a primrose. I must say in their excuse, however, that they have, almost universally, extremely pretty feet. They do not walk well, nor, in fact, do they even appear to advantage when in movement. I know not why this should be, for they have an abundance of French dancing-masters among them, but somehow or other it is the fact. I fancied I could often trace a mixture of affectation and of shyness in their little mincing unsteady step, and the ever-changing position of the hands. They do not dance well; perhaps I should rather say they do not look well when dancing; lovely as their faces are, they cannot, in a position that exhibits the whole person, atone for the want of *tournure*, and for the universal defect in the formation of the bust, which is rarely full, or gracefully formed.

'A lovely and noble city'

AT LENGTH, HOWEVER, we found ourselves alive on board the boat which was to convey us down the Raraton River to New York.

We fully intended to have gone to bed, to heal our bones, on entering the steam-boat, but the sight of a table neatly spread determined us to go to dinner instead. Sin and shame would it have been, indeed, to have closed our eyes upon the scene which soon opened before us. I have never seen the bay of Naples, I can therefore make no comparison, but my imagination is incapable of conceiving anything of the kind more beautiful than the harbour of New York. Various and lovely are the objects which meet the eye on every side, but the naming them would only be to give a list of which, without conveying the faintest idea of the scene. I doubt if even the pencil of Turner could do it justice, bright and glorious as it rose upon us. We seemed to enter the harbour of New York upon waves of liquid gold, and we darted past the green isles which rise from its bosom, like guardian centinels of the fair city, the setting sun stretched his horizontal beams farther and farther at each moment, as if to point out to us some new glory in the landscape.

New York, indeed, appeared to us, even when we saw it by a sober light, a lovely and a noble city. To us who had been so long travelling through half-cleared forests, and sojourning among an 'I'm-as-good-as-you' population, it seemed, perhaps, more beautiful, more splendid, and more refined than it might have done, had we arrived there directly from London; but making every allowance for this, I must still declare that I think New York one of the finest cities I ever saw, and as much superior to every other in the Union (Philadelphia not excepted), as London to Liverpool, or Paris to Rouen. Its advantages of position are, perhaps, unequalled anywhere. Situated on an island, which I think it will one day cover, it rises, like Venice, from the sea, and like that fairest of cities in the days of her glory, receives into its lap tribute of all the riches of the earth.

The southern point of Manhattan Island divides the waters of the harbour into the north and east rivers; on this point stands the city of New York, extending from river to river, and running northward to the extent of three or four miles. I think it covers nearly as much ground as Paris, but is much less thickly peopled. The extreme point is fortified towards the sea by a battery, and forms an admirable point of defence; but in these piping days of peace, it is converted into a public promenade, and one more beautiful, I should suppose, no city could boast. From hence commences the splendid Broadway, as the fine avenue is called, which runs through the whole city. This noble street may vie with any I ever saw, for its length and breadth, its handsome shops, neat awnings, excellent *trottoir*, and well-dressed pedestrians. It has not the crowded glitter of Bond Street equipages, nor the gorgeous fronted palaces of Regent Street; but it is magnificent in its extent, and ornamented by several handsome buildings, some of them surrounded by grass and trees. The Park, in which stands the noble city-hall, is a very fine area. I never found that the most graphic description of a city could give me any feeling of being there; and even if others have the power, I am very sure I have not, of setting churches and squares, and long drawn streets, before the mind's eye. I will not, therefore, attempt a detailed description of this great metropolis of the new world, but will only say that during the seven weeks we stayed there, we always found something new to see and to admire; and were it not so very far from all the old-world things which cling about the heart of an European, I should say that I never saw a city more desirable as a residence.

The dwelling houses of the higher classes are extremely handsome, and very richly furnished. Silk or satin furniture is as often, or oftener, seen than chintz; the mirrors are as handsome as in London; the cheffoniers, slabs, and marble tables as elegant; and in addition, they have all the pretty tasteful decoration of French porcelaine, and or-molu in much greater abundance, because at a much cheaper rate. Every part of their houses is well carpeted, and the exterior finishing, such as steps, railings, and door-frames, are very superior. Almost every house has handsome green blinds on the outside; balconies are not very general, nor do the houses display, externally, so many flowers as those of Paris and London; but I saw many rooms decorated within, exactly like those of an European *petite maitresse*. Little tables, looking and smelling like flower beds, portfolios, nick-nacks, bronzes, busts, cameos, and alabaster vases, illustrated copies of lady-like rhymes bound in silk, and, in short, all the pretty coxcomalities of the drawing-room scattered about with the same profuse and studied negligence as with us.

Thomas Hamilton

younger brother of the metaphysician Sir William Hamilton, was born in Glasgow in 1789 and became an army officer. He settled in Edinburgh on his retirement, wrote a successful novel and contributed to Blackwood. *Men and Manners in America* appeared in 1833. He died in 1842.

Breakfast in a New York hotel

I HAD NEARLY completed my toilet on the morning after my arrival, when the tinkling of a large bell gave intimation, that the hour of breakfast was come. I accordingly descended as speedily as possible to the *salle à manger*, and found a considerable party engaged in doing justice to a meal, which, at first glance, one would scarcely have guessed to be a breakfast. Solid viands of all descriptions loaded the table, while, in the occasional intervals, were distributed dishes of rolls, toast, and cakes of buck-wheat and Indian corn. At the head of the table, sat the landlady, who, with an air of complacent dignity, was busied in the distribution of tea and coffee. A large bevy of negroes were bustling about, ministering with all possible alacrity, to the many wants which were somewhat vociferously obtruded on their attention. Towards the upper end of the table, I observed about a dozen ladies, but by far the larger portion of the company were of the other sex.

The contrast of the whole scene, with that of an English breakfast-table, was striking enough. Here was no loitering or lounging; no dipping into newspapers; no apparent lassitude of appetite; no intervals of repose in mastication; but all was hurry, bustle, clamour, and voracity, and the business of repletion went forward, with a rapidity altogether unexampled. The strenuous efforts of the company were of course, soon rewarded with success. Departures, which had begun even before I took my place at the table, became every instant more numerous, and in a few minutes the apartment had become, what Moore beautifully describes in one of his songs, 'a banquet-hall deserted'. The appearance of the table under such circumstances, was by no means gracious either to the eye or to the fancy. It was strewed thickly with the *disjecta membra* of the entertainment. Here, lay fragments of fish, somewhat odoriferous; there, the skeleton of a chicken; on the right, a mustard-pot upset, and the cloth, *passim*, defiled with stains of eggs, coffee, gravy—but I will not go on with the picture. One nasty custom, however, I must notice. Eggs, instead of being eaten from the shell, are poured into a wine-glass, and after being duly and disgustingly churned up with butter and condiment, the mixture, according to its degree of fluidity, is forthwith either spooned into the mouth, or drunk off like a liquid. The advantage gained by this unpleasant process, I do not profess to be qualified to appreciate, but I can speak from experience, to its sedative effect on the appetite of an unpractised beholder.

Negro children in New York

HAVING RESOLVED TO devote the day to the inspection of schools, I went from that under the superintendence of Professor Griscomb, to another for the education of children of colour. I here found about a hundred boys, in whose countenance might be traced every possible gradation of complexion between those of the swarthy Ethiop and florid European. Indeed several of the children were so fair, that I certainly never should have discovered the lurking taint of African descent. In person they were clean and neat, and though of course the off-spring of the very lowest class of people, there was nothing in their dress or appearance indicative of abject poverty. The master struck me as an intelligent and benevolent man. He frankly answered all my questions, and evidently took pride in the proficiency of his pupils.

It has often happened to me, since my arrival in this country, to hear it gravely maintained by men of education and intelligence, that the Negroes were an inferior race, a link as it were between man and the brutes. Having enjoyed few opportunities of observation on people of colour in my own country, I was now glad to be enabled to enlarge my knowledge on a subject so interesting. I therefore requested the master to inform me whether the results of his experience had led to the inference, that the aptitude of the Negro children for acquiring knowledge was inferior to that of the whites. In reply, he assured me they had not done so; and, on the contrary, declared, that in sagacity, perseverance, and capacity for the acquisition and retention of know-ledge, his poor despised scholars were equal to any boys he had ever known. 'But alas, sir!' said he, 'to what end are these poor creatures taught acquirement, from the exercise of which they are destined to be debarred, by the prejudices of society? It is surely but a cruel mockery to cultivate talents, when in the present state of public feeling, there is no field open for their useful employment. Be his acquirements what they may, a Negro is still a Negro, or, in other words, a creature marked out for degradation, and exclusion from those objects which stimulate the hopes and powers of other white men.'

I observed, in reply, that I was not aware that, in those States in which slavery had been abolished, any such barrier existed as that to which he alluded. 'In the State of New York, for instance,' I asked, 'are not all offices and professions open to the man of colour as well as to the white?'

'I see, sir,' replied he, 'that you are not a native of this country, or you would not have asked such a question.' He then went on to inform me, that the exclusion in question did not arise from any legislative enactment, but from the tyranny of that prejudice, which, regarding the poor black as being of inferior order, works its own fulfilment in making him so . . .

I had become so much interested in the little parti-coloured crowd before me, that I recurred to our former discourse, and enquired of the master, what would probably become of his scholars on their being sent out into the world? Some trades, some description of labour of course were open to them, and I expressed my desire to know what these were. He told me they were few. The class studying navigation, were destined to be sailors; but let their talents be what they might, it was impossible they could rise to be officers of the paltriest merchantman that entered the waters of the United States. The office of cook or steward was indeed within the scope of their ambition; but it was just as feasible for the poor creature to expect to become Chancellor of the State, as mate of a ship. In other pursuits it was the same. Some would become stone-masons, or bricklayers, and to the extent of carrying a hod, or handling a trowel, the course was clear before them; but the office of master-bricklayer was open to them in precisely the same sense as the Professorship of Natural Philosophy. No white artificer would serve under a coloured master. The most degraded Irish emigrant would scout the idea with indignation. As carpenters, shoemakers, or tailors, they were still arrested by the same barrier. In either of the latter capacities, indeed, they might work for people of their own complexion, but no *gentleman* would ever think of ordering garments of any sort from a *schneider* of cuticle less white than his own. Grocers they might be, but then who could conceive the possibility of a respectable household matron purchasing tea or spiceries from a vile 'Nigger?' As barbers, they were more fortunate, and in that capacity might even enjoy the privilege of taking the President of the United States by the nose.

At President Andrew Jackson's levée

ON THE FOLLOWING evening I attended the levée. The apartments were already full before I arrived, and the crowd extended even into the hall. Three—I am not sure that there were not four—large saloons were thrown open on the occasion, and were literally crammed with the most singular and miscellaneous assemblage I had ever seen.

The numerical majority of the company seemed of the class of tradesmen or farmers, respectable men fresh from the plough or counter, who, accompanied by their wives and daughters, came forth to greet their President, and enjoy the splendours of the gala. There were also generals and commodores, and public officers of every description, and foreign ministers and members of Congress, and ladies of all ages and degrees of beauty, from the fair and laughing girl of fifteen, to the haggard dowager of seventy. There were majors in broad cloth and corduroys, redolent of gin and tobacco, and majors' ladies in chintz or russet, with huge Paris ear-rings, and tawny necks, profusely decorated with beads of coloured glass. There were tailors from the board, and judges from the bench; lawyers who opened their mouths at one bar, and the tapster who closed them at another;—in short, every trade, craft, calling, and profession, appeared to have sent its delegates to this extraordinary convention.

For myself, I had seen too much of the United States to expect any thing very different, and certainly anticipated that the mixture would contain all the ingredients I have ventured to describe. Yet after all, I was taken by surprise. There were present at this levée, men begrimed with sweat and filth accumulated in their day's—perhaps their week's —labour. There were sooty artificers, evidently fresh from the forge or the workshop; and one individual, I remember—either a miller or a baker—who, whenever he passed, left marks of contact on the garments of the company. The most prominent group, however, in the assemblage, was a party of Irish labourers, employed on some neighbouring canal, who had evidently been apt scholars in the doctrine of liberty and equality, and were determined, on the present occasion, to assert the full privileges of 'the great unwashed'. I remarked these men pushing aside the more respectable portion of the company with a certain jocular audacity, which put one in mind of the humours of Donnybrook.

A party, composed of the materials I have described, could possess but few attractions. The heat of the apartment was very great, and the odours—certainly not Sabaean—which occasionally affected the nostrils, were more pungent than agreeable. I therefore pushed on in search of the President, in order that, having paid my respects in acknowledgement of a kindness for which I felt really grateful, I might be at liberty to depart. My progress, however, was slow, for the company in the exterior saloons were wedged together in a dense mass, penetrable only at occasional intervals. I looked everywhere for the President as I passed, but without success; but at length a friend, against whom I happened to be jostled, informed me that I should find him at the extremity of the most distant apartment.

The information was correct. There stood the President, whose looks still indicated indisposition, paying one of the severest penalties of greatness; compelled to talk when he had nothing to say, and shake hands with men whose very appearance suggested the precaution of a glove. I must say, however, that under these circumstances, he bore himself well and gracefully. His countenance expressed perfect good-humour; and his manner to the ladies was so full of well-bred gallantry, that having, as I make no doubt, the great majority of the fair sex on his side, the chance of his being unseated at the next election must be very small.

I did not, however, remain long a spectator of the scene. Having gone through the ordinary ceremonial, I scrambled out of the crowd the best way I could, and bade farewell to the most extraordinary scene it had ever been my fortune to witness. It is only fair to state, however, that during my stay in Washington, I never heard the President's levée mentioned in company without an expression of in-dignant feeling on the part of the ladies, at the circumstances I have narrated. To the better order of Americans, indeed, it cannot but be painful that their wives and daughters should thus be compelled to mingle with the very lowest of the people. Yet the evil, whatever may be its extent, is in truth the necessary result of a form of government essentially democratic. Wherever universal suffrage prevails, the people are, and must be, the sole depository of political power. The American President well knows that his only chance of continuance in office, consists in his conciliating the favour of the lowest—and therefore most numerous—order of his constituents. The rich and intelligent are a small minority, and their opinion he may despise. The poor, the un-educated, are, in every country, *the people*. It is to them alone that a public man in America can look for the gratification of his ambition. They are the ladder by which he must mount, or be content to stand on a level with his fellow-men . . .

During the time I was engaged at the levée, my servant remained in the hall through which lay the entrance to the apartments occupied by the company, and on the day following he gave me a few details of a scene somewhat extraordinary, but sufficiently characteristic to merit record. It appeared that the refreshments intended for the company, consisting of punch and lemonade, were brought by the servants, with the intention of reaching the interior saloon. No sooner, however, were the ministers of Bacchus descried to be approaching by a portion of the company, than a rush was made from within, the whole contents of the trays were seized *in transitu*, by a sort of *coup-de-main*; and the bearers having thus rapidly achieved the distribution of their refreshments, had nothing for it but to return for a fresh supply. This was brought, and quite as compendiously despatched, and it at length became apparent, that without resorting to some extraordinary measures, it would be impossible to accomplish the intended voyage, and the more respectable portion of the company would be suffered to depart with dry palates, and in utter ignorance of the extent of the hospitality to which they were indebted.

The butler, however, was an Irishman, and in order to baffle further attempts at intercepting the supplies, had recourse to an expedient marked by all the ingenuity of his countrymen. He procured an escort, armed with sticks, and on his next advance these men kept flourishing their *shillelahs* around the trays, with such alarming vehemence, that the predatory horde, who anticipated repetition of their plunder, were scared from their prey, and, amid a scene of execrations and laughter, the refreshments, thus guarded, accomplished their journey to the saloon in safety.

Men and manners on an Ohio River steamboat

IN REGARD TO the passengers, truth compels me to say, that any thing so disgusting in human shape I had never seen. Their morals and their manners were alike detestable. A cold and callous selfishness, a disregard of all the decencies of society, were so apparent in feature, word, and action, that I found it impossible not to wish that their catalogue of sins had been enlarged by one more—hypocrisy. Of hypocrisy, however, they were not guilty. The conversation in the cabin was interlarded with the vilest blasphemy, not uttered in a state of mental excitement, but with a coolness and deliberation truly fiend-like. There was a Baptist clergyman on board, but his presence did not seem to operate as a restraint. The scene of drinking and gambling had no intermission. It continued day and night. The captain of the vessel, so far from discouraging either vice, was one of the most flagrant offenders in both. He was decidedly the greatest gambler on board; and was often so drunk as to be utterly incapable of taking command of the vessel. There were a few female passengers, but with their presence we were only honoured at meals. At all other times, they prudently confined themselves to their own cabins.

One circumstance may be mentioned, which is tolerably illustrative of the general habits of the people. In every steam-boat there is a *public* comb and hair-brush suspended by a string from the ceiling of the cabin. These utensils are used by the whole body of the passengers, and their condition, the pen of Swift could alone adequately describe. There is no tooth-brush, simply, I believe, because the article is entirely unknown to the American toilet. A common towel, however, passes from hand to hand, and suffices for the perfunctory ablutions of the whole party on board. It was often with great difficulty that I procured the exclusive usufruct of one, and it was evident that the demand was not only unusual but disagreeable.

One day at dinner, my English fellow-traveller, who had resided many years in the United States, enquired whether I observed an ivory hilt protruded from beneath the waistcoat of a gentleman opposite. I answered in the affirmative, and he then informed me that the whole population of the Southern and Western States are uniformly armed with daggers. On my expressing some doubt of this singular fact, he pointed to a number of sticks collected in one corner of the cabin, and offered a wager that every one of these contained either a dagger or a sword. I took the bet, and lost it: and my subsequent observations confirmed the truth of his assertion in every particular. Even in travelling in the State of New York, I afterwards observed that a great number of passengers in stage-coaches and canal boats were armed with this unmanly and assassin-like weapon.

Yankees and southerners compared

THE POLES ARE not more diametrically opposed, than a native of the States south of the Potomac, and a New Englander. They differ in every thing of thought, feeling, and opinion. The latter is a man of regular and decorous habits, shrewd, intelligent, and persevering; phlegmatic in temperament, devoted to the pursuits of gain, and envious of those who are more successful than himself. The former— I speak of the opulent and educated—is distinguished by a high-mindedness, generosity, and hospitality, by no means predictable of his more eastern neighbours. He values money only for the enjoyments it can procure, is fond of gaiety, given to social pleasures, somewhat touchy and choleric, and as eager to avenge an insult as to show a kindness. To fight a duel in the New England States would, under almost any circumstances, be disgraceful. To refuse a challenge, to tolerate even an insinuation derogatory from personal honour, would be considered equally so in the South.

In point of manner, the Southern gentlemen are decidedly superior to all others of the Union. Being more dependent on social intercourse, they are at greater pains perhaps to render it agreeable. There is more spirit and vivacity about them, and far less of that prudent caution, which, however advantageous on the exchange, is by no means pre-possessing at the dinner-table, or in the drawing-room. When at Washington, I was a good deal thrown into the society of members from the South, and left it armed, by their kindness, with a multitude of letters, of which I regret that my hurried progress did not permit me to avail myself. Many of them were men of much accomplish ment, and I think it probable that Englishmen unconnected with business would generally prefer the society of gentlemen of this portion of the Union to any other which the country affords.

Fanny Kemble

a member of the famous family of English actors and actresses, was born in 1809 and went to America with her father's company in 1832. She had a brilliant success on the American stage and two years later married Pierce Butler, the owner of a Georgian plantation who was resident in Philadelphia. The *Journal of Frances Anne Butler* is a record of her American experiences before her marriage. In 1846 she left her husband, returned to the London stage, and was involved in a divorce suit. Her *Journal of a Residence on a Georgian Plantation*, written in 1838–39, was not published until 1863, during the Civil War. Later, she returned to the United States to live in the Berkshires. The American novelist Owen Wister was her grandson. She died in London in 1893.

New York City

Tuesday, September 4th. 1832
New York, America

... THE HOUSES ARE almost all painted glaring white or red; the other favourite colours appear to be pale straw colour and grey. They have all green venetian shutters, which give an idea of coolness, and almost every house has a tree or trees in its vicinity, which looks pretty and garden-like.

Street-behaviour in New York

Friday, Sept. 7th. 1832
New York

... AFTER WALKING NEARLY a mile up Broadway, we came to Canal Street: it is broader and finer than any I have yet seen in New York; and at one end of it, a Christian church, copied from some Pagan temple or other, looked exceedingly well, in the full flood of silver light that streamed from heaven. There were many temptations to look around, but the flags were so horribly broken and out of order, that to do so was to run the risk of breaking one's neck:—this is very bad. The street was very much thronged, and I thought the crowd a more civil and orderly one, than an English crowd. The men did not jostle or push one another, or tread upon one's feet, or kick down one's shoe heels, or crush one's bonnet into one's face, or turn it round upon one's head, all which I have seen done in London streets. There is this to be said: this crowd was abroad merely for pleasure, sauntering along, which is a thing never seen in London; the proportion of idle loungers who frequent the streets there being very inconsiderable, when compared with the number of people going on business through the town. I observed that the young men to-night invariably made room for the women to pass, and many of them, as they drew near us, took the segar from their mouth, which I thought especially courteous. They were all smoking, to a man, except those who were spitting, which helped to remind me of Paris, to which the whole place bore a slight resemblance. The shops appear to me to make no show whatever, and will not bear a comparison with the brilliant display of the Parisian streets, or the rich magnificence of our own, in that respect. The women dress very much, and very much like French women gone mad; they all of them seem to me to walk horribly ill, as if they wore tight shoes.

Freedom of American girls

THE MANNERS OF the young girls of America appear singularly free to foreigners; and until they become better acquainted with the causes which produce so unrestrained a deportment, they are liable to take disadvantageous and mistaken impressions with regard to them. The term which I should say applied best to the tone and carriage of American girls from ten to eighteen, is hoydenish; laughing, giggling, romping, flirting, screaming at the top of their voices, running in and out of shops, and spending a very considerable portion of their time in lounging about in the streets. In Philadelphia and Boston, almost all the young ladies attend classes or day schools; and in the latter place I never went out, morning, noon, or evening, that I did not meet, in some of the streets round the Tremont House, a whole bevy of young school girls, who were my very particular friends, but who, under pretext of going to, or returning from, school, appeared to me to be always laughing, and talking, and running about in the public thoroughfares; a system of education which we should think by no means desirable. The entire liberty which the majority of young ladies are allowed to assume, at an age when in England they would be under strict nursery discipline, appears very extraordinary; they not only walk alone in the streets, but go out into society, where they take a determined and leading part, without either mother, aunt, or chaperon of any sort; custom, which renders such an appendage necessary with us, entirely dispenses with it here; and though the reason of this is obvious enough in the narrow circles of these small towns, where every body knows every body, the manners of the young ladies do not derive any additional charm from the perfect self-possession which they thus acquire. Shyness appears to me to be a quality utterly unknown to either man, woman, or child in America. The girls, from the reasons above stated; and the boys, from being absolutely thrown into the world, and made men of business before they are sixteen, are alike deficient in any thing like diffidence; and I really have been all but disconcerted at the perfect assurance with which I have been addressed, upon any and every subject, by little men and women just half way through their teens. That very common character amongst us, a shy man, is not to be met with in these latitudes. An American conversing on board one of their steam-boats is immediately surrounded, particularly if his conversation, though strictly directed to one individual, is of a political nature; in an instant a ring of spectators is formed round him, and whereas an Englishman would become silent at the very first appearance of a listener, an American, far from seeming abashed at this 'audience', continues his discourse, which thus assumes the nature of an harangue, with perfect equanimity, and feels no annoyance whatever at having unfolded his private opinions of men and matters to a circle of forty or fifty people whom they could in no possible way concern. Speechifying is a very favourite species of exhibition with the men here, by the by; and, besides being self-possessed, they are all remarkably fluent. Really eloquent men are just as rare in this country as in any other, but the 'gift of the gab' appears to me more widely disseminated amongst Americans than any other people in the world. Many things go to make good speakers of them: great acuteness, and sound common sense, sufficient general knowledge, and great knowledge of the world, an intense interest in every political measure, no matter how trivial in itself, no sense of bashfulness, and a great readiness of expression. But to return to the manners of the young American girls:—It is Rousseau, I think, who says, '*Dans un pays ou les moeurs sont pures, les filles seront faciles, et les femmes severes*'. This applies particularly well to the carriage of the American woman. When remarking to a gentleman once the difference between the manners of my own young countrywomen and his, I expressed my disapprobation of the education which led to such a result, he replied, 'You forget the comparatively pure state of morals in our country, which admits of this degree of freedom in our young women, without its rendering them liable to insult or misconstruction.' This is true, and it is most true, for I have seen repeated instances of it, that those very girls, whose manners have been most displeasing to my European ways of feeling, whom I should have pointed out as romps and flirts pre-eminent, not only make excellent wives, but from the very moment of their marriage seem to forsake society, and devote themselves exclusively to household duties and retirement. But that I have seen and known of repeated instances of this, I could scarcely have believed it, but it is the case; and a young American lady, speaking upon this subject, said to me, 'We enjoy ourselves before marriage; but in your country, girls marry to obtain a greater degree of freedom, and indulge in the pleasures and dissipations of society.' She was not, I think, greatly mistaken.

'A darling country for poor folks'

In SPEAKING OF the bad and disagreeable results of the political institutions of this country, as exhibited in the feelings and manners of the lower orders, I have every where dwelt upon those which, from my own disposition, and the opinions and sentiments in which I have been educated, have struck me most, and most unfavourably. But I should be sorry to be so blind, or so prejudiced, as not to perceive the great moral goods which arise from the very same source, and display themselves strongly in the same class of people; *honesty* and *truth*, excellences so great, that the most bigoted worshipper of the forms and divisions of societies in the old world would surely be ashamed to weigh them in the balance against the deference there paid to rank or riches, or even the real and very agreeable qualities of civility and courtesy. Americans (I speak now of the *people*, not the gentlemen and ladies, *they* are neither so honest and true, nor quite so rude,) are indeed independent. Every man that will work a little can live extremely well. No portion of the country is yet overstocked with followers of trades, not even the Atlantic cities. Living is cheap—labour is dear. To conclude, as the Irish woman said, 'It is a darling country for poor folks; for if I work three days in the week, can't I lie in my bed the other three if I please?' This being so, all dealings between handicraftsmen and those who employ them; tradesmen and those who buy of them; servants and those who are served by them; are conducted upon the most entire system of reciprocity of advantage; indeed, if any thing, the obligation appears always to lie in that party which, with us, is generally supposed to confer it. Thus,—my shoemaker, a person with whom I have now dealt largely for two years, said to me the other day, upon my remonstrating about being obliged regularly to come to his shop and unboot, whenever I order a new pair of walking boots—'Well, ma'am, we can keep your measure certainly, *to oblige you*, but as a rule we don't do it for any of our customers, it's so very troublesome.' These people are, then, as I said before, most truly independent; they are therefore never servile, and but seldom civil, but for the very same reason they do not rob you; they do not need to do so; neither do they lie to you, for your favour or displeasure in no way affects their interest. If you entrust to their care materials of any sort to make up, you are sure, no matter how long you may leave them in their hands, or how entirely you may have forgotten the quantity originally given, to have every inch of them returned to you: and you are also generally sure that any question you ask, with regard to the quality of what you purchase, will be answered without any endeavour to impose upon you, or palm upon your ignorance that which is worse for that which is better. Two circumstances, which have come under my own knowledge, will serve to illustrate the spirit of the people; and they are good illustrations to quote, for similar circumstances are of daily and hourly occurrence.

A farmer who is in the habit of calling at our house on his way to market, with eggs, poultry, &c., being questioned as to whether the eggs were new-laid, replied, without an instant's hesitation, 'No, not very fresh ones, *we eat all those ourselves.*'

On returning home late from the play one night, I could not find my slippers any where, and, after some useless searching, performed my toilet for bed without them. The next morning, on enquiring of my maid if she knew any thing of them, she replied with perfect equanimity, that having walked home through the snow, and got her feet extremely wet, she had put them on, and forgotten to restore them to their place before my return. Nobody, I think, will doubt that an English farmer, and an English servant, might sell stale eggs, and use their mistress's slippers; but I think it highly doubtful, that either fact would have been acknowledged with such perfect honesty any where but here. As to the servants here, except the blacks, and the poor Irish bread-hunters who come over, there are scarcely any to be found: the very name seems repugnant to an American; and however high their wages, and easy their situation, they seem hardly to be able to endure the bitterness of subserviency and subordination.

Charleston, South Carolina

IN WALKING ABOUT Charleston, I was forcibly reminded of some of the older country towns in England—of Southampton a little. The appearance of the city is highly picturesque, a word which can apply to none other of the American towns; and although the place is certainly pervaded with an air of decay, it is a genteel infirmity, as might be that of a distressed elderly gentlewoman. It has none of the smug mercantile primness of the Northern cities, but a look of state, as of quondam wealth and importance, a little gone down in the world, yet remembering still its former dignity. The Northern towns, compared with it, are as the spruce citizen rattling by the faded splendors of an old family coach in his new-fangled chariot—they certainly have got on before it. Charleston has an air of eccentricity, too, and peculiarity, which formerly were not deemed unbecoming the wellborn and well-bred gentlewoman, which her gentility itself sanctioned and warranted—none of the vulgar dread of vulgar opinion, forcing those who are possessed by it to conform to a general standard of manners, unable to conceive one peculiar to itself—this 'what-'ll-Mrs-Grundy-say' devotion to conformity in small things and great, which pervades the American body-social from the matter of churchgoing to the trimming of women's petticoats—this dread of singularity, which has eaten up all individuality amongst them, and makes their population like so many moral and mental lithographs, and their houses like so many thousand hideous brick twins.

I believe I am getting excited; but the fact is, that being politically the most free people on earth, the Americans are socially the least so; and it seems as though, ever since that little affair of establishing their independence among nations, which they managed so successfully, every American mother's son of them has been doing his best to divest himself of his own private share of that great public blessing, liberty.

But to return to Charleston. It is in this respect a far more aristocratic (should I say democratic?) city than any I have yet seen in America, inasmuch as every house seems built to the owner's particular taste; and in one street you seem to be in an old English town, and in another in some continental city of France or Italy. This variety is extremely pleasing to the eye; not less so is the intermixture of trees with the buildings, almost every house being adorned, and gracefully screened, by the beautiful foliage of evergreen shrubs. These, like ministering angels, cloak with nature's kindly ornaments the ruins and decays of the mansions they surround; and the latter, time-mellowed (I will not say stained, and a painter knows the difference), harmonize in their forms a coloring with the trees, in a manner most delightful to the eye that knows how to appreciate this species of beauty.

There are several public buildings of considerable architectural pretensions in Charleston, all of them apparently of some antiquity (for the New World), except a very large and handsome edifice which is not yet completed, and which, upon inquiry, we found was indeed for a guardhouse. Its very extensive dimensions excited our surprise; but a man who was at work about it, and who answered our questions with a good deal of intelligence, informed us that it was by no means larger than the necessities of the city required; for that they not unfrequently had between fifty and sixty persons (colored and white) brought in by the patrol in one night.

'But,' objected we, 'the colored people are not allowed to go out without passes after nine o'clock.'

'Yes,' replied our informant, 'but they will do it, nevertheless; and every night numbers are brought in who have been caught endeavouring to evade the patrol.'

This explained to me the meaning of a most ominous tolling of bells and beating of drums, which, on the first evening of my arrival in Charleston, made me almost fancy myself in one of the old fortified frontier towns of the Continent, where the tocsin is sounded, and the evening drum beaten, and the guard set as regularly every night as if an invasion were expected. In Charleston, however, it is not the dread of foreign invasion but of domestic insurrection, which occasions these nightly precautions; and, for the first time since my residence in this free country, the curfew (now obsolete in mine, except in some remote districts, where the ringing of an old church bell at sunset is all that remains of the tyrannous custom) recalled the associations of early feudal times, and the oppressive insecurity of our Norman conquerers. But truly it seemed rather anomalous hereabouts, and nowadays; though, of course, it is very necessary where a large class of persons exists in the very bosom of a community whose interests are known to be at variance and incompatible with those of its other members. And no doubt these daily and nightly precautions are but trifling drawbacks upon the manifold blessings of slavery (for which, if you are stupid, and cannot conceive them, see the late Governor McDuffie's speeches); still I should prefer going to sleep without the apprehension of my servants' cutting my throat in my bed, even to having a guard to prevent their doing so. However, this peculiar prejudice of mine may spring from the fact of my having known many instances in which servants were the trusted and most trustworthy friends of their employers, and entertaining, besides, some old notions of the reciprocal duties of *all* members of families one towards the other.

Why slaves are dirty

OUR SERVANTS—THOSE who have been selected to wait upon us in the house—consist of a man, who is quite a tolerable cook (I believe this is a natural gift with them, as with Frenchmen); a dairy-worker, who churns for us; a laundrywoman; her daughter, our housemaid, the aforesaid Mary; and two young lads of from fifteen to twenty, who wait upon us in the capacity of footmen. As, however, the latter are perfectly filthy in their persons and clothes—their faces, hands, and naked feet being literally incrusted with dirt—their attendance at our meals is not, as you may suppose, particularly agreeable to me, and I dispense with it as often as possible. Mary, too, is so intolerably offensive in her person that it is impossible to endure her proximity, and the consequence is that, among Mr Butler's slaves, I wait upon myself more than I have ever done before. About this same personal offensiveness, the Southerners, you know, insist that it is inherent with the race, and it is one of their most cogent reasons for keeping them as slaves. But, as this very disagreeable peculiarity does not prevent Southern women from hanging their infants at the breasts of Negresses, nor almost every planter's wife and daughter from having one or more little pet blacks sleeping like puppy dogs in their very bedchamber, nor almost every planter from admitting one or several female slaves to the still older intimacy of his bed, it seems to me that this objection to doing them right is not very valid. I cannot imagine that they would smell much worse if they were free, or come in much closer contact with the delicate organs of their white fellow countrymen; indeed, inasmuch as good deeds are spoken of as having a sweet savor before God, it might be supposed that the freeing of the blacks might prove rather an odoriferous process than the contrary. However this may be, I must tell you that this potent reason for enslaving a whole race of people is no more potent with me than most of the others adduced to support the system, inasmuch as, from observation and some experience, I am strongly inclined to believe that peculiar ignorance of the laws of health and the habits of decent cleanliness are the real and only causes of this disagreeable characteristic of the race, thorough ablutions and change of linen, when tried, having been perfectly successful in removing all such objections; and if ever you have come into anything like neighborly proximity with a low Irishman or woman, I think you will allow that the same causes produce very nearly the same effects. The stench in an Irish, Scotch, Italian, or French hovel is quite as intolerable as any I ever found in our Negro houses, and the filth and vermin which abound about the clothes and persons of the lower peasantry of any of those countries as abominable as the same conditions in the black population of the United States. A total absence of self-respect begets these hateful physical results, and in proportion as moral influences are remote, physical evils will abound. Well-being, freedom, and industry induce self-respect, self-respect induces cleanliness and personal attention, so that slavery is answerable for all the evils that exhibit themselves where it exists—from lying, thieving, and adultery, to dirty houses, ragged clothes, and foul smells.

On a Georgia plantation

I HAD A most ludicrous visit this morning from the midwife of the estate—rather an important personage both to master and slave, as to her unassisted skill and science the ushering of all the young Negroes into their existence of bondage is entrusted. I heard a great deal of conversation in the dressing room adjoining mine while performing my own toilet, and presently Mr Butler opened my room door, ushering in a dirty, fat, good-humored looking old Negress, saying: 'The midwife, Rose, wants to make your acquaintance.'

'Oh massa!' shrieked out the old creature, in a paroxysm of admiration, 'where you get this lilly alabaster baby!'

For a moment I looked round to see if she was speaking of my baby; but no, my dear, this superlative apostrophe was elicited by the fairness of *my skin*: so much for degrees of comparison. Now I suppose that if I chose to walk arm in arm with the dingiest mulatto through the streets of Philadelphia, nobody could possibly tell by my complexion that I was not his sister, so that the mere quality of mistress must have had a most miraculous effect upon my skin in the eyes of poor Rose. But this species of outrageous flattery is as usual with these people as with the low Irish, and arises from the ignorant desire, common to both the races, of propitiating at all costs the fellow creature who is to them as a Providence—or rather, I should say, a fate—for 'tis a heathen and no Christian relationship.

Soon after this visit, I was summoned into the wooden porch or piazza of the house, to see a poor woman who desired to speak to me. This was none other than the tall, emaciated-looking Negress who, on the day of our arrival, had embraced me and my nurse with such irresistible zeal. She appeared very ill today, and presently unfolded to me a most distressing history of bodily afflictions. She was the mother of a very large family, and complained to me that, what with child-bearing and hard field labor, her back was almost broken in two. With an almost savage vehemence of gesticulation, she suddenly tore up her scanty clothing, and exhibited a spectacle with which I was inconceivably shocked and sickened. The facts, without any of her corroborating statements, bore tolerable witness to the hardships of her existence. I promised to attend to her ailments and give her proper remedies; but these are natural results, inevitable and irremediable ones, of improper treatment of the female frame; and, though there may be alleviation, there cannot be any cure when once the beautiful and wonderful structure has been thus made the victim of ignorance, folly, and wickedness.

After the departure of this poor woman, I walked down the settlement toward the infirmary or hospital, calling in at one or two of the houses along the row. These cabins consist of one room, about twelve feet by fifteen, with a couple of closets smaller and closer than the staterooms of a ship, divided off from the main room and each other by rough wooden partitions, in which the inhabitants sleep. They have almost all of them a rude bedstead, with the gray moss of the forests for mattress, and filthy, pestilential-looking blankets for covering. Two families (sometimes eight and ten in number) reside in one of these huts, which are mere wooden frames pinned, as it were, to the earth by a brick chimney outside, whose enormous aperture within pours down a flood of air, but little counteracted by the miserable spark of fire, which hardly sends an attenuated thread of lingering smoke up its huge throat. A wide ditch runs immediately at the back of these dwellings, which is filled and emptied daily by the tide. Attached to each hovel is a small scrap of ground for a garden, which, however, is for the most part untended and uncultivated.

Such of these dwellings as I visited today were filthy and wretched in the extreme, and exhibited the most deplorable consequence of ignorance and an abject condition, the inability of the inhabitants to secure and improve even such pitiful comfort as might yet be achieved by them. Instead of the order, neatness, and ingenuity which might convert even these miserable hovels into tolerable residences, there was the careless, reckless, filthy indolence which even the brutes do not exhibit in their lairs and nests, and which seemed incapable of applying to the uses of existence the few miserable means of comfort yet within their reach. Firewood and shavings lay littered about the floors, while the half-naked children were cowering round two or three smouldering cinders. The moss with which the chinks and crannies of their ill-protecting dwellings might have been stuffed was trailing in dirt and dust about the ground, while the back door of the huts, opening upon a most unsightly ditch, was left wide open for the fowls and ducks, which they are allowed to raise, to travel in and out, increasing the filth of the cabin by what they brought and left in every direction.

In the midst of the floor, or squatting round the cold hearth, would be four or five little children from four to ten years old, the latter all with babies in their arms, the care of the infants being taken from the mothers (who are driven afield as soon as they recover from child labor), and devolved upon these poor little nurses, as they are called, whose business it is to watch the infant, and carry it to its mother whenever it may require nourishment. To these hardy human little beings I addressed my remonstrances about the filth, cold, and unnecessary wretchedness of their room, bidding the older boys and girls kindle up the fire, sweep the floor, and expel the poultry. For a long time my very words seemed unintelligible to them, till, when I began to sweep and make up the fire, etc., they first fell to laughing, and then imitating me. The incrustations of dirt on their hands, feet, and faces were my next object of attack, and the stupid Negro practice (by-the-by, but a short time since nearly universal in enlightened Europe) of keeping the babies with their feet bare, and their heads, already well capped by nature with their woolly hair, wrapped in half a dozen hot, filthy coverings.

Thus I traveled down the 'street', in every dwelling endeavouring to awaken a new perception, that of cleanliness, sighing, as I went, over the futility of my own exertions, for how can slaves be improved? Nathless, thought I, let what can be done; for it may be that, the two being incompatible, improvement may yet expel slavery; and so it might, and surely would, if, instead of beginning at the end, I could but begin at the beginning of my task. If the mind and soul were awakened, instead of mere physical good attempted, the physical good would result, and the great curse vanish away; but my hands and feet are tied fast, and this corner of the work is all that I may do. Yet it cannot be but, from my words and actions, some revelations should reach these poor people; and going in and out among them perpetually, I shall teach, and they learn involuntarily a thousand things of deepest import. They must learn, and who can tell the fruit of that knowledge alone, that there are beings in the world, even with skins of a different color from their own, who have sympathy for their misfortunes, love for their virtues, and respect for their common nature—but oh! my heart is full almost to bursting as I walk among these most poor creatures.

The infirmary is a large two-story building, terminating the broad orange-planted space between the two rows of houses which form the first settlement; it is built of whitewashed wood, and contains four large-sized rooms. But how shall I describe to you the spectacle which was presented to me on entering the first of these? But half the case-ments, of which there were six, were glazed, and these were obscured with dirt, almost as much as the other windowless ones were darkened by the dingy shutters, which the shivering inmates had fastened to in order to protect themselves from the cold. In the enormous chimney glimmered the powerless embers of a few sticks of wood, round which, however, as many of the sick women as could approach were cowering, some on wooden settles, most of them on the ground, excluding those who were too ill to rise; and these last poor wretches lay prostrate on the floor, without bed, mattress, or pillow, buried in tattered and filthy blankets, which, huddled round them as they lay strewed about, left hardly space to move upon the floor. And here, in their hour of sickness and suffering, lay those whose health and strength are spent in un-requited labor for us—those who, perhaps even yesterday, were being urged on to their unpaid task—those whose husbands, fathers, brothers, and sons were even at that hour sweating over the earth, whose produce was to buy for us all the luxuries which health can revel in, all the comforts which can alleviate sickness. I stood in the midst of them, perfectly unable to speak, the tears pouring from my eyes at this sad spectacle of their misery, myself and my emotion alike strange and incomprehensible to them. Here lay women expecting every hour the terrors and agonies of childbirth, others who had just brought their doomed offspring into the world, others who were groaning over the anguish and bitter disappointment of miscarriages—here lay some burning with fever, others chilled with cold and aching with rheumatism, upon the hard cold ground, the draughts and dampness of the atmosphere increasing their sufferings, and dirt, noise, and stench, and every aggravation of which sickness is capable, combined in their condition—here they lay like brute beasts, absorbed in physical suffering; unvisited by any of those Divine influences which may ennoble the dispensations of pain and illness, forsaken, as it seemed to me, of all good; and yet, O God, Thou surely hadst not forsaken them! Now pray take notice that this is the hospital of an estate where the owners are supposed to be humane, the overseer efficient and kind, and the Negroes remarkedly well cared for and comfortable.

Poor whites

AFTER DINNER I had a most interesting conversation with Mr King. Among other subjects, he gave me a lively and curious description of the yeomanry of Georgia, more properly termed pinelanders. Have you visions now of well-to-do farmers with comfortable homesteads, decent habits, industrious, intelligent, cheerful and thrifty? Such, however, is not the yeomanry of Georgia. Labor being here the special portion of slaves, it is thenceforth degraded, and considered unworthy of all but slaves. No white man, therefore, of any class puts hand to work of any kind soever. This is an exceedingly dignified way of proving their gentility for the lazy planters who prefer an idle life of semistarvation and barbarism to the degradation of doing anything themselves; but the effect on the poorer whites of the country is terrible. I speak now of the scattered white population, who, too poor to possess land or slaves, and having no means of living in the towns, squat (most appropriately is it so termed) either on other men's land or government districts—always here swamp or pine barren—and claim masterdom over the place they invade till ejected by the rightful proprietors. These wretched creatures will not, for they are whites (and labor belongs to blacks and slaves alone here), labor for their own subsistence. They are hardly protected from the weather by the rude shelters they frame for themselves in the midst of these dreary woods. Their food is chiefly supplied by shooting the wildfowl and venison, and stealing from the cultivated patches of the plantations nearest at hand. Their clothes hang about them in filthy tatters, and the combined squalor and fierceness of their appearance is really frightful.

This population is the direct growth of slavery. The planters are loud in their execrations of these miserable vagabonds; yet they do not see that so long as labor is considered the disgraceful portion of slaves, these free men will hold it nobler to starve or steal than till the earth, with none but the despised blacks for fellow laborers. The blacks themselves —such is the infinite power of custom—acquiesce in this notion, and, as I have told you, consider it the lowest degradation in a white to use any exertion. I wonder, considering the burdens they have seen me lift, the digging, the planting, the rowing, and the walking I do, that they do not utterly condemn me, and, indeed, they seem lost in amazement at it.

Harriet Martineau

born in Norwich in 1802, novelist, economist and translator
of Comte, was one of the most redoubtable of nineteenth-
century English bluestockings. In 1834–36 she visited the
United States, publishing *Society in America* in 1837.
She wrote 52 books in all and was a prolific journalist on
the Radical side in politics. She died in 1876.

Life on a Southern plantation

THE FOLLOWING MAY be considered a pretty fair account of the provision for a planter's table, at this season; and, except with regard to vegetables, I believe it does not vary much throughout the year. Breakfast at seven; hot wheat bread, generally sour; corn bread, biscuits, waffles, hominy, dozens of eggs, broiled ham, beef-steak or broiled fowl, tea and coffee. Lunch at eleven; cake and wine, or liquor. Dinner at two; now and then soup (not good), always roast turkey and ham; a boiled fowl here, a tongue there; a small piece of nondescript meat, which generally turns out to be pork disguised; hominy, rice, hot corn-bread, sweet potatoes; potatoes mashed with spice, very hot; salad and radishes, and an extraordinary variety of pickles. Of these, you are asked to eat everything with everything else. If you have turkey and ham on your plate, you are requested to add tongue, pork, hominy, and pickles. Then succeed pies of apples, squash, and pumpkin; custard, and a variety of preserves as extraordinary as the preceding pickles: pine-apple, peach, limes, ginger, guava jelly, cocoa-nut, and every sort of plums. These are almost all from the West Indies. Dispersed about the table are shell almonds, raisins, hickory, and other nuts; and, to crown the whole, large blocks of ice-cream. Champagne is abundant, and cider frequent. Ale and porter may now and then be seen; but claret is the most common drink. During dinner a slave stands at a corner of a table, keeping off the flies by waving a large bunch of peacock's feathers fastened into a handle,—an ampler fan than those of our grandmothers.

Supper takes place at six, or seven. Sometimes the family sits round the table; but more commonly the tray is handed round, with plates which must be held in the lap. Then follow tea and coffee, waffles, biscuits, sliced ham or hung-beef, and sweet cake. Last of all, is the offer of cake and wine at nine or ten.

The profits of cotton-growing, when I was in Alabama, were thirty-five per cent. One planter whom I knew had bought fifteen thousand dollars' worth of land within two years, which he could then have sold for sixty-five thousand dollars. He expected to make, that season, fifty or sixty thousand dollars of his growing crop. It is certainly the place to become rich in; but the state of society is fearful. One of my hosts, a man of great good-nature, as he shows in the treatment of his slaves, and in his family relations, had been stabbed in the back in the reading-room of the town, two years before, and no prosecution was instituted. Another of my hosts carried loaded pistols for a fortnight, just before I arrived, knowing that he was lain in wait for by persons against whose illegal practices he had given information to a magistrate, whose carri-age was therefore broken in pieces, and thrown into the river. A lawyer with whom we were in company one afternoon, was sent for to take the deposition of a dying man who had been sitting with his family in the shade, when he received three balls in the back from three men who took aim at him from behind trees. The tales of jail-breaking and rescue were numberless; and a lady of Montgomery told me that she had lived there four years, during which time no day, she believed, had passed without some one's life having been attempted, either by duelling or assassination. It will be understood that I describe this region as presenting an extreme case of the material advantages and moral evils of a new settlement, under the institution of slavery. The most prominent relief is the hospitality,—that virtue of young society. It is so remark-able, and to the stranger so grateful, that there is danger of its blinding him to the real state of affairs. In the drawing-room, the piazza, the barouche, all is so gay and friendly, there is such a prevailing hilarity and kindness, that it seems positively ungrateful and unjust to pro-nounce, even in one's own heart, that all this way of life is full of wrong and peril. Yet it is impossible to sit down to reflect, with every order of human beings filling an equal space before one's mental eye, without being struck to the soul with the conviction that the state of society, and no less of individual families, is false and hollow, whether their members are aware of it or not; that they forget that they must be just before they can be generous. The severity of this truth is much softened to sympathetic persons on the spot; but it returns with awful force when they look back upon it from afar.

In the slave quarter of a plantation hereabouts I saw a poor wretch who had run away three times, and been recaptured. The last time he was found in the woods, with both legs frost-bitten above the knees, so as to render amputation necessary. I passed by when he was sitting on the door-step of his hut, and longed to see him breathe his last. But he is a young man, likely to drag out his helpless and hopeless existence for many a dreary year. I dread to tell the rest; but such things must be told sometimes, to show to what a pass of fiendish cruelty the human spirit may be brought by merely witnessing the exercise of irresponsible power over the defenceless.

Chicago

CHICAGO LOOKS RAW and bare, standing on the high prairie above the lake-shore. The houses appeared all insignificant, and run up in various directions, without any principle at all. A friend of mine who resides there had told me that we should find the inns intolerable, at the period of the great land sales, which bring a concourse of speculators to the place. It was even so. The very sight of them was intolerable; and there was not room for our party among them all. I do not know what we should have done, (unless to betake ourselves to the vessels in the harbour,) if our coming had not been foreknown, and most kindly provided for. We were divided between three families, who had the art of removing all our scruples about intruding on perfect strangers. None of us will lose the lively and pleasant associations with the place, which were caused by the hospitalities of its inhabitants.

I never saw a busier place than Chicago was at the time of our arrival. The streets were crowded with land speculators, hurrying from one sale to another. A negro, dressed up in scarlet, bearing a scarlet flag, and riding a white horse with housings of scarlet, announced the times of sale. At every street-corner where he stopped, the crowd flocked round him; and it seemed as if some prevalent mania infected the whole people. The rage for speculation might fairly be so regarded. As the gentlemen of our party walked the streets, store-keepers hailed them from their doors, with offers of farms, and all manner of land-lots, advising them to speculate before the price of land rose higher. A young lawyer, of my acquaintance there, had realized five hundred dollars per day, the five preceding days, by merely making out titles to land. Another friend had realized, in two years, ten times as much money as he had before fixed upon as a competence for life. Of course, this rapid money-making is a merely temporary evil. A bursting of the bubble must come soon. The absurdity of the speculation is so striking, that the wonder is that the fever should have attained such a height as I witnessed. The immediate occasion of the bustle which prevailed, the week we were at Chicago, was the sale of lots, to the value of two

[216]

million dollars, along the course of a projected canal; and of another set, immediately behind these. Persons not intending to game, and not infected with mania, would endeavour to form some reasonable conjecture as to the ultimate value of the lots, by calculating the cost of the canal, the risks from accident, from the possible competition from other places, &c., and, finally, the possible profits, under the most favourable circumstances, within so many years' purchase. Such a calculation would serve as some sort of guide as to the amount of purchase-money to be risked. Whereas, wild land on the banks of a canal, not yet even marked out, was selling at Chicago for more than rich land, well improved, in the finest part of the valley of the Mohawk, on the banks of a canal which is already the medium of an almost inestimable amount of traffic. If sharpers and gamblers were to be the sufferers by the impending crash at Chicago, no one would feel much concerned; but they, unfortunately, are the people who encourage the delusion, in order to profit by it. Many a high-spirited, but inexperienced, young man; many a simple settler, will be ruined for the advantage of knaves.

Others, besides lawyers and speculators by trade, make a fortune in such extraordinary times. A poor man at Chicago had a pre-emption right to some land, for which he paid in the morning one hundred and fifty dollars. In the afternoon, he sold it to a friend of mine for five thousand dollars. A poor Frenchman, married to a squaw, had a suit pending, when I was there, which he was likely to gain, for the right of purchasing some land by the lake for one hundred dollars, which would immediately become worth one million dollars.

There was much gaiety going on at Chicago, as well as business. On the evening of our arrival a fancy fair took place. As I was too much fatigued to go, the ladies sent me a bouquet of prairie flowers. There is some allowable pride in the place about its society. It is a remarkable thing to meet such an assemblage of educated, refined, and wealthy persons as may be found there, living in small, inconvenient houses on the edge of a wild prairie. There is a mixture, of course. I heard of a family of half-breeds setting up a carriage, and wearing fine jewellery. When the present intoxication of prosperity passes away, some of the inhabitants will go back to the eastward; there will be an accession of settlers from the mechanic classes; good houses will have been built for the richer families, and the singularity of the place will subside. It will be like all other new and thriving lake and river ports of America. Meantime I am glad to have seen it in its strange early days.

Milwaukee: population 400

WHILE DR F. went on shore, to see what was to be seen, we had the cabin cleaned out, and took, once more, complete possession of it, for both day and night. As soon as this was done, seven young women came down the companion-way, seated themselves round the cabin, and began to question us. They were the total female population of Milwaukee; which settlement now contains four hundred souls. We were glad to see these ladies; for it was natural enough that the seven women should wish to behold two more, when such a chance offered. A gentleman of the place, who came on board this afternoon, told me that a printing-press had arrived a few hours before; and that a newspaper would speedily appear. He was kind enough to forward the first number to me a few weeks afterwards; and I was amused to see how pathetic an appeal to the ladies of the more thickly-settled districts it contained; imploring them to cast a favourable eye on Milwaukee, and its hundreds of bachelors. Milwaukee had been settled since the preceding November. It had good stores (to judge by the nature and quantity of goods sent ashore from our ship); it had a printing-press and newspaper, before the settlers had had time to get wives. I heard these new settlements sometimes called 'patriarchal': but what would the patriarchs have said to such an order of affairs?

Advantages of the Northern working man

THE MECHANICS OF these northern States appear to me the most favoured class I have ever known. In England, I believe the highest order of mechanics to be, as a class, the wisest and best men of the community. They have the fewest base and narrow interests: they are brought into sufficient contact with the realities of existence, without being hardened by excess toil and care; and the knowledge they have the opportunity of gaining is of the best kind for the health of the mind. To them, if to any, we may look for public and private virtue. The mechanics of

America have nearly all the same advantages, and some others. They have better means of living: their labours are perhaps more honoured; and they are republicans, enjoying the powers and prospects of perfectly equal citizenship. The only respect in which their condition falls below that of English artisans of the highest order is that the knowledge which they have commonly the means of obtaining is not of equal value. The facilities are great: schools, lyceums, libraries, are open to them; but the instruction there is not so good as they deserve. Whenever they have this, it will be difficult to imagine a mode of life more favourable to virtue and happiness than theirs.

There seems to be no doubt among those who know both England and America, that the mechanics of the New World work harder than those of the Old. They have much to do besides their daily handicraft business. They are up and at work early about this; and when it is done, they read till late, or attend lectures; or perhaps have their houses to build or repair, or other care to take of their property. They live in a state and period of society where every man is answerable for his own fortunes; and where there is therefore stimulus to the exercise of every power.

What a state of society it is when a dozen artisans of one town, —Salem,—are seen rearing each a comfortable one-story (or, as the Americans would say, two-story) house, in the place with which they have grown up! when a man who began with laying bricks criticizes, and sometimes corrects, his lawyer's composition; when a poor errand-boy becomes the proprietor of a flourishing store, before he is thirty; pays off the capital advanced by his friends at the rate of 2,000 dollars per month; and bids fair to be one of the most substantial citizens of the place!

Pampering of American women

So MUCH MORE has naturally been observed by travellers of American manners in stages and steam-boats than in private-houses, that all has been said, over and over again, that the subject deserves. I need only testify that I do not think the Americans eat faster than other people, on the whole. The celerity at hotel-tables is remarkable; but so it is in stage-coach travellers in England, who are allowed ten minutes or a quarter of an hour for dining. In private houses, I was never aware of being hurried. The cheerful, unintermitting civility of all gentlemen travellers, throughout the country, is very striking to a stranger. The degree of consideration shown to woman is, in my opinion, greater than is rational, or good for either party; but the manners of an American stage-coach might afford a valuable lesson and example to many classes of Europeans who have a high opinion of their own civilization. I do not think it rational or fair that every gentleman, whether old or young, sick or well, weary or untired, should, as a matter of course, yield up the best places in the stage to any lady passenger. I do not think it rational or fair that five gentlemen should ride on the top of the coach, (where there is no accommodation for holding on, and no resting-place for the feet,) for some hours of a July day in Virginia, that a young lady, who was slightly delicate, might have room to lay her feet, and change her posture as she pleased. It is obvious that, if she was not strong enough to travel on common terms in the stage, her family should have travelled in an extra; or staid behind; or done anything rather than allow five persons to risk their health, and sacrifice their comfort, for the sake of one. Whatever may be the good moral effects of such self-renunciation on the tempers of the gentlemen, the custom is very injurious to ladies. Their travelling manners are anything but amiable. While on a journey, women who appear well enough in their homes, present all the characteristics of spoiled children. Screaming and trembling at the apprehension of danger are not uncommon; but there is something far worse in the cool selfishness with which they accept the best of everything, at any sacrifice to others, and usually, in the south and west, without a word or look of acknowledgement. They are as like spoiled children when the gentlemen are not present to be sacrificed to them;—in the inn parlour, while waiting for meals or the stage; and in the cabin of a steam-boat. I never saw any manner so repulsive as that of many American ladies on board steam-boats. They look as if they supposed you mean to injure them, till you show to the contrary. The suspicious side-glance, or the full stare; the cold, immovable observation; the bristling self-defence the moment you come near; the cool pushing to get the best places,—everything said and done without the least trace of trust or cheerfulness,—these are the disagreeable consequences of the ladies being petted and humoured as they are. The New England ladies, who are compelled by their superior numbers to depend less upon the care of others, are far happier and pleasanter companions in a journey than those of the rest of the country. This shows the evil to be altogether superinduced: and I always found that if I could keep down my spirit, and show that I meant no harm, the apathy began to melt, the pretty ladies forgot their self-defence, and appeared somewhat like what I conclude they are at home, when managing their affairs, in the midst of familiar circumstances. If these ladies would but inquire of themselves what it is that they are afraid of, and whether there is any reason why people should be less cheerful, less obliging, and less agreeable, when casually brought into the society of fifty people, whose comfort depends mainly on their mutual good offices, than among half-a-dozen neighbours at home, they might remove an unpleasant feature of the national manners, and add another to the many charms of their country.

Evil effects of boarding-house life

THE GREATER NUMBER of American women have home and its affairs, wherewith to occupy themselves. Wifely and motherly occupation may be called the sole business of woman there. If she has not that, she has nothing. The only alternative, as I have said, is making an occupation of either religion or dissipation; neither of which is fit to be so used: the one being a state of mind; the other altogether a negation when not taken in alternation with business.

It must happen that where all women have only one serious object, many of them will be unfit for that object. In the United States, as elsewhere, there are women no more fit to be wives and mothers than to be statesmen and generals; no more fit for any responsibility whatever, than for the maximum of responsibility. There is no need to describe such: they may be seen everywhere. I allude to them only for the purpose of mentioning that many of this class shirk some of their labours and cares, by taking refuge in boarding-houses. It is a circumstance very favourable to the character of some American women, that boarding-house life has been rendered compulsory by the scarcity of labour, the difficulty of obtaining domestic service. The more I saw of boarding-house life, the worse I thought of it; though I saw none but the best. Indeed, the degrees of merit in such establishments weigh little in the consideration of the evil of their existence at all. In the best it is something to be secure of respectable company, of a good table, a well-mannered and courteous hostess, and comfort in the private apartments: but the mischiefs of the system throw all these objects into the background.

To begin with young children. There can be no sufficient command of proper food for them; nor any security that they will eat it naturally at the table where fifty persons may be sitting, a dozen obsequious blacks waiting, and an array of tempting dishes within sight. The child is in imminent danger of being too shy and frightened to eat at all, or of becoming greedy to eat too much. Next, it is melancholy to see girls of twelve years old either slinking down beside their parents, and blushing painfully as often as any one of fifty strangers looks towards them; or boldly staring at all that is going on, and serving themselves, like little women of the world. After tea, it is a common practice to hand the young ladies to the piano, to play and sing to a party, composed chiefly of gentlemen, and brought together on no principle of selection except mere respectability. Next comes the mischief to the young married ladies, the most numerous class of women found in boarding-houses. The uncertainty about domestic service is so great, and the economy of boarding-house life so tempting to people who have not provided themselves with house and furniture, that it is not to be wondered at that many young married people use the accommodation provided. But no sensible husband, who could beforehand become acquainted with the liabilities incurred, would willingly expose his domestic peace to the fearful risk. I saw enough when I saw the elegantly dressed ladies repair to the windows of the common drawing-room, on their husbands' departure to the counting-house, after breakfast. There the ladies sit for hours, doing nothing but gossiping with one another, with any gentleman of the house who may happen to have no business, and with visitors. It is true that the sober-minded among the ladies can and do withdraw to their own apartments for the morning: but they complain that they cannot settle to regular employments as they could in a house of their own. Either they are not going to stay long; or they have not room for their books, or they are broken in upon by their acquaintances in the house. The common testimony is, that little can be done in boarding-houses: and if the more sober-minded find it so, the fate of the thoughtless, who have no real business to do, may be easily anticipated. They find a dear friend or two among the boarders, to whom they confide their husbands' secrets. A woman who would do this once would do it twice, or as often as she changes her boarding-house, and finds a new dear friend in each. I have been assured that there is no end to the difficulties in which gentlemen have been involved, both as to their commercial and domestic affairs, by the indiscretion of their thoughtless young wives, amidst the idleness and levities of boarding-house life. As for the gentlemen, they are much to be pitied. Public meals, a noisy house, confinement to one or two private rooms, with the absence of all gratifications of their own peculiar convenience and taste, are but a poor solace to the man of business, after the toils and cares of the day. When to these are added the snares to which their wives are exposed, it may be imagined that men of sense and refinement would rather bear with any domestic inconvenience from the uncertainty and bad quality of help, than give up house-keeping. They would content themselves, if need were, with a bread and cheese dinner, light their own fire, and let their wives dust the furniture a few times in the year, rather than give up privacy, with its securities. I rather think that the gentlemen generally think and feel thus; and that when they break up housekeeping and go to boarding-houses, it is out of indulgence to the wishes of their wives; who, if they were as wise as they should be, would wish it seldomer and less than they do.

Frederick Marryat, Captain R.N.

and one of the best novelists of the sea and of British
naval life during the Napoleonic period, was born in London in
1792. He toured the United States and Canada in 1837–39 and
published his *Diary in America* in the latter year. The nature of
its reception in the United States may be gauged from the fact
that he was burned in effigy in Detroit. He died in 1848.

Luxury in the new towns

In SPEAKING OF the new towns rising so fast in America, I wish the reader to understand that, if he compares them with the country towns of the same population in England, he will not do them justice. In the smaller towns of England you can procure but little, and you have to send to London for any thing good: in the larger towns, such as Norwich, &c., you may procure most things; but, still, luxuries must usually be obtained from the metropolis. But in such places as Buffalo and Cleveland, every thing is to be had that you can procure at New York or Boston. In those two towns on Lake Erie are stores better furnished, and handsomer, than any shops at Norwich, in England; and you will find, in either of them, articles for which, at Norwich, you would be obliged to send to London. It is the same thing at almost every town in America with which communication is easy. Would you furnish a house in one of them, you will find every article of furniture —carpets, stoves, grates, marble chimney-pieces, pier-glasses, pianos, lamps, candelabra, glass, china, &c., in twice the quantity, and in greater variety, than at any provincial town in England.

This arises from the system of credit extended through every vein and artery of the country, and by which English goods are forced, as if with a force-pump, into every available depôt in the Union; and thus, in a town so newly raised, that the stumps of the forest-trees are not only still surrounding the houses, but remain standing in the cellars, you will find every luxury that can be required. It may be asked what becomes of all these goods. It must be recollected that hundreds of new houses spring up every year in the towns, and that the surrounding country is populous and wealthy. In the farm-houses—mean-looking and often built of logs—is to be found not only comfort, but very often luxury.

Whittling

I MAY HERE just as well mention the custom of *whittling*, which is so common in the Eastern States. It is a habit, arising from the natural restlessness of the American when he is not employed, of cutting a piece of stick, or anything else, with his knife. Some are so wedded to it from long custom, that if they have not a piece of stick to cut, they will whittle the backs of the chairs, or any thing within their reach. A yankee shewn into a room to await the arrival of another, has been known to whittle away nearly the whole of the mantel-piece. Lawyers in court whittle away at the table before them; and judges will cut through their own bench. In some courts, they put sticks before noted whittlers to save the furniture. The Down-Easters, as the yankees are termed generally, whittle when they are making a bargain, as it fills up the pauses, gives them time for reflection, and moreover, prevents any examination of the countenance—for in bargaining, like in the game of brag, the countenance is carefully watched, as an index to the wishes. I was once witness to a bargain made between two respectable yankees, who wished to agree about a farm, and in which whittling was resorted to.

They sat down on a log of wood, about three or four feet apart from each other, with their faces turned opposite ways—that is, one had his legs on one side of the log with his face to the East, and the other his legs on the other side with his face to the West. One had a piece of soft wood, and was sawing it with his penknife; the other had an unbarked hiccory stick which he was peeling for a walking-stick . . .

'Well, good morning—and about this farm?'

'I don't know; what will you take?'

'What will you give?'

Silence, and whittle away.

'Well, I should think two thousand dollars, a heap of money for this farm.'

'I've a notion it will never go for three thousand any how.'

'There's a fine farm, and cheaper, on the North side.'

'But where's the sun to ripen the corn?'

'Sun shines on all alike.'

'Not exactly through a Vermont hill, I reckon. The driver offered me as much as I say, if I recollect right.'

[227]

'Money not always to be depended upon. Money not always forth-coming.'

'I reckon, I shall make an elegant 'backy stopper of this piece of sycamore.'

Silence for a few moments. Knives hard at work.

'I've a notion this is as pretty a hiccory stick as ever came out of a wood.'

'I shouldn't mind two thousand five hundred dollars, and time given.'

'It couldn't be more than six months then, if it goes at that price.'

(Pause.)

'Well, that might suit me.'

'What do you say, then?'

'Suppose it must be so.'

'It's a bargain then (*rising up*), come let's liquor on it.'

Spirits and chewing-tobacco

THERE ARE THREE things in great request amongst Americans of all classes,—male, I mean,—to wit, oysters, spirits, and tobacco. The first and third are not prohibited by Act of Congress, and may be sold in the Capitol, but spirituous liquors may not. I wondered how the members could get on without them, but upon this point I was soon enlightened. Below the basement of the building is an oyster-shop and refectory. The refectory has been permitted by Congress upon the express stipulation that no spirituous liquors should be sold there, but law-makers are too often law-breakers all over the world. You go there and ask for a pale sherry, and they hand you gin; brown sherry, and it is brandy; madeira, whisky; and thus do these potent, grave, and reverend signors evade their own laws, beneath the very hall wherein they were passed in solemn conclave.

It appears that tobacco is considered very properly as an article of fashion. At a store, close to the hotel, the board outside informs you that among fashionable requisites to be found there, are gentlemen's shirts, collars, gloves, silk-handkerchiefs, and the best chewing-tobacco. But not only at Washington, but at other large towns, I have seen at silk-mercers and hosiers this notice stuck up in the window— '*Dulcis-*

simus chewing-tobacco'.—So prevalent is the habit of chewing, and so little, from long custom, do the ladies care about it, that I have been told that many young ladies in the South carry, in their work-boxes, &c., pig-tail, nicely ornamented with gold-coloured papers; and when their swains are at fault administer to their wants, thus meriting their affections by such endearing solicitude.

The prairie

AFTER YOU PROCEED south of Prairie du Chien, the features of the Mississippi river gradually change; the bluffs decrease in number and in height, until you descend to Rock Island, below which point they are rarely to be met with. The country on each side now is chiefly composed of variegated rolling prairies, with a less proportion of timber. To describe these prairies would be difficult; that is, to describe the effect of them upon a stranger: I have found myself lost, as it were; and indeed sometimes, although on horseback, have lost myself, having only the sun for my guide. Look round in every quarter of the compass, and there you are as if on the ocean—not a landmark, not a vestige of any thing human but yourself. Instead of sky and water, it is one vast field, bounded only by the horizon, its surface gently undulating like the waves of the ocean; and as the wind (which always blows fresh on the prairies) bows down the heads of the high grass, it gives you the idea of a running swell. Every three or four weeks there is a succession of beautiful flowers, giving a variety of tints to the whole map, which die away and are succeeded by others equally beautiful; and in the spring, the strawberries are in such profusion, that you have but to sit down wherever you may happen to be, and eat as long as you please.

A camp meeting

I WAS INFORMED that a camp meeting was to be held about seven miles from Cincinnati, and, anxious to verify the accounts I had heard of them, I availed myself of this opportunity of deciding for myself. We proceeded about five miles on the high road, and then diverged by a cross-road until we arrived at a steep conical hill, crowned with splendid forest trees without underwood; the trees being sufficiently apart to admit of waggons and other vehicles to pass in every direction. The camp was raised upon the summit of this hill, a piece of table-land comprising many acres. About an acre and a half was surrounded on the four sides by cabins built up of rough boards; the whole area in the centre was fitted up with planks, laid about a foot from the ground, as seats. At one end, but not close to the cabins, was a raised stand, which served as a pulpit for the preachers, one of them praying, while five or six others sat down behind him on benches. There was ingress to the area by the four corners; the whole of it was shaded by vast forest trees, which ran up to the height of fifty or sixty feet without throwing out a branch; and to the trunks of these trees were fixed lamps in every direction, for the continuance of service by night. Outside the area, which may be designated as the church, were hundreds of tents pitched in every quarter, their snowy whiteness contrasting beautifully with the deep verdure and gloom of the forest. These were the temporary habitations of those who had come many miles to attend the meeting, and who remained there from the commencement until it concluded—usually a period of from ten to twelve days, but often much longer. The tents were furnished with every article necessary for cooking; mattresses to sleep upon, &c.; some of them even had bedsteads and chests of drawers, which had been brought in the waggons in which the people of this country usually travel. At a farther distance were all the waggons and other vehicles which had conveyed the people to the meeting, whilst hundreds of horses were tethered under the trees, and plentifully provided with forage. Such were the general outlines of a most interesting and beautiful scene.

Where, indeed, could so magnificent a temple to the Lord be raised as on this lofty hill, crowned as it was with such majestic verdure? Compared with these giants of the forest, the cabins and tents of the multitude appeared as insignificant and contemptible as almost would man himself in the presence of the Deity. Many generations of men must have been mowed down before the arrival of these enormous trees to their present state of maturity; and at the time they sent forth their first shoots, probably there were not on the whole of this continent, now teeming with millions, as many white men as are now assembled on this field. I walked about for some time surveying the panorama, when I returned to the area, and took my seat upon a bench. In one quarter the coloured population had collected themselves; their tents appeared to be better furnished and better supplied with comforts than most of those belonging to the whites. I put my head into one of the tents, and discovered a sable damsel lying on a bed, and singing hymns in a loud voice.

The major portion of those not in the area were cooking the dinners. Fires were burning in every direction: pots boiling, chickens roasting, hams seething; indeed there appeared to be no want of creature comforts.

But the trumpet sounded, as in days of yore, as a signal that the service was about to re-commence, and I went into the area and took my seat. One of the preachers rose and gave out a hymn, which was sung by the congregation, amounting to about seven or eight hundred. After the singing of the hymn was concluded he commenced an extempore sermon: it was good, sound doctrine, and, although Methodism, it was Methodism of the mildest tone, and divested of its bitterness of denunciation, as indeed is generally the case with Methodism in America. I heard nothing which could be considered objectionable by the most orthodox, and I began to doubt whether such scenes as had been described to me did really take place at these meetings. A prayer followed, and after about two hours the congregation were dismissed to their dinners, being first informed that the service would recommence at two o'clock at the sound of the trumpet. In front of the pulpit there was a space railed off, and strewed with straw, which I was told was the *Anxious seat*, and on which sat those who were touched by their consciences or the discourse of the preacher; but, although there were several sitting on it, I did not perceive any emotion on the part of the occupants: they were attentive, but nothing more.

When I first examined the area I saw a very large tent at one corner of it, probably fifty feet long, by twenty wide. It was open at the end, and, being full of straw, I concluded it was used as a sleeping-place for those who had not provided themselves with separate accommodation. About an hour after the service was over, perceiving many people directing their steps towards it, I followed them. On one side of the tent were about twenty females, mostly young, squatted down on the straw; on the other a few men; in the centre was a long form, against which were some other men kneeling, with their faces covered with their hands, as if occupied in prayer. Gradually the numbers increased, girl after girl dropped down upon the straw on the one side, and the men on the other. At last an elderly man gave out a hymn, which was sung with peculiar energy; then another knelt down in the centre, and commenced a prayer, shutting his eyes (as I have observed most clergymen in the United States do when they pray) and raising his hands above his head; then another burst out into a prayer, and another followed him; then their voices became all confused together; and then were heard the more silvery tones of woman's supplication. As the din increased so did their enthusiasm; handkerchiefs were raised to bright eyes, and sobs were intermingled with prayers and ejaculations. It became a scene of Babel; more than twenty men and women were crying out at the highest pitch of their voices, and trying apparently to be heard above the others. Every minute the excitement increased; some wrung their hands and called for mercy; some tore their hair; boys lay down crying bitterly, with their heads buried in the straw; there was sobbing almost to suffocation, and hysterics and deep agony. One young man clung to the form, crying, 'Satan tears at me, but I will hold fast. Help—help, he drags me down!' It was a scene of horrible agony and despair; and, when it was at its height, one of the preachers came in, and, raising his voice high above the tumult, intreated the Lord to receive into his fold those who now repented and would fain return. Another of the ministers knelt down by some young men, whose faces were covered up and who appeared to be almost in a state of phrenzy; and putting his hands upon them, poured forth an energetic prayer, well calculated to work upon their over excited feelings. Groans, ejaculations, broken sobs, frantic motions and convulsions succeeded; some fell on their backs with their eyes closed, waving their hands with a slow motion, and crying out—'Glory, glory, glory!'

American prudery

THEY OBJECT TO everything nude in statuary. When I was at the house of Governor Everett, at Boston, I observed a fine cast of the Apollo

Belvidere, but, in compliance with general opinion, it was hung with drapery, although Governor Everett himself is a gentleman of refined mind and high classical attainments, and quite above such ridiculous sensitiveness. In language it is the same thing: there are certain words which are never used in America, but an absurd substitute is employed. I cannot particularize them after this preface, lest I should be accused of indelicacy myself. I may, however, state one little circumstance, which will fully prove the correctness of what I say.

When at Niagara Falls, I was escorting a young lady with whom I was on friendly terms. She had been standing on a piece of rock, the better to view the scene, when she slipped down, and was evidently hurt by the fall; she had in fact grazed her shin. As she limped a little in walking home, I said, 'Did you hurt your leg much'. She turned from me, evidently much shocked, or much offended; and not being aware that I had committed any very heinous offence, I begged to know what was the reason of her displeasure. After some hesitation, she said that as she knew me well, she would tell me that the word *leg* was never mentioned before ladies. I apologized for my want of refinement, which was attributable to my having been accustomed only to *English* society, and added, that as such articles must occasionally be referred to, even in the most polite circles of America, perhaps she would inform me by what name I might mention them without shocking the company. Her reply was, that the word *limb* was used; 'nay,' continued she, 'I am not so particular as some people are, for I know those who always say limb of a table, or limb of a piano-forte.'

There the conversation dropped; but a few months afterwards I was obliged to acknowledge that the young lady was correct when she asserted that some people were more particular than even she was.

I was requested by a lady to escort her to a seminary for young ladies, and on being ushered into the reception-room, conceive my astonishment at beholding a square piano-forte with four *limbs*. However, that the ladies who visited their daughters, might feel in its full force the extreme delicacy of the mistress of the establishment, and her care to preserve in their utmost purity the ideas of the young ladies under her charge, she had dressed all these four limbs in modest little trousers, with frills at the bottom of them!

Charles Dickens

(1812–1870) visited the United States in 1841, going with extreme enthusiasm and leaving in extreme disillusionment, as the American chapters in *Martin Chuzzlewit* show. The unpopularity into which he fell in America as a result, and as a result also of *American Notes* (1842) did not prevent his being received with great enthusiasm when he undertook his second tour—profits from readings amounted to £20,000—in 1867–68.

'This is not the republic I came to see'

Baltimore, Twenty-second March, 1842.
... MY DEAR MACREADY, I desire to be so honest and just to those who have so enthusiastically and earnestly welcomed me, that I burned the last letter I wrote to you—even to you whom I would speak as to myself—rather than let it come with anything that might seem like an ill-considered word of disappointment. I preferred that you should think me neglectful (if you could imagine anything so wild) rather than I should do wrong in this respect. Still it is of no use. I *am* disappointed. This is not the republic I came to see; this is not the republic of my imagination. I infinitely prefer a liberal monarchy—even with its sickening accompaniments of court circulars—to such a government as this. The more I think of its use and strength, the poorer and more trifling in a thousand aspects it appears in my eyes. In everything of which it has made a boast—excepting its education of the people and its care for poor children—it sinks immeasurably below the level I had placed it upon; and England, bad and faulty as the old land is, and miserable as millions of her people are, rises in the comparison.

You live here, Macready, as I have sometimes heard you imagining! *You!* Loving you with all my heart and soul, and knowing what your disposition really is, I would not condemn you to a year's residence on this side of the Atlantic for any money. Freedom of opinion! Where is it? I see a press more mean, and paltry, and silly, and disgraceful than any country I ever knew. If that is its standard, here it is. But I speak of Bancroft, and am advised to be silent on that subject, for he is 'a black sheep—a Democrat'. I speak of Bryant, and am entreated to be more careful, for the same reason. I speak of international copyright, and am implored not to ruin myself outright. I speak of Miss Martineau, and all parties—Slave Upholders and Abolitionists, Whigs, Tyler Whigs, and Democrats, shower down upon me a perfect cataract of abuse. 'But what has she done? Surely she praised America enough!' 'Yes, but she told us of some of our faults, and Americans can't bear to be told of their faults. Don't split on that rock, Mr Dickens, don't write about America; we are so very suspicious.'

Freedom of opinion! Macready, if I had been born here and had written my books in this country, producing them with no stamp of approval from any other land, it is my solemn belief that I should have lived and died poor, unnoticed, and a 'black sheep' to boot. I never was more convinced of anything than I am of that.

The people are affectionate, generous, open-hearted, hospitable, enthusiastic, good-humoured, polite to women, frank and candid to all strangers, anxious to oblige, far less prejudiced than they have been described to be, frequently polished and refined, very seldom rude or disagreeable. I have made a great many friends here, even in public conveyances, whom I have been truly sorry to part from. In the towns I have formed perfect attachments. I have seen none of the greediness and indecorousness on which travellers have laid so much emphasis. I have returned frankness with frankness; met questions not intended to be rude, with answers meant to be satisfactory; and have not spoken to one man, woman, or child of any degree who has not grown positively affectionate before we parted. In the respect of not being left alone, and of being horribly disgusted by tobacco chewing and tobacco spittle, I have suffered considerably. The sight of slavery in Virginia, the hatred of British feeling upon the subject, and the miserable hints of impotent indignation of the South, have pained me very much! on the last head, of course, I have felt nothing but a mingled pity and amusement; on the other, sheer distress. But however much I like the ingredients of this great dish, I cannot but come back to the point upon which I started, and say that the dish itself goes against the grain with me, and that I don't like it.

You know that I am truly a Liberal. I believe I have as little pride as most men, and I am conscious of not the smallest annoyance from being 'hail fellow well met' with everybody. I have not had greater pleasure in the company of any set of men among the thousands I have received than in that of the carmen of Hertford, who presented themselves in a body in their blue frocks, among a crowd of well-dressed ladies and gentlemen, and bade me welcome through their spokesman. They had all read my books, and all perfectly understood them. It is not these things I have in mind when I say that the man who comes to this country a Radical and goes home again with his opinions unchanged, must be a Radical on reason, sympathy, and reflection, and one who has so well considered the subject that he has no chance of wavering.

Laurence Oliphant

born in 1829, novelist, traveller and diplomat, was in the Crimean
War, the Indian Mutiny, the Chinese War, Garibaldi's invasions of
Italy and the Polish insurrection. He served as private secretary
to Lord Elgin in Washington and China and was Secretary of
Legation in Japan. After a short period as an M.P. he was *The Times*
correspondent in the Franco-German War. Later, in Palestine, he
founded a community of Jewish settlers at Haifa. He published
Minnesota and the Far West in 1855 and died in 1888.

Paddling down the Mississippi

As NEARLY AS possible in the centre of the continent of North America, and at an elevation of about 1800 feet above the level of the sea, extends a tract of pine-covered table-land about 100 miles square, and which probably contains a greater number of small lakes than any other district of the same size in the world. It is called Les Hauteurs des Terres, and is, in fact, the transverse watershed between Hudson's Bay and the St Lawrence waters, and those which run into the Gulf of Mexico. In one of its tiny lakes (Itasca) the Mississippi takes its rise, and flows due south. In another close to it the Red River finds its source, and runs north to Lake Winnipeg; while there are others, not many miles distant in a southerly direction, whose waters have an eastern outlet, and, after a short but rapid course, lose themselves in Lake Superior.

It added no little zest to the enjoyment of a summer evening to feel that we had successfully transferred ourselves and our bark canoe by the long portage through the woods described in the last chapter, from one of these streams to Sandy Lake, which furnishes a tributary to the head waters of the Mississippi. We were now paddling along its silent margin—sometimes hidden by the tall dark shadows which rows of lofty pines fringing the shore threw upon the water—sometimes emerging from them into the full blaze of the setting sun, and rounding long grassy peninsulas which stretched far across the lake—or wending our way through archipelagoes of little wooded islets. Overcome by the fatigues of the day, and the soothing influences of the scene, we lay back upon our blankets, and looked dreamily over the side of the canoe at the gentle ripple, and the evening fly that played upon it, until startled by the sudden plunge of the black bass or the maskelonge; or watched the bright vermillion tinge upon the fantastic outline of the lower clouds fade into a border of pale yellow, and gradually vanish, until roused to fresh energy by these indications of a failing day, and the recollection that the Indian village which was our destination was still some miles distant; and then with vigorous strokes we plied the paddle to the chant of the voyageurs, and shot rapidly along towards the wreath of blue smoke that betokened the wigwam of the

Indian: doubly cheering for us, for we had not seen a human habitation for many days.

It was a solitary hut, with a single upturned canoe before it, and a single mangy cur standing sentinel at the door. Our shouts soon brought to the edge of the lake a wild, half-naked figure, whose long matted hair hung nearly to his waist, and whose naturally dark complexion was increased by a coating of soot. A ragged filthy blanket was his only covering; and he seemed so transfixed with astonishment that he did not for some time recover his faculties sufficiently to enable him to answer our demand for some fresh meat or fish. When we held up a dollar, however, a flood of light poured in upon his bewildered intellects, and he dived into his bark wigwam, and immediately reappeared with a squaw, a papoose, and an armful of fish. The squaw was a degree more dirty and hideous and badly clad than her husband. The infant watched our proceedings with a sort of fixed, unconscious stare, arising probably from an inability to shut its eyes on account of being firmly lashed to a board, after the manner of papooses generally.

Having been fortunate in thus procuring a good supply of fresh bass, we pushed contentedly on, and reached the village just before dark. The scene that here met our eyes was somewhat singular. A collection of wigwams, some conical and some oval in shape like gypsies' tents, were grouped confusedly upon the sandy beach, between which were suspended either fishing-nets, or lines from which hung rows of fish being cured. Two or three ruined log-houses indicated the former residence of white traders; but they had evidently not been tenanted for many years, and were quite dilapidated. A few canoes were fishing off the village; a number more lay upturned upon the edge of the lake, where a knot of persons were collected, evidently watching with some interest so unusual an arrival as a large canoe from the eastern shore with eight paddles. Their curiosity was still further excited when, as we approached nearer, they perceived that four of us were whites. Moreover, there was something novel in our style of paddling, on which, to say the truth, we rather piqued ourselves. The Indians never attempt to keep time, but we commenced at starting to put both voyageurs and Indians into training; and now, at the end of a week's voyage, with twelve hours a-day of practice, we found ourselves in first-rate condition, and, with a 'give way all', dashed past the village in a style that would rather have astonished the 'Leander', much less the unsophisticated Chippeways of Sandy Lake; and then coming gracefully round opposite an amazed missionary, who was standing close to the water surrounded by the youth of his congregation, we 'in bow', and beached our light bark with a violence that seriously imperilled the worthy man's toes. Paddling certainly has this advantage over rowing, that every one sits with his face to the bows to criticize the steering, and take an equal interest with the cockswain in the accidents and incidents of the voyage.

Driving from Dubuque, Iowa, to Illinois

ASCENDING A STEEP hill, we shortly after came upon an interesting family. First, some yards in advance the patriarch appeared, with rounded shoulders and slouching gait, clothed in a negligée buff-coloured suit; his loose hunting-shirt reached nearly to his knees—his wide trousers fell over low fox-coloured shoes—one of his long arms swung by his side, the other supported a heavy rifle—his powder-horn, encased in deer-skin, and his bullet-pouch, ornamented with a squirrel's tail, hung round his coarse sunburnt neck. With long steps and flat Indian tread he stalked past, scarce honouring with a glance of his keen eye our dashing equipage. Behind him came the waggon with the hardy-looking mother, surrounded by a brood of small fry sitting in front, and all their worldly possessions, from a bed-stead to a tea-cup, stowed away inside. There was a big sensible-looking dog keeping watch over all, doubtless a tried and faithful servant, to whom I attached some significance after the description I once heard a Yankee give of the greatest friend he possessed in the world. 'Ah!' he said, 'my friend Sam is a *hull* team and a horse to spare, besides a big dog under the waggon.' It said more for the consistency of Sam's friendship than if he had panegyrized him for half-an-hour in our less forcible Anglican mode of expression. A few hundred yards in the rear came some stray horses and cows, driven by a barefoot lass, with evidently nothing on but a cotton gown, and even that seemed to be an unnatural and disagreeable encumbrance to her lower extremities. The probability is, however, that some stray senator may pick her up on some future day, when the 'diggings' to which she is now bound become thickly populated and progressive. Meantime her father complains of being 'crowded out', and says that he has no longer elbow-room, and that people are settling down under his nose, when the nearest farm to that which he has just left in disgust is at least twenty miles distance by the sectional lines. He is no emigrant from the old country, but moved into Western Illinois when that was the Far West. But he sees crowds of emigrants moving beyond him, and crowds more taking up their location where he once roved in solitary dignity; and that disturbs his peace of mind, and he leaves the cockney atmosphere for the silent prairie far beyond the most distant emigrant, never stopping, perhaps, till he reaches the western borders of Nebraska, where the Indian war-whoop is still heard to recall the experiences of his earlier days, and to keep ever bright the watchful eye, and the listening ear ever attentive, and thus to add to the peaceful occupations of agriculture the excitement incident to a border life.

Thomas Richard Weld

(1813–69) was born in Dublin and became a barrister. His
Vacation Tour of the United States and Canada was published in
1855 and was one of several 'Vacation Tours' he wrote of foreign
countries. He was secretary and librarian of the Royal Society.

Financial advice to the travellers

APPREHENDING THAT MY stock of gold eagles and dollars might run short before arriving at Washington, I called on the agents of Messrs. Coutts, whose letters of credit I held, for the purpose of obtaining a fresh supply. Much to my surprise I was informed a large premium would be required for gold, which I declined paying, and consequently left the counting-house without transacting any business. I mention this in order to show how scarce specie is in the United States, although California pours millions of dollars annually into her treasury. The solution of this apparent paradox is easy. A financial pressure has long been felt throughout the Union, and particularly in the Western States, which have been obliged to send all the specie procurable to Europe to meet obligations; and thus gold was sent out of the country when it was wanted at home for the basis of circulation.

The tourist in the States must take especial care to be provided with gold; otherwise he will not only be subjected to certain loss, but terrible inconvenience and annoyance. The wretched banknotes, of worthless paper commonly called *shin plasters*, are so frequently imitated that, unless the traveller is provided with a 'Bank-Note Reporter', published monthly, and continually consults it, he is sure to be imposed upon. In a recent copy of this periodical, out of 1283 banks by far the largest proportion have had their notes imitated. In several instances ten distinct forgeries are described. The words 'dangerous affair', 'very well executed', 'good imitation of genuine', 'well done', 'close imitation', &c., are frequently attached, showing how cleverly the forgers have operated, and therefore how difficult is detection. On the other hand, many imitations are stated to be exceedingly poor. The effect of this miserable state of things is to cast suspicion on every note; for it appears there are almost as many forgeries in circulation as genuine bank bills. I was constantly witness to disputes between railway conductors and passengers, which, however, invariably ended by the conductor refusing to receive the doubtful notes. . . .

The tourist will therefore see how essential it is for his comfort to avoid American bank-notes. English sovereigns will be generally taken; but the best gold coins are eagles, half-eagles, and dollars, which may be obtained without a premium in the principal Canadian towns and sea-board eastern cities.

Ladies in New York

... I WENT WITH a friend to Taylor's Restaurant, where some three or four hundred persons were supping; it is an enormous establishment, fitted up like a Parisian *café*; but far larger than any of the kind in Paris. Ladies were partaking of refreshments unattended by gentlemen; this is not at all uncommon in New York. One day that I dined at the magnificent and sumptuous Brevoort House with a friend, ladies came into the coffee-room, ordered *recherché* dinners, which they eat a little too speedily for English taste, and departed, without attracting the slightest notice from any one, I believe, but myself. The great deference and respect paid to the fair sex in America, is nowhere more conspicuous than in New York. A lady, young, pretty, and dressed in the gayest costume, may walk through the streets at all hours of the day and night, without running the slightest risk of being annoyed. This is a fact highly honorable to New York; and it is equally honorable that she will not see those humiliating and sad spectacles of an erring sister's shame, which stamp our streets with disgraceful singularity. Let it not be imagined, however, that New York is a virtuous city; I believe, from all I heard, it is far otherwise; but there, as at Paris, profligacy does not offend the eye.

Contrasts in Richmond, Virginia

... I MUST GIVE a sketch of an interesting sight which I witnessed in the afternoon. I was on my way to the Armoury, when I met Captain Dimmock. 'You are fortunate,' he observed, 'for the ceremony of an adult negro baptism has just commenced.' Proceeding towards the James River, we soon fell in with crowds of negroes going to the

[247]

scene of attraction; and on coming within sight of the water, we beheld the banks covered by thousands of blacks of both sexes. A small wooden house near the river contained numerous candidates for baptismal regeneration, clad in linen trousers, and a shirt. They were led into the stream, and received by the officiating minister and his assistants, who, after a short prayer, plunged them deep beneath the water. Before immersion the assembled multitude sang at the top of their voices spirit-stirring hymns. The sudden transition from the swelling and not inharmonious chorus to profound silence, had a curious effect; for the minister, whom I recognized as the preacher I heard in the morning,—

—'Stretch'd his arms and call'd
Across the tumult, and the tumult fell.'

Every eye was on him, and the moment a negro emerged from the water, a mighty cry arose from the excited multitude, welcoming a brother's advent into their fold. It was a touching spectacle. For all present were firmly persuaded salvation attended the ceremony, which in spirit at least lifted the souls of these poor bondsmen above the power of oppression.

Not, assuredly, greater is the contrast between a fair landscape illumined by brilliant summer sunshine, and steeped in the purple gloom of an impending thunder-storm, than that presented by the baptismal scene on the banks of the James River and the Richmond slave market.

I visited this place with mingled feelings of sadness and curiosity. The market consists of three human shambles, situated in the lower part of the town, far from the dwellings of the whites, easily distinguished by red flags over the entrances, to which are attached particulars of the slaves for sale. The number greatly varies, sometimes amounting to about fifty, and occasionally falling to one or two. On the day of my visit, fourteen males, and seven female 'likely' slaves, with their children, were advertised to be sold by auction. The first establishment I entered, consisted of a large barn-like room, about forty feet square, furnished with rude wooden benches and chairs; a platform for the display of the human goods; a desk, and a screen across the upper end of the room. The floor, walls, and indeed every object, were befouled by tobacco juice. About a score of ill-looking fellows were present, engaged, with scarcely an exception, in perpetual chewing and whittling. The benches, chairs, and all the woodwork, exhibited abundant marks how vigorously the latter practice had been carried on. The pillars were in many cases nearly severed. One man, who had tilted his chair back, was whittling one of the raised legs, with such energy of purpose, as to speedily threaten the amputation of that most important member of a chair's economy. By degrees more people arrived. When about fifty were present, the slaves were brought in from the neighbouring jail, where they had been confined. There were four men and two girls. The former were immediately led behind the screen, stripped stark naked, and examined with great minuteness. Marks were criticized with the knowing air assumed by horse dealers, and pronounced to be the results of flogging, vermin, or scrofula. Little value was apparently attached to the answers of the slaves, though considerable pains were taken to ascertain their ages, (of which, by the way, they were generally very ignorant,) and the cause of their sale; with one exception, none could assign any reason. The exceptional case was a youth, who stated he was the slave of a tobacco manufacturer, and that although his master treated him well, the overseer was harsh and cruel, and frequently beat him. In proof of this he exhibited a scar on his shoulder. His master, he added, had consented to allow him to be sold. The women were more tenderly dealt with. Personal examination was confined to the hands, arms, legs, bust, and teeth. Searching questions were put respecting their age, and whether they had children. If they replied in the negative, their bosoms were generally handled in a repulsive and disgusting manner. When sufficient time had been given for the examination of the slaves, the auctioneer left his desk, and desired his assistant, who was a slave, to bring up the first lot. This was a male negro about thirty years of age, who had been working on a tobacco plantation. He was ordered to ascend the platform, and the auctioneer stood on a chair by his side. The assistant now tucked up the slave's trousers, bared his neck and breast, and the sale commenced. 'Here,' said the auctioneer, 'is a likely young nigger, used to all sorts of farm work; what will ye bid, gentlemen? He's worth a thousand dollars. Who'll bid? come, 500 dollars to begin. Thank ye sir; 500 dollars—500 doll'r —doll'r—doll'r—' (uttered with bewildering rapidity), '500 doll'r— doll'r—doll'r: 600, thank ye sir.' Here the bidding hung fire, and the auctioneer, after expatiating on the good qualities of the lot, ordered him to be walked up and down the room before the people, who now amounted to about 200. During his progress, he was frequently stopped by the parties who examined him. On returning to the platform, the biddings were renewed with greater spirit, until they reached 858 dollars, at which sum the man was sold. The next lot—also a male, who stated he was worn out, and unable to do good work, though apparently under fifty years of age—sold for 630 dollars; the third male, about thirty years old, who had been working in a plantation, for 940 dollars; and the fourth, the young man who was sold at his own request, for 750 dollars. In all these cases the same process was gone through, each slave being trotted up and down the room precisely like a horse. Now came the women's turn. The first put up was a good-looking girl, gaily-dressed, her hair adorned with ribbons,—who, according to her statement, was nineteen years old, and was skilful in the use of her needle. 'Can you make shirts?' was a question put to her by a dozen men. 'Yes,' she replied, 'and wash them too.' The auctioneer expatiated at great length on the excellent qualities of this 'prime lot', for which he expected 1000 dollars at least. He obtained more—the first bid was 500, and she was knocked down for 1005. The second woman, aged twenty-five, who had been a domestic servant, realized only 700 dollars, on account of some scars on her shoulders, which a man near me was confident were produced by the whip. As all the slaves present were now sold, I thought business was over in this establishment; but just as the last woman was led away, a mulatto entered the room with another woman followed by two little children about three and four years old, and carrying a third still younger in her arms. These were the children announced for sale. The circumstances of this woman, or lot, as she and the children were called, being brought in alone, led me to suppose there was some distinction between her and the preceding slaves like those just sold; but in appearance the difference was great. She was a remarkably handsome mulatto, and her children were nearly, if not fully, as white as the fairest Americans. If any doubt existed in my mind respecting the revolting nature of this human traffic, the case of this woman would have determined my judgement. Her story was brief: she was not married, and the man whose passions had made her his mistress as well as slave, willed that she should be sold with *his* children. More she would not divulge; nor would she answer questions relative to her occupation. All attempts at extracting further information were met by a scornful refusal to divulge ought of her past life, and when her small soft hands and bosom were examined, on which her infant was reposing, her eyes flashed fire, and I sincerely believe, had a knife been within her grasp she would have plunged it in the

[250]

hearts of her tormentors. Followed by her two little children, who clung to her dress like scared lambs, shrinking from the gaze of the rough men who pressed round them, she ascended the platform, and the auctioneer recommenced his business. Whether he dreaded a scene, or that he deemed it unnecessary, I am unable to say; but he limited his prefatorial harangue to the simple announcement that he had a fine young woman to offer, with her children, who would not be sold separate, adding that in a few years the boys would be fit for work. What could he say of her, whose heart's finest affections were perhaps at that moment lacerated to satisfy the greed of a man? He set a high price on the woman and her children, declaring he expected at least 2500 dollars for the lot. The first bid was 800; languid biddings succeeded, until the amount reached 900 dollars. The woman was then ordered down, and followed by her little children, was made to walk up and down the room. On resuming her place on the platform, the biddings became a little brisker; but as no eloquence on the part of the auctioneer could raise them above 1100 dollars, the lot was withdrawn. I was informed the woman alone would have realized more than this amount, but there is a strong aversion against purchasing white children.

William Makepeace Thackeray

(1811–63) made two lecture tours of the United States, the first in 1852–53, when he delivered 'The English Humourists of the Eighteenth Century', the second in 1855–56, when his theme was 'The Four Georges'. It was on his second visit that he began his research for *The Virginians*, the sequel to *Esmond*, which ends in colonial Virginia.

From Thackeray's letters

December 1 (1852)

... I HAVE HAD no time or courage to see anything though, except here
and there a little sight on my way. The queerest was one of the Albany
Steamers—called the Francis Skiddy. Fancy Vauxhall glorified fresh
gilt decorated, carpeted and afloat and theres this wonderful ark. It's
an immense moving saloon 200 feet long with little state-rooms in each
side furnished some of them in such a way that the Duchess of Suther-
land herself never had any thing so grand to sleep in—white brocade silk
curtains and gold bullion hangings and velvet carpets and porcelain ye
Gods such porcelain!—this what they call the bridal chamber—Fancy a
lean yellow tobacco chewing youth, with a gold ring on his dirty hands
and a *goatee* on his chin, leading a pretty frail (I mean in stature only)
overdressed bride into this! and their going to settle in a New York
boarding house till he can get money enough to set up housekeeping.
He may be an omnibus driver or a millionaire in the next 5 or 10
years. Every chance is open to everybody. Everybody seems his neighbour's equal. They begin without a dollar and make fortunes in 5
years—a young lawyer of 26 just married to a beautiful young wife
told me he had made 100000 dollars and began without a cent at 21.
Then his sons will very likely spend or lose the money and his grandson be rich again—the wheel is always whirring and turning—the
pace is awful. No man lives in his fathers house—a house 20 years old
is worn out and used up. Broadway is never without barricades
houses are always being torn down there and it makes you tipsy to
walk in the place—it gives my brain a whirl as I think of it—I feel as
if this was getting like a sentence for a book: & I'm not a going to
write one. Stop Pennyaliner! Wo-o-o!

Last night at Bancrofts was a first chop 'Upper Ten' party of 16 or
18 in my honour. What I am pleased to find is that the people are a
hundred times pleasanter and more refined here than when with us
imitating our manners and sulking or pushing in our world. I have met
very many very pleasant and clever men and women naturally witty
and extremely good natured among one another. There's nothing to
sneer at some usages different to ours, but a manliness and fairness that

puts our society to shame often. I like to see the equality, I wince a little at first when a Shopman doesn't say 'Sir' or a coachman says 'Help that man with his luggage'—but y not? I'm sure its right that Society shd. be as it is here, that no harm should attach to a man for any honest way of working for his bread, and that a man should be allowed to be poor. We allow certain men to be poor at home, but not every one. . . .

Philadelphia. Jan. 17. 1853

. . . There are 500000 in this city abou hw. we know so little—theres one street with shops on each side 6 miles long—theres New York with 700000—Boston, Cincinatti scores more vast places—only beginning too and evidently in their very early youth whereas we are past our prime most likely. Empires more immense than any the old world has known are waiting their time here. In 10 years we shall cross to Europe in a week and for 5L; in 50 the population will treble that of Britain—Everybody prospers. There are scarce any poor. For hundreds of years more there is room and food and work for whoever comes. In travelling in Europe our confounded English pride only fortifies itself; and we feel that we are better than 'those foreigners' but it's worth while coming here that we may think small beer of ourselves afterwards. Greater nations than ours ever have been, are born in America and Australia—and Truth will be spoken and Freedom will be practised, and God will be worshipped among them, as they never have been with the antiquarian trammels that bind us in the Old World. I look at this, and speculate on this bright Future, as an Astronomer of a Star; and admire and worship the beautiful goodness of God.

Philadelphia, Jan. 23

. . . There's something simple in the way these kind folks regard a man; they read our books as if we were Fielding, and so forth. The other night some men were talking of Dickens and Bulwer as if they were equal to Shakespeare, and I was pleased to find myself pleased at hearing them praised. The prettiest girl in Philadelphia, poor soul, has read *Vanity Fair* twelve times. I paid her a great big compliment yesterday, about her good looks of course, and she turned round delighted to her friend and said, 'Ai most tallut', that is something like the pronunciation . . . And what do you think? One of the prettiest girls in Boston is to be put under my charge to go to a marriage at Washington next

[255]

week. We are to travel together all the way alone—only, only, I'm not going. Young people when they are engaged here, make tours alone; fancy what the British Mrs Grundy would say at such an idea!

There was a young quakeress at the lecture last night, listening about Fielding. Lord! Lord. how pretty she was! There are hundreds of such everywhere, airy looking little things, with magnolia—no not magnolia, what is that white flower you make bouquets of, camilla or camilia—complexions, and not lasting much longer . . .

Richmond, Virginia. March 3. 1853

This is the very prettiest friendliest and pleasantest little town I have seen in these here parts: but I did not see Washington's house on the Potomac for I was too late for the morning boat and obliged to come on by night. The streets swarm with negroes the Inn servants are all slaves—Well, I have never seen in my life so many happy looking people—the little nigger-children trotting about the Streets are the queerest grotesque little imps, they all look well fed and are in the main kindly treated—But it is the dearest and worst kind of service in the end. I dined yesterday with a gentleman who has but a wife and one child and has 12 servants to wait upon these 3. They are not so well attended as we are at Kensington. The plate was all dirty &c: and the lady told me her housekeeper an Englishwoman does as much work as all the women servants put together. The care & expense of these slaves is prodigious: you can't part with them as with an English bad servant, you must keep them and keep them comfortably when they are old & ill—The outcry against the practice has done this good perhaps that it has piqued the slave-holders into being *extra*-good to their servants. And for freeing them—Bon Dieu it is an awful measure to contemplate—there are three millions of them. You must indemnify not only the master but the slave whom you set free. The practice of the country (not the law) is strongly against separating families, and a man is held infamous who does such a crime. The people are no worse than we are whom they taunt about the frightful state and tyranny exercised over our poor—We acquiesce perforce in the state of things so do they—And until Nature affords some outlet for the evil, as with us when the Colonies have carried off multitudes of our poor and raised the wages of those who remain at home, slaves these poor dark folks must remain: as slaves they have been ever since their race (for what we know) began. Here the best workmen among them can put by as much as 25L or 30L in a year—they tell me—and at their church on

Sunday where 2000 of them go, you see the finest dressed women and the queerest grand bonnets &c.

Savannah, Georgia March 14–19
... Yesterday I drove out to a negro settlement on a Mr Faversham's plantation and saw: this let's see—(this is a bad pen Eyre Crowe has got the good one and I don't like to deprive him of it).

Picture of negroes

I can't draw it, I can't draw without the drawing pen—but it was the first negro village, and it gave me a sensation. I went into their houses: they are not uncomfortable—they have half a pound of bacon a day, plenty of flour, nice treacle and a little tobacco—they are kindly treated that's the truth—no planter but is anxious you should see his people at any hour and unknown to him if you like—Of course there are bad and savage masters too, but the general condition is far from unhappy. They are no more fit for freedom than a child of 10 years old is fit to compete in the struggle of life with grown up folks; and the physiologists who take that side of the question say they never can be.

New York. November 20. 1855
In both visits to America I have found the effects of the air here the same ... I sleep 3 hours less than in England, making up however with a heavy long sleep every 4th night or so. . . . There is some electric influence in the air & sun here wh. we dont experience on our side of the globe. Under this Sun people cant sit still people can't ruminate over their dinners dawdle in their studies and be lazy and tranquil!— they must keep moving, rush from one activity to another, jump out of sleep and to their business, have lean eager faces—I want to dash into the street now. At home after breakfast I want to read my paper leisurely and then get to my books and work. The men here read surprisingly—one tells me, a busy man keeping a great Store in the City that he does all his reading in the railway-cars as he comes in & out from his country residence daily. Fancy an English City Grocer reading Tennyson & Browning on his way from Brighton to Broad Street every day! A look over the Times, a snooze for the rest of the journey wd. be enough for him.

New Orleans. March 10. 1856
... What did I do yesterday? Yesterday we took the horse railway 3 or 4 miles to the suburb called — then crossed the Mississippi in the steam

ferry-boat to a little Dutch town built on tother side; then walked along the river by swamps by plantations by ruined wooden houses by groups of negroes by kind German folks walking in their Sunday clothes, by enormous steamers, by lines of ships moored along the vast river banks under the sweetest blue sky to another ferry opposite Canal Street, and here we were landed at a great plain covered with millions of bales of cotton. Sunday as it was the enormous steamers were busy in discharging into the arms of scores of big fellows who roll them away to the ships wh. carry them to England. We met a black preacher walking with a friend and swaggering with a most delightful majesty—we heard another black gentleman reading prayers out of a great book, and saw him swagger out of the hut when his devotions were over—as for the little black children they ruin me in 5 cent pieces. A man came up to me in the street & asked me if I could sign him any one who wanted to buy a farm hand? It was because I looked like a Kentucky farmer my friends tell me, that this obliging offer was made to me—If one of these imps wd. remain little I think I would buy him and put him into buttons as a page for the young ladies—but presently he will become big, lazy, lying, not sweet smelling doing the 4th of a white mans work and costing more to keep. No we wont buy a black imp . . .

On the Mississippi. Easter Saturday & Sunday I lay my hand on a letter begun to you on the 28 January in a country tavern in North Carolina (where our engine broke down Sir, and our engine had broke down the day before sir—) and I had written down the first page when our conductor tapped me on the shoulder and told me to get ready—a new engine had come to our relief.

If it had been pleasant to write you would have had a fulfilment of my promise ere this—but it isn't. The journey, the incidents on it, the people I see along the road, the business I am on are all as disagreeable as can be. From Richmond in Virginia I have travelled say 1500 miles of railway—one endless swamp of pines, sand, loghouses, niggers, in dirty cars, amongst dirty passengers, spitting, chewing, cutting their gums with their penknives, the young ones cursing outrageously—not unfriendly in the main—The hotel life is disgusting, rows all night, gongs banging at all hours to the dirty meals, knives down everybody's throat, dirty bucks straddling over the balconies their dirty boots as high as their heads, the bar-rooms resounding with blasphemies—not one pretty aspect of nature for those hundreds of miles except now and then a melancholy ragged vista of pines or live oaks fringed with a dreary funereal moss—nothing picturesque in the so called cities—only great straight streets of tenements chiefly wood—pigs cows and negroes sauntering about them—about the stores the hotels and the barrooms a little more life. Im not speaking of Charleston Mobile & New Orleans these are great towns—the first like Europe with an aristocracy and a very pleasant society, ruling patriarchally over its kind black vassals hospitable, tolerably lettered, keeping aloof from politics as almost all the gentlemen of the States are forced to do. As for the negroes, if laughter indicates happiness, I have never seen people so happy as the negroes in the towns, never met a country gentleman but he has been eager that I should go to his plantation & see how his people were cared for—I have no doubt that, at no period of time, since wool first grew on human skulls, negroes have never been so well off as those now in America. This does not make Slavery right: but—but I cant mend it, and so leave it. The awful day for the Institution will be not now when a good negro is worth 1200$, and you know an animal of such value *can't* be ill-treated, but when white labor begins to undersell them at cotton & sugar work. Then the 'beautiful relation betwixt owner & servant' will pretty soon come to an end—O it will be a terrible day when 5 or 6 millions of these blacks have to perish and give place to the white man wanting work—but theres a long day for that yet, the West has to be filled ere the white mans hand turns against the black man—after your time and mine after Englands perhaps in ½ a dozen generations when this the Great Empire of the world numbers 120 millions of citizens (and *esses*) at least when our old Europe is worn out, who knows whether the Great Republic may not colonize with its negroes the vacant British Isles? Put the case & is it the least improbable? that despotic Europe coalesces and fights against England alone— —we battle tooth and nail, we know that old Hardinge & Co and H.R.H. Prince Albert and the Horse Guards cant save us, we let loose the dogs of war, we become interested in the suffering nationalities and suddenly sympathize with the oppressed peoples—whatever the issue of that inevitable conflict, *our* England perishes, our dear old orderly absurd wise unjust just illiberal fanatical free England goes to the deuce, and something quite different remains after conflagration.— Hullo! Whither is the prophetic Spirit carrying me? There has been a fellow lecturing at my heels, and over me in the same towns sometimes, on the battle of Armageddon and how the US are clearly foretold in the Apocalypse; that England & the European powers are to do battle with America & to be defeated in the great valley of the Mississippi after wh. the Reign of Righteousness is comfortably to ensue—I suppose some of his divine furor has leaked through from his lecture room to my pulpit—and hadn't I better tear off this page at once?

Well Sir, I have been up the Alabama River 3½ days say 600 miles and now up the Mississippi near 1000—these remarks were begun off the city of Memphis and tomorrow we shall reach Cairo DV and in my life have seen nothing more dreary & funereal than these streams. The nature and the people oppress me and are repugnant to me . . . but I go out forward and the view gives me pain and I come back—I don't like that great fierce strong impetuous ugliness.

With what a company bon Dieu! I was drawing a picture for the girls of the opposite side of the table in the Alabama Steamer with every man with his knife down his throat—Yesterday on this boat (the Thomas Small) every woman had her knife down her's too. I vow every one. Men constantly do without pocket handkerchiefs (there's one elegant way of operating with one forefinger applied to one nostril wh. I'll show any company of ladies when I get home)—After the ladies had done the giantess (who's travelling and very likely going to perform at the same fair as myself) had her dinner and she swallowed her victuals with the help of her knife too it looked quite small in her hand. She is with the Bearded Lady who has a little boy of 3 who has also got very handsome whiskers and a little girl of 6 who seems to me rather pensive because her chin is quite smooth (I think the late Mr Addison wd. have made something out of that incident, don't you?) the Bearded Lady the Giantess & the English Lecturer all rowing in the same boat is pleasant to reflect on. O how sick I am of the House of Hanover—As for George IV I think him a contemptible imposter & say so but I think those who come to hear me go away with a soft heart for George II, & they all applaud when speak up as I do with all my heart for the Queen . . .

Isabella Bishop

(1832–1904) was not for nothing a relation of Mary Kingsley,
for like her, she was one of those intrepid Victorian ladies who
strode the four quarters of the earth doing good works.
She built five hospitals and an orphanage in the East.
She published *The English Woman in America* in 1856.

Railway travelling in the West

SOME TIME AFTERWARDS, while travelling for two successive days and nights in an unsettled district in the west, on the second night, fairly overcome with fatigue, and unable, from the crowded state of the car, to rest my feet on the seat in front, I tried unsuccessfully to make a pillow for my head by rolling up my cloak, which attempts being perceived by a working mechanic, he accosted me thus: 'Stranger, I guess you're almost used up? Maybe you'd be more comfortable if you could rest your head.' Without further parley he spoke to his companion, a man in a similar grade in society; they both gave up their seats, and rolled a coat round the arm of the chair, which formed a very comfortable sofa; and these two men stood for an hour and a half, to give me the advantage of it, apparently without any idea that they were performing a deed of kindness. I met continually with these acts of hearty unostentatious good nature. I mention these in justice to the lower classes of the United States, whose rugged exteriors and uncouth vernacular render them peculiarly liable to be misunderstood.

Chicago

CHICAGO IS CONNECTED with the western rivers by a sloop canal—one of the most magnificent works ever undertaken. It is also connected with the Mississippi at several points by railroad. It is regularly laid out with wide airy streets, much more cleanly than those of Cincinnati. The wooden houses are fast giving place to lofty substantial structures of brick, or a stone similar in appearance to white marble, and are often six stories high. These houses, as in all business streets in the American cities, are disfigured, up to the third story, by large glaring sign-boards containing the names and occupations of their residents. The side walks are of wood, and, wherever they are made of this unsubstantial material, one frequently finds oneself stepping into a hole, or upon the end of a board which tips up under one's feet. The houses are always let in flats, so that there are generally three stores one above the other. These stores are very handsome, those of the outfitters particularly so, though the quality of goods displayed in the streets gives them rather a barbaric appearance. The side walks are literally encumbered with bales of scarlet flannel, and every other article of an emigrant's outfit. At the out-fitters' stores you can buy anything, from a cart-nail to a revolver; from a suit of oilskin to a paper of needles. The streets present an extraordinary spectacle. Everything reminds that one is standing on the very verge of western civilization.

The roads are crowded to an inconvenient extent with carriages of curious construction, waggons, carts, and men on horseback, and the side-walks with eager foot-passengers. By the side of a carriage drawn by two or three handsome horses, a creaking waggon with a white tilt, drawn by four heavy oxen, may be seen—Mexicans and hunters dash down the crowded streets at full gallop on mettlesome steeds, with bits so powerful as to throw their horses on their haunches when they meet with any obstacle. They ride animals that look too proud to touch the earth, on high-peaked saddles, with pistols in their holsters, short stirrups, and long cruel-looking Spanish spurs. They wear scarlet caps or palmetto hats, and high jackboots. Knives are stuck into their belts, and light rifles are slung behind them. These picturesque beings—the bullock-waggons setting out for the Far West—the medley of different nations and costumes in the streets—make the city a spectacle of great interest.

The deep hollow roar of the locomotive, and the shrill scream from the steamboat, are heard here all day; a continuous stream of life ever bustles through the city, and, standing as it does on the very verge of western civilization, Chicago is a vast emporium of the trade of the districts east and west of the Mississippi.

American passion for oysters

THE AMOUNT OF oysters eaten in New York surprised me, although there was an idea at the time of my visit that they produced the cholera, which rather checked any extraordinary excesses in this curious fish. In the business streets of New York the eyes are greeted continuously with the words 'Oyster Saloon', painted in large letters on the basement story. If the stranger's curiosity is sufficient to induce him to dive down a flight of steps into a subterranean abode, at the first glance rather suggestive of robbery, one favourite amusement of the people may be seen in perfection. There is a counter at one side, where two or three persons, frequently blacks, are busily engaged in opening oysters for their customers, who swallow them with astonishing relish and rapidity. In a room beyond, brightly lighted by gas, family groups are to be seen, seated at round tables, and larger parties of friends, enjoying basins of stewed oysters; while from some mysterious recess the process of cookery makes itself distinctly audible. Some of these saloons are highly respectable, while many are just the reverse. But the consumption of oysters is by no means confined to the saloons: in private families an oyster supper is frequently a nightly occurrence; the oysters are dressed in the parlour by an ingenious and not inelegant apparatus. So great is the passion for this luxury, that the consumption of it during the season is estimated at 3500 lb. a day.

American temperance

THE APPARENTLY TEMPERATE habits in the United States form another very pleasing feature to dwell upon. It is to be feared that there is a considerable amount of drunkenness among the English, Irish, and Germans, who form a large portion of the American population; but the temperate tea-drinking, water-drinking habits of the native Americans are most remarkable. In fact, I only saw one intoxicated person in the States, and he was a Scotch fiddler. At the hotels, even when sitting down to dinner in a room with four hundred persons, I never on any occasion saw more than two bottles of wine on the table, and I know from experience that in many private dwelling-houses there is no fermented liquor at all. In the West, more especially at the rude hotels where I stopped, I never saw wine, beer, or spirits upon the table; and the spectacle gratified me exceedingly, of seeing fierce-looking, armed, and bearded men, drinking frequently in the day of that cup 'which cheers, but not inebriates'. Water is a beverage which I never enjoyed in purity and perfection before I visited America. It is provided in abundance in the cars, the hotels, the waiting-rooms, the steamers, and even the stores, in crystal jugs or stone filters, and it is always iced. This may be either the result or the cause of the temperance of the people.

Thomas Colley Grattan

born in Dublin in 1792, was an historical novelist, historian and travel-writer. Appointed British Consul to Massachusetts in 1839, he published *Civilized America* twenty years later. He died in 1864.

Boston

BOSTON HAS THE reputation—and its inhabitants are not a little proud thereat—of being the most 'English-like' city in the Union. Such is the prevalent idea, and in certain respects it is correct. The people are of nearly unmixed British descent. The early settlers of New England generally, and of this their capital in particular, were exclusively so. And so they remained until within the last thirty or forty years, during which a considerable accession of Irish has taken from the population its entirely Anglo-Saxon character; and, in the opinion of the majority, its purity has consequently much deteriorated. That point I will not stop to discuss; but I will merely remark that the cross between the Hibernian and the Yankee produces a breed intelligent and active, with a dash of frankness that the purely national race has no pretensions to.

With the exception just stated, there are, almost literally, no foreigners resident in Boston. I know but one English merchant, not a naturalized citizen, who frequented 'Change'; but two Frenchmen, two or three Germans, a couple of Greeks, one Sicilian, a Russian, and a Swede, who were the vice-consuls of their respective countries. There may be half-a-dozen German and Italian music and dancing masters. Among the artisans and shopkeepers are a few Europeans. The mass of Irish labourers completes the list; but as the latter form the lowest order of the community, and are totally confined to their own haunts, I may safely say, that there are no foreign settlers in Boston at all known in the more elevated circles of society. It is a common saying, that a Scotchman cannot thrive in New England, the Yankees being 'too cannie for him'. There are, nevertheless, some highly respectable Scotch tradesmen among the citizens of Massachusetts. Even a Jew, it is remarked, with more apparent truth, would have no chance there. Boston does not, I believe, contain one individual Israelite. But the very resemblances in character and habits between the Hebrew and the Yankee are very remarkable, and very soon become obvious. The latter shows many tendencies towards a relapse into Judaism and a return to the Mosaic law. The Old Testament is more congenial than the New to *his* Christianity. Its maxims and doctrines are constantly appealed to. The exclusive characteristics of the Jews are very common, and the great prevalence of Hebrew in comparison with Christian names is one of the most striking peculiarities of a people eminently pharisaical.

American street-scenes

THE STREETS OF the 'Atlantic cities', as the seaport towns are called, are altogether deficient in the air of lounging and lazy life, which well-dressed men of leisure and the many varieties of *vagabondage* give to the towns of the Continent, and, in a minor degree, to those of the British Isles. But there is much bustle and business-like vivacity. The thoroughfares are full of well-clad, plain-looking, serious-visaged men, and women in all the gaudiness of over-dressed pretension. The flaunting air of these ladies, their streaming feathers and flowers, silks and satins of all colours, and a rapid, dashing step as they walk along, singly or in couples, give foreigners a widely mistaken notion of them. They look, in fact, like so many nymphs of the *pavé*; for no other class of females in Europe are at all like them; and many awkward mistakes take place in consequence. But in proportion as the American ladies lose much of the retiring modesty so becoming in their sex, by this habit of independent promenading, the streets gain largely, in the glare and glitter of the fair *piétons*.

The perils of central heating

THE METHOD OF heating many of the best houses is a terrible grievance to persons not accustomed to it, and a fatal misfortune to those who are. Casual visitors are nearly suffocated, and constant occupiers killed. An enormous furnace in the cellar sends up, day and night, streams of hot air, through apertures and pipes, to every room in the house. No spot is free from it, from the dining-parlour to the dressing-closet. It meets you the moment the street-door is opened to let you in, and it rushes after you when you emerge again, half-stewed and parboiled, into the wholesome air. The self-victimized citizens, who have a preposterous affection for this atmosphere, undoubtedly shorten their lives by it. Several elderly gentlemen of my acquaintance, suddenly cut off, would assuredly have had a verdict of 'died of a furnace' pronounced on their cases, had a coroner been called, and had a jury decided on fair evidence. But no citizen is inclined to condemn the instrument which every one in 'high life' patronizes, and which is congenial to the frigid temperament of all classes. Half the sickness in the Atlantic cities, north of Washington, is to be attributed to the extreme heat of the houses, without which the cold external air would do good instead of harm. Large fires of Anthracite coal and close stoves are common, in houses of moderate pretensions, where the cruel luxury of a furnace is not found. And independent of the mischief done to the health of both sexes and all ages, there is something inexpressibly cheerless, whether it be in Germany, Holland, or the United States, in the look of a house heated by a furnace, particularly if the rooms have grates unfilled and useless.

The inauguration of President William Henry Harrison

UNDER A SALUTE of artillery, and the loud shouts of the crowd, the solemnity broke up, and the long procession returned to the President's official dwelling, the White House, which Harrison now entered as temporary tenant, little thinking that the ceremony which had just given him his title to possession also set the seal on his frail tenure of life. The exposure and fatigue he had gone through on that occasion, laid the germs of the disease which carried him off exactly a month from that day.

But the labours of the day were by no means at an end. Crowds pressed in to pay their respects and their court in the promiscuous enthusiasm of pleasure at the President's elevation, and in hope at the prospect of their own. Many of these partisans shared the hospitable dinner of their chief; and at a large and brilliant public ball in the evening, the indefatigable President again made his appearance early, and for hours went the rounds of a hundred little circles, all so many eddies of delight in which he sported unrestrained. At this ball there were full a thousand persons. As the price of the tickets was as high as ten dollars each, it might be supposed that the company would have been somewhat select. But it formed a most curious mixture, being composed of contingents from all parts of the Union. And strange varieties they were. Groups of fine ladies from Boston, New York, Baltimore, and Philadelphia, overloaded with ornament and in flaunting colours, were contrasted with specimens from the wild West, in dresses as gaudy in pattern, but more uncouth in cut. The hanging sleeves and flowing flounces in satin and gauze, with rich embroidery and lace garnitures, were opposed to tight muslin or cotton gowns made in defiance of all modern taste, while flowers, feathers, and the most fantastic combinations of head-gear, threw an air of inconceivable burlesque over the whole display. Female beauty, in every shape and hue which the country could furnish, was there, from the bright-skinned New Englander to the New Orleans brunette; while sprigs of dandyism from the Atlantic cities were in amusing contrast with rough western men, or down-east delegates, in the glorious equality of semi-civilization. The uniforms of diplomatists and military and naval officers gave their usual bright relief to the mass of black cloth coats and black satin vests. The building was large and straggling and of rude construction. The walls were covered with mere whitewash which, with a profusion of spermaceti lights, threw an intense glare upon the crowded company, and I think I never saw so true a picture on a large scale of elation and enjoyment as was presented by this motley assembly.

Mysteries of childbirth

As EVERY EUROPEAN must be struck with the absence of youthful spirit which characterizes the population of the United States, so does the progress of population itself appear to the stranger a very mysterious matter. Few give themselves the trouble to search for statistical details of its aggregate increase. The newspapers, which are in every one's hands, abstain, on a point of delicacy, from ever announcing the birth of a child; while marriages and deaths occupy their columns without reserve. The impression, therefore, at first is—at least it was mine—on looking over the daily journals, that the wealthier orders of society, who in Europe are sure to have every addition to their families announced to the public, are in America a very unprolific class. This idea was much strengthened by the extreme rarity of the appearance which indicates an increase of population. Neither the shadow nor the substance of such a coming event is shown to the vulgar gaze. No lady allows herself to be publicly seen while she is visibly *enceinte*. A rigid confinement to her house, and even to her 'chamber', is observed for a considerable time preceding her confinement, which thus bears a double signification, while her delivery is of a two-fold nature—from her maternal burden, and from a term of solitary imprisonment.

It has frequently happened to me to miss ladies from the parties of the circle in which we moved, and on inquiring after them from some mother or sister, to be told they were 'in the country', or 'visiting', and on meeting them, in probably a year or more, to find them accompanied by a nurse with a fine, fat baby, or they themselves holding some little waddling 'responsibility' (to use one of their favourite words for designating children) of whose existence I had never heard.

American servants

INCONSISTENT AS IT may appear to be with the pride of personal independence, inherent in the republican, it is certainly true that domestic service is not considered so disgraceful in the United States, as it is felt to be in the United Kingdom. I have often seen a contrary remark made by travellers; but I know them to be mistaken. An American youth or 'young lady' will go to service willingly, if they can be better paid for it than for teaching in a village school, or working on a farm or in a factory. Many girls prefer the latter occupation, because the high rate of wages soon enables them to lay by a larger sum than they could possibly save in the same space of time as 'chamber girls' or 'sempstresses'. But those who do prefer going to service, and the observation applies to both sexes, assuredly feel less degraded by it than persons in a similar condition in any other part of the world.

There are several causes for this. In the first place they satisfy themselves that they are *helps*, not servants—that they are going to work with (not for) Mr so and so, not going to service—they call him and his wife their *employers*, not their master and mistress—they bargain for great privileges as to receiving their friends, going out, and coming in—they consider themselves entitled to, and will insist on, sharing all the delicacies consumed in the family, and, above all things, they have their conviction that the persons they serve, or their parents, or some of their immediate connections, have been themselves in the very position *they* now occupy; and the male or female servant whose father is an independent farmer and proprietor of his land, is quite satisfied that such a position entitles him and them to a perfect feeling of political equality with any other person in the country. This innate sentiment of independence, when modified by a good sense and a fair share of education, which is common to most persons of that class, qualifies them, in my opinion, to make very good servants, when properly managed.

I have had ample opportunities for observation, in families with whom we were intimate, in hotels innumerable, and in our own actual service; and everything has satisfied me that, if well treated, the native Americans are the best servants in the country; and according to my experience the best I have ever known, in the qualities which I consider among the most essential. They are regular, quiet, good-tempered, sober; all knowing how to read and write, and every one looking forward to some better condition in life, for which they seem to prepare themselves by economy and good conduct. They are not conscious of having forfeited their self-respect, from the manner in which they choose to view their condition, in comparison with that of their employers. They can consequently afford, without any sacrifice of self-importance, to be respectful to those whom they serve. It is only those who wince under the sensitiveness I have before described, and sensitiveness is rare in the Yankee temperament, who give themselves relief by insolence to others. Native American servants undoubtedly take great liberties in comparison with those of Europe, as to the distribution of their time. Engaged to do a certain quantity of work, it is always understood that when it is done they are free to do with themselves what they like. They do not hold themselves obliged to ask leave for the disposal of their extra time, which they frequently employ (the females I mean) in needlework of various kinds, for their own benefit. It is very common to see a cook or a chamber-girl at work, making a set of shirts, or the like, for persons not in their employer's family. They do not stand on much ceremony as to giving warning, if it suits them to quit. They do not in general form attachments to their employers, any more than a labourer or mechanic who hires himself for a certain piece of task work or to complete a job. A servant who will make herself useful, which implies in England a disposition to turn his hand to all things from regard to the family, is almost unknown in Yankee-land. The affections are not strong there, and they are certainly less so between employers and helps, than between any other classes of individuals in the community—except, perhaps, between parents and children.

And here is the true source of the never-ending lamentations about the badness of servants and the miseries of housekeeping, which form the chief staple of complaint on the part of the ladies and gentlemen of America. The employers having no confidence in persons whom they hire for a temporary purpose, treat them with extreme distrust. They have nothing in common. The interests of each are altogether matters of a separate feeling. The employer does not inquire into those of the helps, and the help takes no care of those of the master. The greatest apprehension of the latter is that the former may not have a fitting sense of the difference between them—may not treat them with sufficient deference—may take undue liberties with them. There is consequently no ease of manner, no security of position on the part of the employer; and there is nothing so easily detected as a forced reserve. Its natural effect on those towards it is assumed is to create an antagonist influence, which soon amounts to dislike. So that the help who discovers in his employer an air of false importance, is sure to pay it back with an assumption of equality.

To escape as much as possible from this evil, the majority of persons prefer Irish servants to native helps. With those they are under less restraint; they can treat them with greater kindness with less risk of compromising their dignity; they have a chance of meeting gratitude in return for good treatment, and fidelity for trustingness. These uneducated immigrants readily admit the superiority of those they serve, without inquiring into their origin or their earlier occupations. In fact, the grand desideratum of the wealthier class is thus in a certain degree realized. They establish, at least in their own household, an acknowledged graduation of ranks, which they so vainly sigh for on a more extended scale.

But these Irish servants, so agreeable in this regard, are, with some exceptions, of a very indifferent order as attendants. They have rarely lived in the same capacity in Europe, the great majority having adopted this line on arriving in America, without any previous training. Many of the men are deserters from the British army in Canada, and the other

British provinces, and these, from their former habits of discipline, are not badly adapted to the great hotels, where a regular system of drill and duty is strictly preserved; but as they are generally volatile and fond of variety, they change about from one place to another, and, as private and public houses employ them alike, they have all the air and manner of waiters, and you rarely see in a family a domestic that gives the notion of his belonging to a fixed and reputable service. The Irish women, on the other hand, who have learned their little knowledge in the United States, are rarely anything but very indifferent. The cooks particularly know little or nothing of their art; they adopt the thick, greasy, salt sauces common to the country; they roast or boil a joint in the ordinary fashion, but are altogether ignorant of the lighter and more graceful appurtenances of a repast.

The applications which designate house servants with us are not used in America. There are none such, for instance, as those of butler, valet, own man, footman, page. Steward, or groom of the chambers, are of course not to be expected, belonging, even in England, only to a scale of establishments which has no existence in the New World. A man servant in America is in the best houses called a waiter, and it gives great offence to a European ear to hear a gentleman at a dinner-table call to the servant of a host, 'Waiter, get me a piece of the beef,' 'Waiter, hand me the casters.' A most ludicrous, yet unmeant sarcasm on the abuse of military titles exists in the appellation of 'kitchen colonels', given by servants in America to men servants in families.

Coloured men are not much employed as permanent house servants in the northern and eastern parts of the Union. But extra attendants for both private and public parties are almost entirely chosen from them. They are a very respectable class, and excellent for such employment, being not so independent and indifferent in manner as the native white men, nor as bustling and fidgetty as the Irish. The greatest annoyance from the latter class arises from their over anxiety to serve and oblige. They give one no rest at table, but in accordance with the usual taste of the native Americans of all classes, are constantly putting every possible incongruity before or beside you; offering you, for instance, cranberry sauce with your fish, maccaroni with mutton chops, vegetables of any and every kind with stewed oysters, and so on . . .

With respect to female servants, they are on the most limited plan. There are no housekeepers or ladies' maids. The lady herself does all the duties of the former, those of the latter are performed, jointly and severally, by the 'sempstress' and the chamber girl, the regular employment of the first of whom is to do the 'sewing', the latter to attend to the bedrooms, or, in American phrase, to 'fix the chambers'. Needlework of all kinds is, I believe, called 'sewing' throughout the United States. Ladies do very much to assist their female servants in their ordinary duty, making beds, 'fixing' the rooms, making puddings, ironing, making up linen, etc. Servants are thus really justified in giving to themselves the favourite designation of 'helps'. Even in the Atlantic cities they frequently make it a point, on entering into a service, that the ladies of the family share with them such kind of work as I have specified. I dare say that condition will be more rigidly enforced by the native domestics in proportion as democratic principles spread and become permanent. Nursery governesses are unknown, the mothers performing some of the multifarious business expected from that over-worked class of young women in England; but teaching the young idea how to spell or write does not enter into the list of maternal duties. Ladies keeping house in America are indeed little better than upper servants. The whole superintendence of the indoor work depends on them. And very often do they assist in all that is going on, in laundry, pantry, nursery, and kitchen. The husbands invariably go to market. No woman does any of that essential business beyond giving an order at the 'Grocery', or the 'Provision store'. It is not easy to know the secrets of the scheme of domestic economy, followed by so very close and cautious a community. But a strict avoidance of needless expense, a great distrust of servants, and a mean system of locking up and doling out, are, I am inclined to believe, its general characteristics, though there, I am satisfied, many exceptions exist. The cook is a very independent and irresponsible person. She has none of the importance of housekeeping, but she is without its cares; little being required from her she has little to look after; the meals of the family prepared, her time is her own. Between the regular hours she goes where she chooses, and if she be a person of the least pretensions in her profession, she fixes her own time for everything, and upon the slightest deviation from the arrangement, which might interfere with her plans for going to meeting on Sunday, or to lectures on week days, she quits her place without notice, frequently while the dinner is half dressed, and the company waiting for it in vain. In general, these cooks are wretchedly bad; chiefly Irishwomen, who knew little at home beyond boiling potatoes, they learn their art in America, and nothing can be worse than the Yankee taste in all that concerns the *cuisine*. They have in eating, as in speaking or dressing, a great love of finery. A simple gravy is distasteful to them;

thick sauces, and highly salted and over-spiced dishes, with quantities of pickles, are the common style. The cook catches the taste of the employer, and the unfortunate foreigner who would model his *cuisine* on that of France or even of England, suffers constant annoyance and disappointment.

Anthony Trollope

(1815–1882) Visited the United States briefly in 1858 on his way back to England from the West Indies. He went again in 1861, explaining in his *Autobiography* that 'my mother had thirty years previously written a very popular, but, as I thought, a somewhat unjust book about our cousins over the water. She had seen what was distasteful in the manners of a young people, but had hardly recognized their energy. I had entertained for many years an ambition to follow her footsteps there, and to write another book.' His own criticism of *North America* (1862) was that it 'was a true book. But it was not well done. It is tedious and confused, and will hardly, I think, be of future value to those who wish to make themselves acquainted with the United States.' Modern opinion of the book may very well be different.

Rhode Island

WE HIRED SADDLE-HORSES, and rode out nearly the length of the island. It was all very well, but there was little in it remarkable either as regards cultivation or scenery. We found nothing that it would be possible either to describe or remember. The Americans of the United States have had time to build and populate vast cities, but they have not yet had time to surround themselves with pretty scenery.

Outlying grand scenery is given by nature; but the prettiness of home scenery is a work of art. It comes from the thorough draining of land, from the planting and subsequent thinning of trees, from the controlling of waters, and constant use of minute patches of broken land. In another hundred years or so Rhode Island may be, perhaps, as pretty as the Isle of Wight.

American hotels

I CANNOT SAY that I like hotels in those parts, or indeed the mode of life at American hotels in general. In order that I may not unjustly defame them, I will commence these observations by declaring that they are cheap to those who choose to practise the economy which they encourage, that the viands are profuse in quantity and wholesome in quality, that the attendance is quick and unsparing, and that travellers are never annoyed by that grasping greedy hunger and thirst after francs and shillings which disgrace in Europe many English and many continental inns. All this is, as must be admitted, great praise; and yet I do not like American hotels.

One is in a free country and has come from a country in which one has been brought up to hug one's chains—so at least the English traveller is constantly assured—and yet in an American inn one can never do as one likes. A terrific gong sounds early in the morning, breaking one's sweet slumbers, and then a second gong sounding some thirty minutes later, makes you understand that you must proceed to breakfast, whether you be dressed or no. You certainly can go on with your toilet and obtain your meal after half an hour's delay. Nobody actually scolds you for so doing, but the breakfast is, as they say in this country, 'through'.

You sit down alone, and the attendant stands immediately over you. Probably there are two so standing. They fill your cup the instant it is empty. They tender you fresh food before that which had disappeared from your plate has been swallowed. They begrudge you no amount that you can eat or drink; but they begrudge you a single moment that you sit there neither eating nor drinking. This is your fate if you're late, and therefore as a rule you are not late.

In that case you form one of a long row of eaters who proceed through their work with a solid energy that is past all praise. It is wrong to say that Americans will not talk at their meals. I never met but few who would not talk to me, at any rate till I got to the Far West; but I have rarely found that they would address me first.

The dinner comes early; at least it always does so in New England, and the ceremony is much of the same kind. You came there to eat, and the food is pressed on you almost ad nauseam. But as far as one can see there is no drinking. In these days, I am quite aware that drinking has become improper, even in England. We are apt at home to speak of wine as a thing tabooed, wondering how our fathers lived and swilled. I believe that as a fact we drink as much as they did; but nevertheless that is our theory.

I confess, however, that I like wine. It is very wicked, but it seems to me that my dinner goes down better with a glass of sherry than without it. As a rule I always did get it at hotels in America. But I had no comfort with it. Sherry they do not understand at all. Of course I am only speaking of hotels. Their claret they get exclusively from Mr Gladstone, and looking at the quality, have a right to quarrel even with Mr Gladstone's price.

But it is not the quality of the wine that I hereby intend to subject to ignominy, so much as the want of any opportunity for drinking it. After dinner, if all that I hear be true, the gentlemen occasionally drop into the hotel bar and 'liquor up'. Or rather this is not done specially after dinner, but without prejudice to the hour at any time that may be found desirable. I also have 'liquored up', but I cannot say that I enjoy the process. I do not intend hereby to accuse Americans of drinking too much, but I maintain that what they do drink, they drink in the most uncomfortable manner that the imagination can devise.

Milwaukee and the frontier mind

MILWAUKEE IS A pleasant town, a very pleasant town, containing 45,000 inhabitants. How many of my readers can boast that they know anything of Milwaukee, or even have heard of it? To me its name was unknown until I saw it on huge railway placards stuck up in the smoking-rooms and lounging halls of all American hotels. It is the big town of Wisconsin, whereas Madison is the capital. It stands immediately on the western shore of Lake Michigan, and is very pleasant.

Why it should be so, and why Detroit should be the contrary, I can hardly tell; only I think that the same verdict would be given by any English tourist. It must always be borne in mind that 10,000 or 40,000 inhabitants in an American town, and especially in any new western town, is a number which means much more than would be implied by any similar number as to an old town in Europe. Such a population in America consumes double the amount of beef which it would in England, wears double the amount of clothes, and demands double as much of the comforts of life. If a census could be taken of the watches it would be found, I take it, that the American population possessed among them nearly double as many as would the English; and I fear also that it would be found that many more of the Americans were readers and writers by habit.

In any large town in England it is probable that a higher excellence of education would be found than in Milwaukee, and also a style of life into which more of refinement and more of luxury had found its way. But the general level of these things, of material and intellectual well-being—of beef, that is, and book learning—is no doubt infinitely higher in a new American than in an old English town. Such an animal as a beggar is as much unknown as a mastodon. Men out of work and in want are almost unknown.

I do not say that there are none of the hardships of life—and to them I will come by-and-by; but want is not known as a hardship in these towns, nor is that dense ignorance in which so large a proportion of our town populations is still steeped. And then the town of 40,000 inhabitants is spread over a surface which would suffice in England for a city of four times the size. Our towns in England—and the towns, indeed, of Europe generally—have been built as they have been wanted.

No aspiring ambition as to hundreds of thousands of people warmed the bosoms of their first founders. Two or three dozen men required habitations in the same locality, and clustered them together closely. Many such have failed and died out of the world's notice. Others have thriven, and houses have been packed on to houses till London and Manchester, Dublin and Glasgow have been produced. Poor men have built, or have had built for them, wretched lanes; and rich men have erected grand palaces. From the nature of their beginnings such has, of necessity, been the manner of their creation.

But in America, and especially in western America, there has been no such necessity and there is no such result. The founders of cities have had the experience of the world before them. They have known of sanitary laws as they began. That sewerage, and water, and gas, and good air would be needed for a thriving community has been to them as much a matter of fact as are the well understood combinations between timber and nails, and bricks and mortar. They have known that water carriage is almost a necessity for commercial success, and have chosen their sites accordingly.

Broad streets cost as little, while land by the foot is not as yet of value to be regarded, as those which are narrow; and therefore the sites of towns have been prepared with noble avenues, and imposing streets. A city at its commencement is laid out with an intention that it shall be populous. The houses are not all built at once, but there are the places allocated for them. The streets are not made, but there are the spaces.

Many an abortive attempt at municipal greatness has so been made and then all but abandoned. There are wretched villages with huge straggling parallel ways which would never grow into towns. They are the failures—failures in which the pioneers of civilization, frontier men as they call themselves, have lost their tens of thousands of dollars. But when the success comes, when the happy hit has been made, and the ways of commerce have been truly foreseen with a cunning eye, then a great and prosperous city springs up, ready made, as it were, from the earth.

Such a town is Milwaukee, now containing 45,000 inhabitants, but with room apparently for double that number; with room for four times that number, were men packed as closely there as they are with us.

In the principal business streets of all these towns one sees vast buildings. They are usually called blocks, and are often so dominated in large letters on their front, as Portland Block, Devereux Block, Buel's Block. Such a block may face to two, three, or even four streets, and, as I presume, has generally been a matter of one special speculation. It may be divided into separate houses, or kept for a single purpose, such as that of an hotel, or grouped into shops below, and into various sets of chambers above.

I have had occasion in various towns to mount the stairs within these blocks, and have generally found some portion of them vacant—have sometimes found the greater portion of them vacant. Men build on an enormous scale, three times, ten times as much as is wanted. The only measure of size is an increase on what men have built before.

Monroe P. Jones, the speculator, is very probably ruined, and then begins the world again, nothing daunted. But Jones' block remains, and gives to the city in its aggregate a certain amount of wealth. Or the block becomes at once of service and finds tenants. In which case Jones probably sells it and immediately builds two others twice as big.

That Monroe P. Jones will encounter ruin is almost a matter of course; but then he is none the worse for being ruined. It hardly makes him unhappy. He is greedy of dollars with a terrible covetousness; but he is greedy in order that he may speculate more widely. He would sooner have built Jones' tenth block, with a prospect of completing a twentieth, than settle himself down at rest for life as the owner of a Chatsworth or a Woburn. As for his children he has no desire of leaving them money. Let the girls marry. And for the boys—for them it will be good to begin as he began. If they cannot build blocks for themselves, let them earn their bread in the blocks of other men.

So Monroe P. Jones, with his million dollars accomplished, advances on to a new frontier, goes to work again on a new city, and loses it all. As an individual I differ very much from Monroe P. Jones. The first block accomplished, with an adequate rent accruing to me as the builder, I fancy that I should never try a second. But Jones is undoubtedly the man for the West. It is that love of money to come, joined to a strong disregard for money made, which constitutes the vigorous frontier mind, the true pioneering organization. Monroe P. Jones would be a great man to all posterity, if only he had a poet to sing of his valour.

American workmen

THE LABOURING IRISH in these towns eat meat seven days a week, but I have met many a labouring Irishman among them who has wished himself back in his old log cabin. Industry is a good thing, and there is no bread so sweet as that which is eaten in the sweat of a man's brow, but labour carried to excess wearies the mind as well as the body and the sweat that is ever running makes the bread bitter.

There is, I think, no task-master over free labour so exacting as an American. He knows nothing of hours, and seems to have that idea of a man which a lady always has of a horse. He thinks that he will go for ever. I wish those masons in London who strike for nine hours' work for ten hours' pay could be driven to the labour market of western America for a spell. And moreover, which astonished me, I have seen men driven and hurried, as it were, forced at their work, in a manner which to an English workman would be intolerable.

This surprised me much, as it was at variance with our—or perhaps I should say with my—preconceived ideas as to American freedom. I had fancied that an American citizen would not submit to be driven— that the spirit of the country if not the spirit of the individual would have made it impossible. I thought that the shoe would have pinched quite on the other foot. But I found that such driving did exist; and American masters in the West with whom I had an opportunity of discussing the subject all admitted it.

'Those men'll never half move unless they're driven,' a foreman said to me once as we stood together over some twenty men who were at their work. 'They kinder look for it, and don't well know how to get along when they miss it.'

But there is worse even than this. Wages in these regions are what we should call high. An agricultural labourer will earn perhaps fifteen dollars a month and his board and a town labourer will earn a dollar a day. A dollar may be taken as representing four shillings, though it is in fact more. Food in these parts is much cheaper than in England, and therefore the wages must be considered as very good.

In making, however, a just calculation it must be borne in mind that clothing is dearer than in England and that much more of it is necessary. The wages nevertheless are high, and will enable the labourer to save money—if only he can get them paid. The complaint that wages are held back and not even ultimately paid is very common. There is no fixed rule for satisfying all such claims once a week; and thus debts to labourers are contracted and when contracted are ignored.

With us there is a feeling that it is pitiful, mean almost beyond expression, to wrong a labourer of his hire. We have men who go in debt to tradesmen perhaps without a thought of paying them—but when we speak of such a one who has descended into the lowest mire of insolvency, we say that he has not paid his washerwoman. Out there in the West the washerwoman is as fair game as the tailor, the domestic servant as the wine merchant. If a man be honest he will not willingly take either goods or labour without payment and it may be hard to prove that he who takes the latter is more dishonest than he who takes the former; but with us there is a prejudice in favour of one's washerwoman by which the western mind is not weakened.

'They certainly have to be smart to get it,' a gentleman said to me whom I taxed on the subject. 'You see on the frontier a man is bound to be smart. If he ain't smart he'd better go back East—perhaps as far as Europe. He'll do there.'

New York—and the American face

No OTHER AMERICAN city is so intensely American as New York. It is generally considered that the inhabitants of New England, the Yankees properly so called, have the American characteristics of physiognomy in the fullest degree. The lantern jaws, the thin and lithe body, the dry face on which there has been no tint of the rose since the baby's long clothes were first abandoned, the harsh, thick hair, the thin lips, the intelligent eyes, the sharp voice with the nasal twang—not altogether harsh, though sharp and nasal—all these traits are supposed to belong especially to the Yankee. Perhaps it was so once, but at present they are, I think, more universally common in New York than in any other part of the States. Go to Wall Street, the front of the Astor House, and the regions about Trinity Church, and you will find them at their fullest perfection.

What circumstances of blood or food, of early habit or subsequent education, have created for the latter-day American his present physiognomy? It is as completely marked, as much his own, as is that of any race under the sun that has bred in and in for centuries. But the American owns a more mixed blood than any other race known. The chief stock is English, which is itself so mixed that no man can trace its ramifications. With this are mingled the bloods of Ireland, Holland, France, Sweden and Germany. All this has been done within but a few years, so that the Americans may be said to have no claims to any national type of face.

Nevertheless, no man has a type of face so clearly national as the American. He is acknowledged by it all over the continent of Europe, and on his own side of the water is gratified by knowing that he is never mistaken for his English visitor. I think it comes from the hot-air pipes and from dollar worship. In the Jesuit his mode of dealing with things divine has given a peculiar cast of countenance and why should not the American be similarly moulded by his special aspirations? As to the hot-air pipes, there can, I think, be no doubt that to them is to be charged the murder of all rosy cheeks throughout the States. If the effect was to be noticed simply in the dry faces of the men about Wall Street, I should be very indifferent to the matter. But the young ladies of Fifth Avenue are in the same category. The very pith and marrow of life is baked out of their young bones by the hot-air chambers to which they are accustomed. Hot air is the great destroyer of American beauty.

New York schools

AND AS TO the schools, it is almost impossible to mention them with too high a praise. I am speaking here specially of New York, though I might say the same of Boston, or of all New England. I do not know any contrast that would be more surprising to an Englishman, up to that moment ignorant of the matter, than that which he would find by visiting first of all a free school in London, and then a free school in New York. If he would also learn the number of children that are educated gratuitously in each of the two cities, and also the number in each which altogether lack education, he would, if susceptible of statistics, be surprised also at that.

But seeing and hearing are always more effective than mere figures. The female pupil at a free school in London is, as a rule, either a ragged pauper or a charity girl, if not degraded at least stigmatized by the badges and dress of the Charity. We Englishmen know well the type of each, and have a fairly correct idea of the amount of education which is imparted to them. We see the results afterwards when the same girls become our servants, and the wives of our grooms and porters.

The female pupil at a free school in New York is neither a pauper nor a charity girl. She is dressed with the utmost decency. She is perfectly cleanly. In speaking to her, you cannot in any degree guess whether her father has a dollar a day, or three thousand dollars a year. Nor will you be enabled to guess by the manner in which her associates treat her. As regards her manner to you, it is always the same as though her father were in all respects your equal.

New York: Central Park

BUT THE GLORY of New York is the Central Park—its glory in the mind of all New Yorkers of the present day. The first question asked of you is whether you have seen Central Park, and the second is as to what you think of it. It does not do to say simply that it is fine, grand, beautiful, and miraculous. You must swear by cock and pie that it is more fine, more grand, more beautiful, more miraculous than anything else of the kind anywhere. Here you encounter, in its most annoying form, that necessity for eulogium which presses you everywhere. For, in truth, taken as it is at present, the Central Park is not fine, nor grand, nor beautiful. As to the miracle, let that pass. It is perhaps as miraculous as some other great latter-day miracles.

But the Central Park is a very great fact, and affords a strong additional proof of the sense and energy of the people. It is very large, being over three miles long, and about three-quarters of a mile in breadth. When it was found that New York was extending itself, and becoming one of the largest cities of the world, a space was selected between Fifth and Seventh Avenues, immediately outside the limits of the city as then built, but nearly in the centre of the city as it is intended to be built. The ground around it became at once of great value; and I do not doubt that the present fashion of the Fifth Avenue about Twentieth Street will in course of time move itself up to the Fifth Avenue as it looks, or will look, over the Park at Seventieth, Eightieth, and Ninetieth Streets. The great waterworks of the city bring the Croton River, whence New York is supplied, by an aqueduct over the Harlem river into an enormous reservoir just above the Park; and hence it shall come to pass that there will be water not only for sanitary and useful purposes, but also for ornament.

At present the Park, to English eyes, seems to be all road. The trees are not grown up, and the new embankments, and new lakes, and new ditches, and new paths give to the place anything but a picturesque appearance. The Central Park is good for what it will be, rather than for what it is. The summer heat is so very great that I doubt whether the people of New York will ever enjoy such verdure as our parks show. But there will be a pleasant assemblage of walks and waterworks, with fresh air and fine shrubs and flowers immediately within reach of the citizens. All that art and energy can do will be done, and the Central Park doubtless will become one of the great glories of New York. When I was expected to declare that St James's Park, Green Park, Hyde Park, and Kensington Gardens, altogether were nothing to it, I confess that I could only remain mute.

Washington, D.C.

THE POLITICAL LEADERS of the country have done what they could for Washington. The pride of the nation has endeavoured to sustain the character of its chosen metropolis. There has been no rival, soliciting favour on the strength of other charms. The country has all been agreed on the point since the father of the country first commenced the work. Florence and Rome in Italy have each their pretensions but in the States no other city has put itself forward for the honour of entertaining Congress.

And yet Washington has been a failure. It is commerce that makes great cities, and commerce has refused to back the General's choice. New York and Philadelphia, without any political power, have become great among the cities of the earth. They are beaten by none except by London and Paris. But Washington is but a ragged, unfinished collection of unbuilt broad streets, as to the completion of which there can now, I imagine, be but little hope. Of all places that I know it is the most ungainly and most unsatisfactory—I fear I must also say the most presumptuous in its pretensions. There is a map of Washington accurately laid down; and taking that map with him in his journeyings a man may lose himself in the streets, not as one loses oneself in London between Shoreditch and Russell Square, but as one does so in the deserts of the Holy Land, between Emmaus and Arimathea.

In the first place no one knows where the places are, or is sure of their existence, and then between their presumed localities the country is wild, trackless, unbridged, uninhabited, and desolate. Massachusetts Avenue runs the whole length of the city, and is inserted on the maps as a full-blown street, about four miles in length. Go there, and you will find yourself not only out of town, away from the fields, but you will find yourself beyond the fields, in an uncultivated, undrained wilderness. Tucking your trousers up to your knees you will wade through the bogs, you will lose yourself among rude hillocks, you will be out of reach of humanity. The unfinished dome of the Capitol will loom before you in the distance, and you will think that you approach the ruins of some western Palmyra. If you are a sportsman, you will desire to shoot snipe within sight of the President's house. There is much unsettled land within the States of America, but I think none so desolate in its state of nature as three-fourths of the ground on which is supposed to stand the city of Washington.

The city of Washington is something more than four miles long, and is something more than two miles broad. The land apportioned to it is nearly as compact as may be, and it exceeds in area the size of a parallelogram four miles long by two miles broad. These dimensions are adequate for a noble city, for a city to contain a million of inhabitants. It is impossible to state with accuracy the actual population of Washington, for it fluctuates exceedingly. The place is very full during Congress, and very empty during the recess. By which I mean it to be understood that those streets which are blessed with houses, are full when Congress meets. I do not think that Congress makes much difference to Massachusetts Avenue. I believe that the city never contains as many as eighty thousand, and that its permanent residents are less than sixty thousand.

Thirsting after civil words

THOUGH I HAD felt Washington to be disagreeable as a city, yet I was almost sorry to leave it when the day of my departure came. I had allowed myself a month for my sojourn in the capital, and I had stayed a month to the day. Then came the trouble of packing up, the necessity of calling on a long list of acquaintances one after another, the feeling that bad as Washington might be, I might be going to places that were worse, a conviction that I should get beyond the reach of my letters, and a sort of affection which I had acquired for my rooms. My landlord, being a coloured man, told me he was sorry I was going. Would I not remain? Would I come back to him? Had I been comfortable? Only for so and so and so and so, he would have done better for me. No white American citizen, occupying the position of landlord, would have condescended to such comfortable words. I knew the man did not in truth want me to stay, as a lady and gentleman were waiting to go up in the moment I went out; but I did not the less value the assurance.

One hungers and thirsts after such civil words among American citizens in this class. The clerks and managers at hotels, the officials at railway stations, the cashiers at banks, the women in the shops—ah! they are the worst of all. An American woman who is bound by her position to serve you—who is paid in some shape to supply your wants, whether to sell you a bit of soap or bring you a towel in your bedroom at an hotel—is, I think, of all human creatures, the most insolent. I certainly had a feeling of regret at parting with my coloured friend— and some regret also as regards a few that are white.

Slaves in Kentucky

A FARM IN that part of the States depends, and must depend, on slave-labour. The slaves are a material part of the estate, and as they are regarded by the law as real property an inheritor of land has no alternative but to keep them. A gentleman in Kentucky does not sell his slaves. To do so is considered low and mean, and is opposed to the aristocratic conditions of the country. A man who does so willingly, puts himself beyond the pale of good fellowship with his neighbours. A sale of slaves is regarded as a sign almost of bankruptcy. When a man owns more slaves than he needs, he hires them out by the year; and when he requires more than he owns, he takes them on hire by the year. Care is taken in such hirings not to remove a married man away from his home. The price paid for a Negro's labour at the time of my visit was about a hundred dollars or twenty pounds, for the year; but this price was extremely low in consequence of the war disturbances. The usual price has been fifty or sixty per cent above this. The man who takes the Negro on hire feeds him, clothes him, provides him with a bed, and supplies him with medical attention.

I went into some of their cottages on the estate which I visited, and was not in the least surprised to find them preferable in size, furniture, and all material comforts to the dwellings of most of our own agricultural labourers. Any comparison between the material comfort of a Kentucky slave and an English ditcher and delver would be preposterous. The Kentucky slave never wants for clothing fitted to the weather. He eats meat twice a day, and has three good meals; he knows no limit but his own appetite; his work is light; he has many varieties of amusement; he has instant medical attention at all periods of necessity for himself, his wife, and his children. Of course he pays no rent, fears no banker and knows no hunger. I would not have it supposed that I conceive slavery with all these comforts to be equal to freedom without them; nor do I conceive that the Negro can be made equal to the white man. But in discussing the condition of the Negro, it is necessary that we should understand what are the advantages of which abolition would deprive him, and in what condition he has been placed by the daily receipt of such advantages. If a Negro slave wants new shoes, he asks for them, and receives them, with the undoubted simplicity of a child. Such a state of things has its picturesque patriarchal side; but what would be the state of such a man if he were emancipated tomorrow?

The Westerner

As REGARDS THE people of the West, I must say that they were not such as I expected to find them. With the Northerns we are more or less intimately acquainted. Those Americans whom we meet in our own country, or on the Continent, are generally from the North, or if not so they have that type of American manners which has become familiar to us. They are talkative, intelligent, inclined to be social, though frequently not sympathetically social with ourselves; somewhat *soi-disant*, but almost invariably companionable. As the traveller goes south into Maryland and Washington, the type is not altered to any great extent. The hard intelligence of the Yankee gives place gradually to the softer, and perhaps more polished manner of the Southern. But the change thus experienced is not so great as that between the American of the western and the American of the Atlantic States.

In the West I found the men gloomy and silent—I might almost say sullen. A dozen of them will sit for hours round a stove, speechless. They chew tobacco and ruminate. They are not offended if you speak to them, but they are pleased. They answer with monosyllables, or, if it be practicable, with a gesture of the head. They care for nothing of the graces—or shall I say, for the decencies of life. They are essentially a dirty people. Dirt, untidiness, and noise, seem in nowise to afflict them. Things are constantly done before your eyes, which should be done and might be done behind your back. No doubt we daily come into the closest contact with matters which, if we saw all that pertains to them, would cause us to shake and shudder. In other countries we do not see all this, but in the western States we do. I have eaten in Bedouin tents, and have been ministered to by Turks and Arabs. I have sojourned in the hotels of old Spain, and of Spanish America. I have lived in Connaught, and have taken up my quarters with monks of different nations. I have, as it were, been educated to dirt, and taken out my degree in outward abominations. But my education had not reached a point which would enable me to live at my ease in the western States. A man or woman who could do that may be said to have graduated in the highest honours, and to have become absolutely invulnerable, either through the sense of touch, or by the eye, or by the nose.

No men love money with a more eager love than these western

men, but they bear the loss of it as an Indian bears his torture at the stake. They are energetic in trade; speculating deeply whenever speculation is possible; but nevertheless they are slow in motion, loving to loaf about. They are slow in speech, preferring to sit in silence, with the tobacco between their teeth. They drink, but are seldom drunk to the eye; they begin it early in the morning, and take it in a solemn, sullen, ugly manner, standing always at a bar; swallowing their spirits, and saying nothing as they swallow it. They drink often, and to great excess; but they carry it off without noise, sitting down and ruminating over it with the everlasting cud between their jaws. I believe that a stranger might go to the West, and passing from hotel to hotel through a dozen of them might sit for hours at each in the large everlasting public hall, and never have a word addressed to him.

I cannot part from the West without saying in its favour that there is a certain manliness about its men, which gives them a dignity of their own. It is shown in that very difference of which I have spoken. Whatever turns up the man is still there—still unsophisticated and still unbroken. It has seemed to me that no race of men requires less outward assistance than these pioneers of civilization. They rarely amuse themselves. Food, newspapers, and brandy-smashes suffice for life; and while these last the man is still there in his manhood. The fury of the mob does not shake him, nor the stern countenance of his present martial tyrant. Alas! I cannot stick to my text by calling him a just man. Intelligence, energy, and endurance are his virtues. Dirt, dishonesty, and morning drinks are his vices.

The immigrant transformed

. . . There is the fact. The Irishman when he expatriates himself to one of those American States loses much of that affectionate, confiding, master-worshipping nature which makes him so good a fellow when at home. But he becomes more of a man. He assumes a dignity which he has never known before. He learns to regard his labour as his own property. That which he earns he takes without thanks, but he desires to take no more than he earns. To me he has perhaps become less pleasant than he was. But to himself—! It seems to me that such a man must feel himself half a god, if he has the power of comparing what he is with what he was.

It is right that all this should be acknowledged by us. When we speak of America and her institutions we should remember that she has given to our increasing population rights and privileges which we could not give—which as an old country we probably never can give. That self-asserting, obtrusive independence which so often wounds us is, if viewed aright, but an outward sign of those good things which a new country has produced for its people. Men and women do not beg in the States—they do not often offend you with tattered rags; they do not complain to heaven of starvation; they do not crouch to the ground for halfpence. If they are poor they are not abject in their poverty. They read and write. They walk like human beings made in God's form. They know that they are men and women, owing it to themselves and to the world that they should earn their bread by their labour, but feeling that when earned it is their own. If this be so—if it be acknowledged that it is so—should not such knowledge in itself be sufficient testimony of the success of the country and of her institutions?

Windham Thomas Wyndham-Quin

fourth Earl of Dunraven (1841–1926), Irish politician, racehorse-breeder, yachtsman and sportsman, visited the United States several times, in the last capacity. *The Great Divide: Travels in the Yellowstone Park in the Summer of 1874* appeared in 1876.

Squaw-men in Montana

IN THE AFTERNOON we passed quite a patriarchal camp, composed of
two men with their Indian wives and several children; half a dozen
powerful savage-looking dogs and about fifty horses completed the
party. They had been grazing their stock, hunting and trapping, leading
a nomad, vagabond and delicious life—a sort of mixed existence,
half hunter half herdsman, and had collected a great pile of deer-
hides and beaver-skins. They were then on their way to settlements
to dispose of their peltry, and to get stores and provisions; for they,
too, were proceeding to look for comfortable winter quarters, 'down
the river or up the cañon'.

Encountering people in these solitudes is like meeting a suspicious sail
at sea when your country is at war, and you are uncertain as to the
character, nationality, intentions, size and strength of the stranger. The
latter point is the most important to clear up. Man is the most
dangerous beast that roams the forest, and the first idea that enters
the mind in meeting him or seeing his traces is one of hostility; you take
it for granted that he is an enemy and to be guarded against, until
you ascertain that he is a friend and can be trusted. It is therefore
advisable in such cases to heave-to and reconnoitre, and make signals.
The number of horses staggered us at first, but we soon discovered that
the strangers were white, and, moreover, that there were only two men
in camp; and without more ado we rode in and made friends. What a
lot of mutually interesting information was given and received! We
were outward bound and had the news, and the latitude and the
longitude. They were homeward bound, had been wandering for
months, cut off from all means of communication with the outside
world, and had but the vaguest notion of their position on the globe.

But, though ignorant of external matters and what was going on in
the settlements, they had not lost all desire for information. It seems
natural to suppose that a man condemned to a long sojourn in the
wilds would become quite careless of everything but the wants and
necessities of his daily life. But with the United Stateans, at any rate,
this is not the case. An American, although he lives with an Indian
woman in the forests or on the plains, never quite loses his interest

[296]

in politics and parties; and these two squaw-men were very anxious to hear all about electioneering matters, and to know whether anything important had taken place on the great question that was convulsing their world—that is, the few detached settlements in Montana; namely, whether Virginia City should continue to be the capital, or whether her mantle should be taken from her shoulders and transferred to the back of her more prosperous rival, Helena. They wanted to know also how far it was to Bozeman, and how the place lay by compass.

These men looked very happy and comfortable. Unquestionably the proper way for a man to travel with ease and luxury in these deserts is for him to take unto himself a helpmate chosen from the native population. No amount of art, industry, and study can rival the instinct displayed by savages in making themselves comfortable, and in utilizing for their own benefit all the accidents of Nature. Nobody can choose a camp as they can; nobody knows how to make a fire so quickly or so well; nobody can so wisely pick a shady cool place in summer heat, or choose one sheltered from wind and storms in winter. With an Indian wife to look after his bodily comforts, a man may devote himself to hunting, fishing, or trapping without a thought or care. He may make his mind quite easy about all household matters. His camp will be well-arranged, the tent-pegs driven securely home, the stock watered, picketed, and properly cared for, a good supper cooked, his bed spread out, and everything made comfortable; his clothes and hunting-gear looked after, the buttons sewn on his shirt— if he has got any shirt or any buttons; and all the little trivial incidents of life which, if neglected, wear out one's existence, he will find carefully attended to by a willing and affectionate slave.

They had a lot to tell us also about their travels and adventures, about the wood and water supply, and the abundance or deficiency of game. So we sat down on the bales of beaver-skins and retailed all the civilized intelligence we could think of; and the women came and brought us embers for our pipes, and spread our robes for us and made us at home; and the little fat, chubby children, wild and shy as young wolves, peered at us from behind the tent out of their round, black, beady eyes.

Robert Louis Stevenson

(1850 94) went to California in 1879 in order to marry
Mrs Fanny Osbourne, whom he had met in France. Out of
his experiences in the Far West he wrote *The Amateur Emigrant*,
Across the Plains and *The Silverado Squatters*. He returned
to the United States in 1887–88, living at Saranac Lake, a health
resort in the Adirondacks, where he wrote *The Master of
Ballantrae*.

Notes by the Way to Council Bluffs

Monday.—It was, if I remember rightly, five o'clock when we were all signalled to be present at the Ferry Depot of the railroad. An emigrant ship had arrived at New York on the Saturday night, another on the Sunday morning, our own on Sunday afternoon, a fourth early on Monday; and as there is no emigrant train on Sunday, a great part of the passengers from these four ships was concentrated on the train by which I was to travel. There was a babel of bewildered men, women, and children. The wretched little booking office, and the baggage-room, which was not much larger, were crowded thick with emigrants, and were heavy and rank with the atmosphere of dripping clothes. Open carts full of bedding stood by the half-hour in the rain. A bearded, mildewed little man, whom I take to have been an emigrant agent, was all over the place, his mouth full of brimstone, blustering and interfering. It was plain that the whole system, if system there was, had utterly broken down under the strain of so many passengers.

My own ticket was given me at once, and an oldish man, who preserved his head in the midst of this turmoil, got my baggage registered, and counselled me to stay quietly where I was till he should give me the word to move. I had taken along with me a small valise, a knapsack, which I carried on my shoulders, and in the bag of my railway rug the whole of 'Bancroft's History of the United States' in six fat volumes. It was as much as I could carry with convenience even for short distances, but it insured me plenty of clothing, and the valise was at that moment, and often after, useful for a stool. I am sure I sat for an hour in the baggage-room, and wretched enough it was; yet, when at last the word was passed to me, and I picked up my bundles and got under way, it was only to exchange discomfort for downright misery and danger.

I followed the porters into a long shed reaching downhill from West Street to the river. It was dark, the wind blew clean through it from end to end; and here I found a great block of passengers and baggage, hundreds of one and tons of the other. I feel I shall have a difficulty to make myself believed; and certainly the scene must have been exceptional, for it was too dangerous for daily repetition. It was a tight jam; there was no fairway through the mingled mass of brute and living obstruction. Into the upper skirts of the crowd, porters, infuriated by hurry and overwork, clove their way with shouts. I may say that we stood like sheep, and that the porters charged among us like so many maddened sheep-dogs; and I believe these men were no longer answerable for their acts. It mattered not what they were carrying, they drove straight into the press, and when they could get no farther, blindly discharged their barrowful. With my own hand, for instance, I saved the life of a child as it sat upon its mother's knee, she sitting on a box; and since I heard of no accident, I must suppose that there were many similar interpositions in the course of the evening. It will give some idea of the state of mind to which we were reduced if I tell you that neither the porter nor the mother of the child paid the least attention to my act. It was not till some time after that I understood what I had done myself, for to ward off heavy boxes seemed at the moment a natural incident of human life. Cold, wet, clamour, dead opposition to progress, such as one encounters in an evil dream, had utterly daunted the spirits. We had accepted this purgatory as a child accepts the conditions of the world. For my part I shivered a little, and my back ached wearily; but I believe I had neither a hope nor a fear, and all the activities of my nature had become tributary to one massive sensation of discomfort.

At length, and after how long an interval I hesitate to guess, the crowd began to move, heavily straining through itself. About the same time some lamps were lighted, and threw a sudden flare over the shed. We were being filtered out into the river boat for Jersey City. You may imagine how slowly this filtering proceeded, through the dense, choking crush, every one overladen with packages or children, and yet under the necessity of fishing out his ticket by the way; but it ended at length for me, and I found myself on deck, under a flimsy awning, and with a trifle of elbowroom to stretch and breathe in. This was on the starboard; for the bulk of the emigrants stuck hopelessly on the port side, by which we had entered. These poor people were under a spell of stupor, and did not stir a foot. It rained as heavily as ever, but the wind now came in sudden claps and capfuls, not without danger to a boat so badly ballasted as ours; and we crept over the river in the darkness, trailing one paddle in the water like a wounded duck, and passed ever and again by huge, illuminated steamers running many knots, and heralding their approach by strains of music. The contrast between these pleasure embarkations and our own grim vessel, with her list to port and her freight of wet and silent emigrants, was of that glaring description which we count too obvious for the purposes of art.

The landing at Jersey City was done in a stampede. I had a fixed sense of calamity, and, to judge by conduct, the same persuasion was common to us all. A panic of selfishness, like that produced by fear, presided over the disorder of our landing. People pushed, and elbowed, and ran, their families following how they could. Children fell, and were picked up, to be rewarded by a blow. One child, who had lost her parents, screamed steadily and with increasing shrillness, as though verging towards a fit; an official kept her near him, but no one else seemed so much as to remark her distress; and I am ashamed to say that I ran among the rest. I was so weary that I had twice to make a halt and set down my bundles in the hundred yards or so between the pier and the railway station, so that I was quite wet by the time that I got under cover. There was no waiting-room; the cars were locked; and for at least another hour, or so it seemed, we had to camp upon the draughty, gas-lit platform. I sat on my valise, too crushed to observe my neighbours; but as they were all cold, and wet, and weary, and driven stupidly crazy by the mismanagement to which we had been subjected, I believe they can have been no happier than myself. I bought half a dozen oranges from a boy, for oranges and nuts were the only refection to be had. As only two of them had even a pretence of juice, I threw the other four under the cars, and beheld, as in a dream, grown people and children groping on the track after my leavings.

At last we were admitted into the cars, utterly dejected, and far from dry. For my own part, I got out a clothes-brush, and brushed my trousers as hard as I could, till I had dried them and warmed my blood into the bargain; but no one else, except my next neighbour, to whom I lent the brush, appeared to take the least precaution. As they were, they composed themselves to sleep. I had seen the lights of Philadelphia, and been twice ordered to change carriages and twice countermanded, before I allowed myself to follow their example.

Tuesday.—When I awoke, it was already day; the train was standing idle; I was in the last carriage, and, seeing some others strolling to and fro about the lines, I opened the door and stepped forth, as from a caravan by the wayside. We were near no station, nor even, as far as I could see, within reach of any signal. A green, open, undulating country stretched away upon all sides. Locust trees and a single field

[302]

of Indian corn gave it a foreign grace and interest; but the contours of the land were soft and English. It was not quite England, neither was it quite France; yet like enough either to seem natural in my eyes. And it was in the sky, and not upon the earth, that I was surprised to find a change. Explain it how you may, and for my part I cannot explain it at all, the sun rises with a different splendour in America and Europe. There is more clear gold and scarlet in our old country mornings, more purple, brown, and smoky orange in those of the new. It may be from habit, but to me the coming of day is less fresh and inspiring in the latter; it has a duskier glory, and more nearly resembles sunset; it seems to fit some subsequential, evening epoch of the world, as though America were in fact, and not merely in fancy, farther from the orient of Aurora and the springs of the day. I thought so then, by the railroad-side in Pennsylvania, and I have thought so a dozen times since in far distant parts of the continent. If it be an illusion, it is one very deeply rooted, and in which my eyesight is an accomplice.

Soon after a train whisked by, announcing and accompanying its passage by the swift beating of a sort of chapel-bell upon the engine; and it was for this we had been waiting, we were summoned by the cry of 'All aboard!' and went on again upon our way. The whole line, it appeared, was topsy-turvy; an accident at midnight having thrown all the traffic hours in arrear. We paid for this in the flesh, for we had no meals all that day. Fruit we could buy upon the cars; and now and then we had a few minutes at some station with a meagre show of rolls and sandwiches for sale; but we were so many and so ravenous that, though I tried at every opportunity, the coffee was always exhausted before I could elbow my way to the counter.

Our American sunrise had ushered in a noble summer's day. There was not a cloud; the sunshine was baking; yet in the woody river valleys among which we wound our way, the atmosphere preserved a sparkling freshness till late in the afternoon. It had an inland sweetness and variety to one newly from the sea; it smelt of woods, rivers, and delved earth. These, though in so far a country, were airs from home. I stood on the platform by the hour; and, as I saw, one after another, pleasant villages, carts upon the highway and fishers by the stream, and heard cockcrows and cheery voices in the distance, and beheld the sun no longer shining blankly on the plains of ocean, but striking among shapely hills and his light dispersed and coloured by a thousand accidents of form and surface, I began to exult with myself upon this rise in life like a man who had come into a rich estate. And when I asked the name of the river from the brakesman, and heard that it was called the Susquehanna, the beauty of the name seemed to be part and parcel of the beauty of the land. As when Adam with divine fitness named the creatures, so this word Susquehanna was at once accepted by the fancy. That was the name, as no other could be, for that shining river and desirable valley.

None can care for literature in itself who do not take a special pleasure in the sound of names; and there is no part of the world where nomenclature is so rich, poetical, humorous, and picturesque as the United States of America. All times, races, and languages have brought their contribution. Pekin is in the same State with Euclid, with Bellefontaine, and with Sandusky. Chelsea, with its London associations of red brick, Sloane Square, and the King's Road, is own suburb to stately and primeval Memphis; there they have their seat, translated names of cities, where the Mississippi runs by Tennessee and Arkansas; and both, while I was crossing the continent, lay, watched by armed men, in the horror and isolation of a plague. Old, red Manhattan lies, like an Indian arrow-head under a steam factory, below anglified New York. The names of the States and Territories themselves form a chorus of sweet and most romantic vocables: Delaware, Ohio, Indiana, Florida, Dakota, Iowa, Wyoming, Minnesota, and the Carolinas; there are few poems with a nobler music for the ear: a songful, tuneful land; and if the new Homer shall arise from the Western continent, his verse will be enriched, his pages sung spontaneously, with the names of states and cities that would strike the fancy in a business circular.

Late in the evening we were landed in a waiting-room at Pittsburg. I had now under my charge a young and sprightly Dutch widow with her children; these I was to watch over providentially for a certain distance farther on the way; but as I found she was furnished with a basket of eatables, I left her in the waiting-room to seek a dinner for myself.

I mention this meal, not only because it was the first of which I had partaken for about thirty hours, but because it was the means of my first introduction to a coloured gentleman. He did me the honour to wait upon me after a fashion, while I was eating; and with every word, look and gesture marched me farther into the country of surprise. He was indeed strikingly unlike the negroes of Mrs Beecher Stowe, or the Christy Minstrels of my youth. Imagine a gentleman, certainly somewhat dark, but of a pleasant warm hue, speaking English with a slight and rather odd foreign accent, every inch a man of the world, and armed with manners so patronizingly superior that I am at a loss to name their parallel in England. A butler perhaps rides as high over the unbutlered, but then he sets you right with a reserve and a sort of sighing patience which one is often moved to admire. And again, the abstract butler never stoops to familiarity. But the coloured gentleman will pass you a wink at a time; he is familiar like an upperform boy to a fag; he unbends to you like Prince Hal with Poins and Falstaff. He makes himself at home and welcome. Indeed, I may say, this waiter behaved himself to me throughout that supper much as, with us, a young, free, and not very self-respecting master might behave to a good-looking chambermaid. I had come prepared to pity the poor negro, to put him at his ease, to prove in a thousand condescensions that I was no sharer in the prejudice of race; but I assure you I put my patronage away for another occasion, and had the grace to be pleased with that result.

Seeing he was a very honest fellow, I consulted him upon a point of etiquette: if one should offer to tip the American waiter? Certainly not, he told me. Never. It would not do. They considered themselves too highly to accept. They would even resent the offer. As for him and me, we had enjoyed a very pleasant conversation; he, in particular, had found much pleasure in my society; I was a stranger; this was exactly one of these rare conjectures. . . . Without being very clear-seeing, I can still perceive the sun at noonday; and the coloured gentleman deftly pocketed a quarter.

San Francisco

FANCY APART, SAN FRANCISCO is a city beleaguered with alarms. The lower parts, along the bay side, sit on piles; old wrecks decaying, fish dwelling unsunned, beneath the populous houses; and a trifling subsidence might drown the business quarters in an hour. Earthquakes are not only common, they are sometimes threatening in their violence; the fear of them grows yearly on a resident; he begins with indifference, ends in sheer panic; and no one feels safe in any but a wooden house. Hence it comes that, in that rainless clime, the whole city is built of timber—a woodyard of unusual extent and complication; that fires spring up readily, and served by the unwearying trade-wind, swiftly spread; that all over the city there are fire-signal boxes; that the sound of the bell, telling the number of the threatened ward, is soon familiar to the ear; and that nowhere else is the art of the fireman carried to so nice a point.

Next, perhaps, in order of strangeness to the rapidity of its appearance, is the mingling of the races that combine to people it. The town is essentially not Anglo-Saxon; still more essentially not American. The Yankee and the Englishman find themselves alike in a strange country. There are none of these touches—not of nature, and I dare scarcely say of art—by which the Anglo-Saxon feels himself at home in so great a diversity of lands. Here, on the contrary, are airs of Marseilles and of Pekin. The shops along the street are like the consulates of different nations. The passers-by vary in feature like the slides of a magic-lantern. For we are here in that city of gold to which adventurers congregated out of all the winds of heaven; we are in a land that till the other day was ruled and peopled by the countrymen of Cortes; and the sea that laves the piers of San Francisco is the ocean of the East and of the isles of summer. There goes the Mexican, unmistakeable; there the blue-clad Chinaman with his white slippers; there the soft-spoken, brown Kanaka, or perhaps a waif from far-away Malaya. You hear French, German, Italian, Spanish, and English indifferently. You taste the food of all nations in the various restaurants; passing from a French *prix-fixe* where every one is French, to a roaring German ordinary where every one is German; ending, perhaps, in a cool and silent Chinese tea-house. For every man, for every race and nation, that city is a foreign city; humming with foreign tongues and customs; and yet each and all have made themselves at home. The Germans have a German theatre and innumerable beer-gardens. The French Fall of the Bastille is celebrated with squibs and banners, and marching patriots, as noisily as the American Fourth of July. The Italians have their dear domestic quarter, with Italian caricatures in the windows, Chianti and polenta in the taverns. The Chinese are settled as in China. The goods they offer for sale are as foreign as the lettering on the signboard of the shop: dried fish from the China seas; pale cakes and sweetmeats—the like, perhaps, once eaten by Badroubadour; nuts of unfriendly shape; ambiguous, outlandish vegetables, misshapen, lean, or bulbous—telling of a country where the trees are not as our trees,

[306]

and the very back-garden is a cabinet of curiosities. The joss-house is hard by, heavy with incense, packed with quaint carvings and the paraphernalia of a foreign ceremonial. All these you behold, crowded together in the narrower arteries of the city, cool, sunless, a little mouldy, with the unfamiliar faces at your elbow, and the high, musical sing-song of that alien language in your ears. Yet the houses are of Occidental build; the lines of a hundred telegraphs pass, thick as ship's rigging, overhead, a kite hanging among them, perhaps, or perhaps two, one European, one Chinese, in shape and colour; mercantile Jack, the Italian fisher, the Dutch merchant, the Mexican vaquero, go hustling by; at the sunny end of the street, a thoroughfare roars with European traffic; and meanwhile, high and clear, out breaks perhaps the San Francisco fire-alarm, and people pause to count the strokes, and in the station of the double fire-service you know that the electric bells are ringing, the traps opening, and clapping to, and the engine, manned and harnessed, being whisked into the street, before the sound of the alarm has ceased to vibrate on your ear . . .

With all this mass of nationalities, crime is common. There are rough quarters where it is dangerous o'nights; cellars of public entertainment which the wary pleasure-seeker chooses to avoid. Concealed weapons are unlawful, but the law is continually broken. One editor was shot dead while I was there; another walked the streets accompanied by a bravo, his guardian angel. I have been quietly eating a dish of oysters in a restaurant, where, not more than ten minutes after I left, shots were exchanged and took effect; and one night about ten o'clock, I saw a man standing watchfully at a street-corner with a long Smith-and-Wesson glittering in his hand behind his back. Somebody had done something he should not, and was being looked for with a vengeance. It is odd, too, that the seat of the last vigilance committee I know of—a mediaeval *Vehmgericht*—was none other than the Palace Hotel, the world's greatest caravanserai, served by lifts and lit with electricity; where, in the great glazed court, a band nightly discourses music from a grove of palms. So do extremes meet in this city of contrasts: extremes of wealth and poverty, apathy and excitement, the conveniences of civilization and the red justice of Judge Lynch . . .

The great net of straight thoroughfares lying at right angles, east and west and north and south, over the shoulders of Nob Hill, the hill of palaces, must certainly be counted the best part of San Francisco. It is there that the millionaires are gathered together vying with each other in display. From thence, looking down over the business wards of the city, we can descry a building with a little belfry, and that is the Stock Exchange, the heart of San Francisco: a great pump we might call it, continually pumping up the savings of the lower quarters into the pockets of the millionaires upon the hill. But these same thoroughfares that enjoy for awhile so elegant a destiny have their lines prolonged into more unpleasant places. Some meet their fate in the sands; some must take a cruise in the ill-famed China quarters; some run into the sea; some perish unwept among pig-sties and rubbish-heaps.

Nob Hill comes, of right, in the place of honour; but the two other hills of San Francisco are more entertaining to explore. On both there are a world of old wooden houses snoozing together all forgotten. Some are of the quaintest design, others only romantic by neglect and age. Some have been almost undermined by new thoroughfares, and sit high up on the margin of the sandy cutting, only to be reached by stairs. Some are curiously painted, and I have seen one at least with ancient carvings panelled in its wall. Surely they are not of Californian building, but far voyagers from round the stormy Horn, like those who sent for them and dwelt in them at first. Brought to be the favourites of the wealthy, they have sunk into these poor, forgotten districts, where, like old town toasts, they keep each other silently in countenance. Telegraph Hill and Rincon Hill, these are the two dozing quarters that I recommend to the city dilettante. There stand these forgotten houses, enjoying the unbroken sun and quiet. There, if there were such an author, would the San Francisco Fortuné de Boisgobey pitch the first chapter of his mystery. But the first is the quainter of the two, and commands, moreover, a noble view. As it stands at the turn of the bay, its skirts are all waterside, and round from North Reach to the Bay Front you can follow doubtful paths from one quaint corner to another. Everywhere the same tumble-down decay and sloppy progress, new things yet unmade, old things tottering to their fall; everywhere the same out-at-elbows, many-nationed loungers at dim, irregular grog-shops; everywhere the same sea-air and isleted sea-prospect; and for a last and more romantic note, you have on the one hand Tamalpais standing high in the blue air, and on the other the tail of that long alignment of three-masted, full-rigged, deep-sea ships that make a forest of spars along the eastern front of San Francisco. In no other port is such a navy congregated. For the coast trade is so trifling, and the ocean trade from round the Horn so large, that the smaller ships are swallowed up, and can do nothing to confuse the majestic order of these merchant princes. In an age when the ship-of-the-line is already a thing of the past, and we can never again hope to go coasting in a cock-boat between the 'wooden walls' of a squadron at anchor, there is perhaps no place on earth where power and beauty of sea architecture can be so perfectly enjoyed as in this bay.

Matthew Arnold

(1822–1888) visited the United States in 1883 and then in 1886. Regarded as the archetype of the superior, supercilious Englishman, he received the full treatment from the American press. His conclusions on America, based on lectures delivered there, were published as *Civilization in the United States* in 1888.

Civilization in the United States

PERHAPS IT IS not likely that any one will now remember what I said three years ago here about the success of the Americans in solving the political and social problem. I will sum it up in the briefest possible manner. I said that the United States had constituted themselves in a modern age; that their institutions complied well with the form and pressure of those circumstances and conditions which a modern age presents. Quite apart from all question how much of the merit for this may be due to the wisdom and virtue of the American people, and how much to their good fortune, it is undeniable that their institutions do work well and happily. The play of their institutions suggests, I said, the image of a man in a suit of clothes which fits him to perfection, leaving all his movements unimpeded and easy; a suit of clothes loose where it ought to be loose, and sitting close where its sitting close is an advantage; a suit of clothes able, moreover, to adapt itself naturally to the wearer's growth, and to admit of all enlargements as they successively arise.

So much as to the solution, by the United States, of the political problem. As to the social problem, I observed that the people of the United States were a community singularly free from the distinction of classes, singularly homogeneous; that the division between rich and poor was consequently less profound there than in countries where the distinction of classes accentuates that division. I added that I believed there was exaggeration in the reports of their administrative and judicial corruption; and altogether, I concluded, the United States, politically and socially, are a country living prosperously in a natural modern condition, and conscious of living prosperously in such a condition. And being in this healthy case, and having this healthy consciousness, the community there uses its understanding with the soundness of health; it in general, as to its own political and social concerns, sees clear and thinks straight. Comparing the United States with ourselves, I said that while they are in this natural and healthy condition, we on the contrary are so little homogeneous, we are living with a system of classes so intense, with institutions and a society so little modern, so unnaturally complicated, that the whole action of our minds is hampered and falsened by it; we are in consequence wanting in lucidity, we do not see clear or think straight, and the Americans have here much the advantage of us.

Yet we find an acute and experienced Englishman saying that there is no country, calling itself civilized, where one would not rather live than in the United States, except Russia! The civilization of the United States must somehow, if an able man can think thus, have short-comings, in spite of the country's success and prosperity. What is civilization? It is the humanization of man in society, the satisfaction for him, in society, of the true law of human nature. Man's study, says Plato, is to discover the right answer to the question *how to live*? our aim, he says, is very and true life. We are more or less civilized as we come more or less near to this aim, in that social state which the pursuit of our aim essentially demands. But several elements of powers, as I have often insisted, go to build up a complete human life. There is the power of conduct, the power of intellect and knowledge, the power of beauty, the power of social life and manners; we have instincts responding to them all, requiring them all. And we are perfectly civilized only when all these instincts in our nature, all these elements in our civilization, have been adequately recognized and satisfied. But of course this adequate recognition and satisfaction of all the elements in question is impossible; some of them are recognized more than others, some of them more in one community, some in an-other; and the satisfactions found are more or less worthy.

And meanwhile, people use the term *civilization* in the loosest pos-sible way, for the most part attaching to it, however, in their own mind some meaning connected with their own preferences and ex-periences. The most common meaning thus attached to it is perhaps that of satisfaction, not of all the main demands of human nature, but of the demand for the comforts and conveniences of life, and of this demand as made by the sort of person who uses the term.

Now we should always attend to the common and prevalent use of an important term. Probably, Sir Lepel Griffin had this notion of the comforts and conveniences of life much in his thoughts when he re-proached American civilization with its shortcomings. For men of his kind, and for all that large number of men, so prominent in this country and who make their voice so much heard, men who have been at the public schools and universities, men of the professional and official class, men who do the most part of our literature and our journalism, America is not a comfortable place of abode. A man of this sort has in England everything in his favour; society appears organized expressly for his advantage. A Rothschild or a Vanderbilt can buy his way anywhere, and can have what comforts and luxuries he likes whether in America or in England. But it is in England that an income of from three or four to fourteen or fifteen hundred a year does so much for its possessor, enables him to live with so many of the conveniences of far richer people. For his benefit, his benefit above all, clubs are organized and hansom cabs ply; service is abundant, porters stand waiting at the railway stations. In America all luxuries are dear except oysters and ice; service is in general scarce and bad; a club is a most expensive luxury; the cab-rates are prohibitive—more than half the people who in England would use cabs must in America use the horse-cars, the tram. The charges of tailors and mercers are about a third higher than they are with us ...

On the other hand, for that immense class of people whose income is less than three or four hundred a year, things in America are favourable. It is easier for them there than in the Old World to rise and to make their fortune; but I am not now speaking of that. Even without making their fortune, even with their income below three or four hundred a year, things are favourable to them in America, society seems organized there for their benefit. To begin with, the humbler kind of work is better paid in America than with us, the higher kind worse. The official, for instance, gets less, his office-keeper gets more. The public ways are abominably cut up by rails and blocked with horse-cars; but the inconvenience is for those who use private carriages and cabs, the convenience is for the bulk of the community who but for the horse-cars would have to walk. The ordinary railway cars are not delightful, but they are cheap, and they are better furnished and in winter are warmer than third-class carriages in England. Luxuries are, as I have said, very dear—above all, European luxuries; but a working man's clothing is nearly as cheap as in England, and plain food is on the whole cheaper. Even luxuries of a certain kind are within a labouring man's easy reach. I have mentioned ice, I will mention fruit also. The abundance and cheapness of fruit is a great boon to people of small incomes in America. Do not believe the Americans when they extol their peaches as equal to any in the world; they are not to be compared to peaches grown under glass. Do not believe that the American Newtown pippins appear in the New York and Boston fruit-shops as they appear in those of London and Liverpool; or that the Americans have any pear to give you like the Marie Louise. But what labourer, or artisan,

[314]

or small clerk, ever gets hot-house peaches, or Newtown pippins, or Marie Louise pears? Not such good pears, apples, and peaches as those, but pears, apples, and peaches by no means to be despised, such people and their families in America get in plenty.

Well, now, what would a philosopher or a philanthropist say in this case? Which would he say was the more civilized condition—that of the country where the balance of advantage, as to the comforts and conveniences of life, is greatly in favour of the people with incomes below three hundred a year, or that of the country where it is greatly in favour of those with incomes above that sum?

Many people will be ready to give an answer to that question without the smallest hesitation. They will say that they are, and that all of us ought to be, for the greatest happiness of the greatest number. However, the question is not one which I feel bound now to discuss and answer. Of course, if happiness and civilization consist in being plentifully supplied with the comforts and conveniences of life, the question presents little difficulty. But I believe neither that happiness consists, merely or mainly, in being plentifully supplied with the comforts and convenience of life, nor that civilization consists in being so supplied; therefore I leave the question unanswered.

I prefer to seek some other and better tests by which to try the civilization of the United States. I have often insisted on the need of more equality in our own country, and on the mischiefs caused by inequality over here. In the United States there is not our intense division of classes, our inequality. Let me mention two points in the system of social life and manners over there in which this equality seems to me to have done good. The first is a mere point of form, but it has significance. Every one knows it is the established habit with us in England, if we write to people supposed to belong to the class of gentlemen, of addressing them by the title of *Esquire*, while we keep *Mr* for people not supposed to belong to that class. If we think of it, could one easily find a habit more ridiculous, more offensive? The title of *Esquire*, like most of our titles, comes out of the great frippery shop of the Middle Age; it is alien to the sound taste and manner of antiquity, when men said Pericles and Camillus. But unlike other titles, it is applied or withheld quite arbitrarily. Surely, where a man has no specific title proper to him, the one plain title of *Master* or *Mr* is enough, and we need not be cumbered with a second title of *Esquire*, now quite unmeaning, to draw an invidious and impossible line of distinction between those who are gentlemen and those who are not; as if we actually wished to provide a source of embarrassment for the sender of a letter, and of mortification for the receiver of it . . .

The other point goes deeper. Much may be said against the voices and intonation of American women. But almost every one acknowledges that there is a charm in American women—a charm which you find in almost all of them, wherever you go. It is the charm of a natural manner, a manner not self-conscious, artificial, and constrained. It may not be a beautiful manner always, but it is almost always a natural manner, a free and happy manner; and this gives pleasure. Here we have, undoubtedly, a note of civilization, and an evidence, at the same time, of the good effect of equality upon social life and manners. I have often heard it observed that a perfectly natural manner is as rare among English women of the middle classes as it is general among American women of like condition with them. And so far as the observation is true, the reason of its truth no doubt is, that the English woman is living in the presence of an upper class, as it is called—in presence, that is, of a class of woman recognized as being the right thing in style and manner, finding this or that to be amiss with it, this or that to be vulgar. Hence self-consciousness and constraint in her. The American woman lives in presence of no such class; there may be circles trying to pass themselves off as such a class, giving themselves airs as such, but they command no recognition, no authority. The American woman in general is perfectly unconcerned about their opinion, is herself, enjoys her existence, and has consequently a manner happy and natural. It is her great charm; and it is moreover, as I have said, a real note of civilization, and one which has to be reckoned to the credit of American life, and of its equality.

But we must get nearer still to the heart of the question raised as to the character and worth of American civilization. I have said how much the word civilization really means—the humanization of man in society; his making progress there towards his true and full humanity. Partial and material achievement is always being put forward as civilization. We hear a nation called highly civilized by reason of its industry, commerce, and wealth, or by reason of its liberty or equality, or by reasons of its numerous churches, schools, libraries, and newspapers. But there is something in human nature, some instinct of growth, some law of perfection, which rebels against this narrow account of the matter. And perhaps what human nature demands in civilization, over and above all those obvious things which first occur to our thoughts—what human nature, I say, demands in civilization, is best described by the word *interesting*. Here is the extraordinary charm of the old Greek civilization—that it is so *interesting*. Do not tell me only, says human nature, of the magnitude of your industry and commerce; of the beneficence of your institutions, your freedom, your equality; of the great and growing number of your churches and schools, libraries and newspapers; tell me also if your civilization—which is the grand name you give to all this development—tell me if your civilization is *interesting* . . .

Now, the great sources of the *interesting* are distinction and beauty: that which is elevated and that which is beautiful. Let us take the beautiful first, and consider how far it is present in American civilization. Evidently this is that civilization's weak side. There is little to nourish and delight the sense of beauty there. In the long-settled States east of the Alleghanies the landscape in general is not interesting, the climate harsh and in extremes. The Americans are restless, eager to better themselves and to make fortunes; the inhabitant does not strike his roots lovingly down into the soil, as in rural England. In the valley of the Connecticut you will find farm after farm which the Yankee settler has abandoned in order to go West, leaving the farm to some new Irish immigrant. The charm of beauty which comes from ancientness and permanence of rural life the country could not yet have in a high degree, but it has it in an even less degree than might be expected. Then the Americans come originally, for the most part, from that great class in English society amongst whom the sense for conduct and business is much more strongly developed than the sense for beauty. If we in England were without the cathedrals, parish churches, and castles of the catholic and feudal age, but had only the towns and buildings which the rise of our middle class has created in the modern age, we should be in much the same case as the Americans. . . . In general, where the Americans succeed best in their architecture—in that art so indicative and educative of a people's sense for beauty—is in the fashion of their villa cottages in wood. These are often original and at the same time very pleasing, but they are pretty and coquettish, not beautiful. Of the really beautiful in the other arts, and in literature, very little has been produced there as yet . . .

So much as to beauty, as to the provision, in the United States, for the sense of beauty. As to distinction, and the interest which human nature seeks from enjoying the effect made upon it by what is elevated, the case is much the same. There is very little to create such an effect, very much to thwart it. Goethe says somewhere that 'the thrill of awe is the best thing humanity has':

Das Schaudern ist der Menschheit bestes Theil.

But, if there be a discipline in which the Americans are wanting, it is the discipline of awe and respect. An austere and intense religion imposed on their Puritan founders the discipline of respect, and so provided for them the thrill of awe; but this religion is dying out. The Americans have produced plenty of men strong, shrewd, upright, able, effective; very few who are highly distinguished. Alexander Hamilton is indeed a man of rare distinction; Washington, though he has not the mental distinction of Pericles or Caesar, has true distinction of style and character. But these men belong to the pre-American age. Lincoln's recent American biographers declare that Washington is but an Englishman, an English officer; the typical American, they say, is Abraham Lincoln. Now Lincoln is shrewd, sagacious, humorous, honest, courageous, firm; he is a man with qualities deserving the most sincere esteem and praise, but he has not distinction.

In truth everything is against distinction in America, and against the sense of elevation to be gained through admiring and respecting it. The glorification of 'the average man', who is quite a religion with statesmen and publicists there, is against it. The addiction to 'the funny man', who is a national misfortune there, is against it. Above all, the newspapers are against it.

It is often said that every nation has the government it deserves. What is much more certain is that every nation has the newspapers it deserves. The newspaper is the direct product of the want felt; the supply answers closely and inevitably to the demand. I suppose no one knows what the American newspapers are, who has not been obliged, for some length of time, to read either those newspapers or none at all. Powerful and valuable contributions occur scattered about in them. But on the whole, and taking the total impression and effect made by them, I should say that if one were searching for the best means to efface and kill in a whole nation the discipline of respect, the feeling for what is elevated, one could not do better than take the American newspapers . . .

The Americans used to say to me that what they valued was news, and that this their newspapers gave them. I at last made the reply: 'Yes, news for the servants' hall!' I remember that a New York newspaper, one of the first I saw after landing in the country, had a long account, with the prominence we should give to the illness of the German Emperor or the arrest of the Lord Mayor of Dublin, of a young woman who had married a man who was a bag of bones, as we say, and who used to exhibit himself as a skeleton; of her growing horror in living with this man, and finally of her death. All this in the most minute detail, and described with all the writer's powers of rhetoric. This has always remained by me as a specimen of what the Americans call news ...

I once declared that in England the born lover of ideas and of light could not but feel that the sky over his head is of brass and iron. And so I say that, in America, he who craves for the *interesting* in civilization, he who requires from what surrounds him satisfaction for his sense of beauty, his sense for elevation, will feel the sky over his head to be of brass and iron. The human problem, then, is as yet solved in the United States most imperfectly; a great void exists in the civilization over there: a want of what is elevated and beautiful, of what is interesting.

The want is grave; it was probably, though he does not exactly bring it out, influencing Sir Lepel Griffin's feelings when he said that America is one of the last countries in which one would like to live. The want is such as to make any educated man feel that many countries, much less free and prosperous than the United States, are yet more truly civilized; have more which is interesting, have more to say to the soul; are countries, therefore, in which one would rather live.

The want is graver because it is so little recognized by the mass of Americans; nay, so loudly denied by them. If the community over there perceived the want and regretted it, sought for the right ways of remedying it, and resolved that remedied it should be; if they said, or even if a number of leading spirits amongst them said: 'Yes, we see what is wanting to our civilization, we see that the average man is a danger, we see that our newspapers are a scandal, that bondage to the common and ignoble is our snare; but under the circumstances our civilization could not well have been expected to begin differently. What you see are *beginnings*, they are crude, they are too predominantly material, they omit much, leave much to be desired—but they could not have been otherwise, they have been inevitable, and we will rise above them'; if the Americans frankly said this, one would have not a word to bring against it. One would *then* insist on no shortcoming, one would accept their admission that the human problem is at present quite insufficiently solved by them, and would press the matter no further. One would congratulate them on having solved the political problem and the social problem so successfully, and only remark, as I have said already, that in seeing clear and thinking straight on *our* political and social questions, we have great need to follow the example they set us on theirs.

But now the Americans seem, in certain manners, to have agreed, as a people, to deceive themselves, to persuade themselves that they have what they have not, to cover the defects of their civilization by boasting, to fancy that they well and truly solve, not only the political and social problem, but the human problem too. One would say that they do really hope to find in tall talk and inflated sentiment a substitute for that real sense of elevation which human nature, as I have said, instinctively craves—and a substitute which may do as well as the genuine article. The thrill of awe, which Goethe pronounces to be the best thing humanity has, they would fain create by proclaiming themselves at the top of their voices to be 'the greatest nation on earth', by assuring one another, in the language of their national historian, that 'American democracy proceeds in its ascent as uniformly and majestically as the laws of being, and is as certain as the decrees of eternity'.

Or, again, far from admitting that their newspapers are a scandal, they assure one another that their newspaper press is one of their most signal distinctions. Far from admitting that in literature they have as yet produced little that is important, they play at treating American literature as if it were a great independent power; they reform the spelling of the English language by the insight of their average man. For every English writer they have an American writer to match. And him good Americans read; the Western States are at this moment being nourished and formed, we hear, on the novels of a native author called Roe, instead of those of Scott and Dickens. Far from admitting that their average man is a danger, and that his predominance has brought about a plentiful lack of refinement, distinction, and beauty, they declare in the words of my friend Colonel Higginson, a prominent critic at Boston, that 'Nature said, some years since: "Thus far the English is my best race, but we have had Englishmen enough; put in one drop more of nervous fluid and make the American". And with that drop a new range of promise opened on the human race, and a lighter, finer, more highly organized type of mankind was born.'

The worst of it is, that all this tall talk and self-glorification meets with hardly any rebuke from sane criticism over there. I will mention, in regard to this, a thing which struck me a good deal. A Scotchman who has made a great fortune in Pittsburg, a kind friend of mine, one of the most hospitable and generous of men, Mr Andrew Carnegie, published a year or two ago a book called *Triumphant Democracy*, a most splendid picture of American progress. The book is full of valuable information, but religious people thought that it insisted too much on mere material progress, and did not enough set forth America's deficiencies and dangers. And a friendly clergyman in Massachusetts, telling me how he regretted this, and how apt the Americans are to shut their eyes to their own dangers, put into my hands a volume written by a leading minister among the Congregationalists, a very prominent man, which he said supplied a good antidote to my friend Mr Carnegie's book. The volume is entitled *Our Country*. I read it through. The author finds in evangelical Protestantism, as the orthodox Protestant sects present it, the grand remedy for the deficiencies and dangers of America. On this I offer no criticism; what struck me, and that on which I wish to lay stress, is, the writer's entire failure to perceive that such self-glorification and self-deception as I have been mentioning is one of America's dangers, or even that it *is* self-deception at all. He himself shares in all the self-deception of the average man among his countrymen, he flatters it. In the very points where a serious critic would find the Americans most wanting he finds them superior; only they require to have a good dose of evangelical Protestantism added. 'Ours is the elect nation,' preaches this reformer of American faults—'ours is the elect nation for the age to come. We are the chosen people.' Already, says he, we are taller and heavier than other men, longer lived than other men, richer and more energetic than other men, above all, 'of finer nervous organization' than other men. Yes, this people, who endure to have the American newspaper for their daily reading, and to have their habitation in Briggsville, Jacksonville, and Marcellus—this people is of finer, more delicate nervous organization than other nations!

. . . Common-sense criticism, I repeat, of all this hollow stuff there is in America next to none. There are plenty of cultivated, judicious, delightful individuals there. They are our hope and America's hope; it is through their means that improvement must come. They know perfectly well how false and hollow the boastful stuff talked is; but they let the storm of self-laudation rage, and say nothing. For political opponents and their doings there are in America hard words to be heard in abundance; for the real faults in American civilization, and for the foolish boasting which prolongs them, there is hardly a word of regret or blame, at least in public. Even in private, many of the most cultivated Americans shrink from the subject, are irritable and thin-skinned when it is canvassed. Public treatment of it, in a cool and sane spirit of criticism, there is none.

To sum up, then. What really dissatisfies in American civilization is the want of the *interesting*, a want due chiefly to the want of those elements of the interesting, which are elevation and beauty.. And the want of these elements is increased and prolonged by the Americans being assured that they have them when they have them not. And it seems to me that what the Americans now most urgently require, is not so much a vast additional development of orthodox Protestantism, but rather a steady exhibition of sane and cool criticism by their men of light and leading over there. And perhaps the very first step of such men should be to insist on having for America, and to create if need be, better newspapers.

To us, too, the future of the United States is of incalculable importance. Already we feel their influence much, and we shall feel it more. We have a good deal to learn from them; we shall find in them, also, many things to beware of, many points in which it is to be hoped our democracy may not be like theirs. As our country becomes more democratic, the malady here may no longer be that we have an upper class materialized, a middle class vulgarized, and a lower class brutalized. But the predominance of the common and ignoble, born of the predominance of the average man, is a malady too. That the common and ignoble is human nature's enemy, that, of true human nature, distinction and beauty are needs, that a civilization is insufficient where these needs are not satisfied, faulty where they are thwarted, is an instruction of which we, as well as the Americans, may greatly require to take fast hold, and not let go. We may greatly require to keep, as if it were our life, the doctrine that we are failures after all, if we cannot eschew vain boasting and vain imaginations, eschew what flatters in us the common and ignoble, and approve things that are truly excellent.

Sir Henry Lepel Griffin

(1840–1908) served in the Bengal Civil Service and in 1885 was British Envoy Extraordinary to Pekin. *The Great Republic* appeared in 1884.

Niagara

THE ONLY SIGHT which, in American eyes, disputes the pre-eminence
of the Chicago slaughter-yards is Niagara, and there may be some
who would unhesitatingly assign it the palm. Its chief beauty consists
in its being the largest waterfall in the world, with greater capacity
than any other for producing by water-power those manufactured
abominations which, as American fabrics or novelties, are gradually
debasing the taste of the civilized world. Its one drawback is that the
left bank of the Niagara river being English territory and the main
body of the fall being situated therein, Americans are unable to claim
a monopoly in this natural marvel for the States. It is fortunate for
posterity that the Canadian English have control over the finer portion
of the Niagara scenery, as this alone protects it from such ruin as
vulgarity and greed combined can bring on nature. On a small island,
midway across the American fall, the authorities of the State of New
York—whose names I would hand down to eternal infamy were I not
convinced that, being New York officials, they are already as infamous
as it is possible for officials to be—have permitted the erection of a
paper-mill, hideous in its architectural deformity, and blighting with a
curse the beauty of Niagara. It is not possible to describe the effect that
this building has upon a sensitive visitor. The outrage on good taste
is so extreme, and the state of nervous irritation induced by the unconscious vandalism of the American people is so acute, that I am disposed
to consider a visit to Niagara a source of more pain than pleasure. This
mill is the outward and visible sign, blazoned voluntarily to the world,
of American Philistinism. The Boston journals may announce the
advent of the millennium of good taste; Messrs James and Howells
and White may set forth their poor platitudes to prove the cultured
and refined sentiments of their countrymen; but the Niagara paper-mill
raises its tall chimney high above the everlasting roar of the torrent to
give them all the lie.

Nor is this the only outrage on good taste at Niagara. The torture of
the paper-mill ceases with the daylight, and its presence may be forgotten. The traveller then, in frantic search for an emotion, may hope
to wander alone to the edge of the avalanche of waters, and there

commune with such soul as waiters, rival touts, and coachmen may have allowed him to retain. In the solemn moonlight the wonderful pageant seems more weird and mysterious than ever. But what is this new and unknown effect of the moonbeams? Is it—yes, it is—the coloured limelight, red, green and blue, thrown upon the hoary fleece of Niagara by American cockneys! In sheer disgust and exasperation the traveller turns his back on the insult and retires sulkily to bed . . .

On the whole, and always excepting the Chicago pig-shambles, I am disposed to think Niagara the sight best worth seeing in America, though I will never return there until the paper-mill shall have been removed. I will not attempt to describe the indescribable, and would merely note for the benefit of future travellers that the effect of Niagara is as follows. On the first day it is distinctly disappointing: the roar of the waters is not so loud, the fall so high, or the current so fierce as was imagined. On the second day this natural though irrational disappointment had been gradually and unconsciously swallowed up by the waterfall, which has become omnipresent, tremendous, and soul-absorbing. On the third day Niagara has grown a monster so oppressive to soul and sense that the visitor hurries from the place with the feeling that another day's communing with the waters would make him mad. Such, at any rate, were my sensations, and I found them almost identical with those of my three fellow travellers.

The last, though by no means the least, annoyance connected with Niagara is the all-pervading presence of brides. When a young American's fancy lightly turns to thoughts of love, he vibrates to Niagara as the needle to the pole. Here he brings his bride for the honeymoon, whether from the facilities offered for suicide, or for other and more recondite reasons, unconnected with the beauty of the scenery, I know not; though my belief, founded on prolonged observation, is that the choice is due to the fact that Niagara is the place in the world where two persons, who have nothing to say to each other, can remain silent without embarrassment for the longest period of time, the noise of the water forbidding all but pantomimic conversation. However this may be, brides and bridegrooms are everywhere to be seen, making demonstrative if silent love under every tree and on every point of danger overhanging the torrent. There are perhaps earthly conditions in which the identity of a bride may remain concealed, for other women besides her are demonstrative in their affection and wear new frocks. But Niagara, with its most perpendicular descents to the river, is peculiarly favourable to the display of the feminine foot and ankle; and the bride invariably wears new boots, which is done by no other sane woman on a country excursion. The time to visit Niagara is in the early spring or in the late autumn, before the arrival, or after the departure, of tourists, and when all hotels save one are closed.

Oscar Wilde

(1854–1900) made a lecture-tour of the United States in 1883. It
was when going through the New York Custom House that he
is supposed to have said: 'I have nothing to declare except my
genius.' 'Impressions of America' was delivered as a lecture
on his return to London.

Impressions of America

I FEAR I cannot picture America as altogether an Elysium—perhaps, from the ordinary standpoint I know but little about the country. I cannot give its latitude or longitude; I cannot compute the value of its dry goods, and I have no very close acquaintance with its politics. These are matters which may not interest you, and they certainly are not interesting to me.

The first thing that struck me on landing in America was that if the Americans are not the most well-dressed people in the world, they are the most comfortably dressed. Men are seen there with the dreadful chimney-pot hat, but there are very few hatless men; men wear the shocking swallow-tail coat, but few are to be seen with no coat at all. There is an air of comfort in the appearance of the people which is a marked contrast to that seen in this country, where, too often, people are seen in close contact with rags.

The next thing particularly noticeable is that everybody seems in a hurry to catch a train. This is a state of things which is not favourable to poetry or romance. Had Romeo or Juliet been in a constant state of anxiety about trains, or had their minds been agitated by the question of return-tickets, Shakespeare could not have given us those lovely balcony scenes which are so full of poetry and pathos.

America is the noisiest country that ever existed. One is waked up in the morning, not by the singing of the nightingale, but by the steam whistle. It is surprising that the sound practical sense of the Americans does not reduce this intolerable noise. All Art depends upon exquisite and delicate sensibility, and such continual turmoil must ultimately be destructive of the musical faculty.

There is not so much beauty to be found in American cities as in Oxford, Cambridge, Salisbury or Winchester, where are lovely relics of a beautiful age; but still there is a good deal of beauty to be seen in them now and then, but only where the American has not attempted to create it. Where the Americans have attempted to produce beauty they have signally failed. A remarkable characteristic of the Americans is the manner in which they have applied science to modern life.

This is apparent in the most cursory stroll through New York. In

[328]

England an inventor is regarded almost as a crazy man, and in too many instances invention ends in disappointment and poverty. In America an inventor is honoured, help is forthcoming, and the exercise of ingenuity, the application of science to the work of man, is there the shortest road to wealth. There is no country in the world where machinery is so lovely as in America.

I have always wished to believe that the line of strength and the line of beauty are one. That wish was realized when I contemplated American machinery. It was not until I had seen the water-works at Chicago that I realized the wonders of machinery; the rise and fall of the steel rods, the symmetrical motion of the great wheels is the most beautifully rhythmic thing I have ever seen. One is impressed in America, but not favourably impressed, by the inordinate size of everything. The country seems to try to bully one into a belief in its power by its impressive bigness.

I was disappointed with Niagara—most people must be disappointed with Niagara. Every American bride is taken there, and the sight of the stupendous waterfall must be one of the earliest, if not the keenest, disappointments in American married life. One sees it under bad conditions, very far away, the point of view not showing the splendour of the water. To appreciate it really one has to see it from underneath the fall, and to do that it is necessary to be dressed in a yellow oil-skin, which is as ugly as a mackintosh—and I hope none of you ever wears one. It is a consolation to know, however, that such an artist as Madame Bernhardt has not only worn that yellow, ugly dress, but has been photographed in it.

Perhaps the most beautiful part of America is the West, to reach which, however, involves a journey by rail of six days, racing along tied to an ugly tin kettle of a steam engine. I found but poor consolation for this journey in the fact that the boys who infest the cars and sell everything that one wants to eat—or should not eat—were selling editions of my poems vilely printed on a kind of grey blotting paper, for the low price of ten cents. Calling these boys on one side I told them that though poets like to be popular they desire to be paid, and selling editions of my poems without giving me a profit is dealing a blow at literature which must have a disastrous effect on poetical aspirants. The invariable reply that they made was that they themselves made a profit out of the transaction and that was all they cared about.

It is a popular superstition that in America a visitor is invariably addressed as 'Stranger'. I was never once addressed as 'Stranger'. When I went to Texas I was called 'Captain'; when I got to the centre of the country I was addressed as 'Colonel', and, on arriving at the borders of Mexico, as 'General'. On the whole, however, 'Sir', the old English method of addressing people is the most common.

It is, perhaps, worth while to note that what many people call Americanisms are really old English expressions which have lingered in our colonies while they have been lost in our own country. Many people imagine that the term 'I guess', which is so common in America, is purely an American expression, but it was used by John Locke in his work 'The Understanding', just as we now use 'I think'.

It is in the colonies, and not in the mother country, that the old life of the country really exists. If one wants to realize what English Puritanism is—not at its worst (when it is very bad), but at its best, and then it is not very good—I do not think one can find much of it in England, but much can be found about Boston and Massachusetts. We have got rid of it. America still preserves it, to be, I hope, a short-lived curiosity.

San Francisco is a really beautiful city. China Town, peopled by Chinese labourers, is the most artistic town I have ever come across. The people—strange, melancholy Orientals, whom many people would call common, and they are certainly very poor—have determined that they will have nothing about them that is not beautiful. In the Chinese restaurant, where these navvies meet to have supper in the evening, I found them drinking tea out of china cups as delicate as the petals of a rose-leaf, whereas at the gaudy hotels I was supplied with a delf cup an inch and a half thick. When the Chinese bill was presented it was made out on rice paper, the account being done in Indian ink as fantastically as if an artist had been etching little birds on a fan.

Salt Lake City contains only two buildings of note, the chief being the Tabernacle, which is in the shape of a soup-kettle. It is decorated by the only native artist, and he has treated religious subjects in the naïve spirit of the early Florentine painters, representing people of our own day in the dress of the period side by side with people of Biblical history who are clothed in some romantic costume.

The building next in importance is called Amelia Palace, in honour of one of Brigham Young's wives. When he died the present president of the Mormons stood up in the Tabernacle and said that it had been revealed to him that he was to have Amelia Palace, and that on this subject there were to be no more revelations of any kind!

From Salt Lake City one travels over great plains of Colorado and up the Rocky Mountains, on the top of which is Leadville, the richest city in the world. It has also got the reputation of being the roughest, and every man carries a revolver. I was told that if I went there they would be sure to shoot me or my travelling manager. I wrote and told them that nothing that they could do to my travelling manager would intimidate me. They are miners—men working in metals, so I lectured them on the Ethics of Art. I read them passages from the autobiography of Benvenuto Cellini and they seemed much delighted. I was reproved by my hearers for not having brought him with me. I explained that he had been dead for some little time which elicited the enquiry 'Who shot him?' They afterwards took me to a dancing saloon where I saw the only rational method of art criticism I have ever come across. Over the piano was printed a notice:

PLEASE DO NOT SHOOT THE
PIANIST.
HE IS DOING HIS BEST.

The mortality among pianists in that place is marvellous. Then they asked me to supper, and having accepted, I had to descend a mine in a rickety bucket in which it was impossible to be graceful. Having got into the heart of the mountain I had supper, the first course being whisky, the second whisky and the third whisky.

I went to the Theatre to lecture and I was informed that just before I went there two men had been seized for committing a murder, and in that theatre they had been brought on to the stage at eight o'clock in the evening, and then and there tried and executed before a crowded audience. But I found these miners very charming and not at all rough.

Among the more elderly inhabitants of the South I found a melancholy tendency to date every event of importance by the late war. 'How beautiful the moon is tonight,' I once remarked to a gentleman who was standing next to me. 'Yes,' was his reply, 'but you should have seen it before the war.'

So infinitesimal did I find the knowledge of Art, west of the Rocky Mountains, that an art patron—one who in his day had been a miner—actually sued the railroad company for damages because the plaster cast of Venus of Milo, which he had imported from Paris, had been delivered minus the arms. And, what is more surprising still, he gained his case and the damages.

Pennsylvania, with its rocky gorges and woodland scenery, reminded me of Switzerland. The prairie reminded me of a piece of blotting-paper.

The Spanish and French have left behind them memorials in the beauty of their names. All the cities that have beautiful names derive them from the Spanish or the French. The English people give intensely ugly names to places. One place had such an ugly name that I refused to lecture there. It was called Grigsville. Supposing I had founded a school of Art there—fancy 'Early Grigsville'. Imagine a School of Art teaching 'Grigsville Renaissance'.

As for slang I did not hear much of it, though a young lady who had changed her clothes after an afternoon dance did say that 'after the heel kick she had shifted her day goods'.

American youths are pale and precocious, or sallow and supercilious, but American girls are pretty and charming—little oases of pretty unreasonableness in a vast desert of practical common-sense.

Every American girl is entitled to have twelve young men devoted to her. They remain her slaves and she rules them with charming nonchalance.

The men are entirely given to business; they have, as they say, their brains in front of their heads. They are also exceedingly acceptive of new ideas. Their education is practical. We base the education of children entirely on books, but we must give a child a mind before we can instruct the mind. Children have a natural antipathy to books—handicraft should be the basis of education. Boys and girls should be taught to use their hands to make something, and they would be less apt to destroy and be mischievous.

In going to America one learns that poverty is not a necessary accompaniment to civilization. There at any rate is a country that has no trappings, no pageants and no gorgeous ceremonies. I saw only two processions—one was the Fire Brigade preceded by the Police, the other was the Police preceded by the Fire Brigade.

Every man when he gets to the age of twenty-one is allowed to vote, and thereby immediately acquires his political education. The Americans are the best politically educated people in the world. It is well worth one's while to go to a country which can teach us the beauty of the word FREEDOM and the value of the thing LIBERTY.